Lifeguarding

Lifeguarding

A Memoir of Secrets, Swimming, and the South

Catherine McCall

 Harmony Books / New York

This is a true story.
Some of the names have been changed.

Copyright © 2006 by Catherine McCall

All rights reserved.
Published in the United States by Harmony Books, an imprint of the Crown
Publishing Group, a division of Random House, Inc., New York.
www.crownpublishing.com

Harmony Books is a registered trademark and the Harmony Books colophon is a
trademark of Random House, Inc.

Library of Congress Cataloging-in-Publication Data

McCall, Catherine (Catherine West)
  Lifeguarding : a memoir of secrets, swimming, and the South/Catherine
McCall.—Ist ed.
  I. McCall, Catherine (Catherine West).   2. Swimmers—Kentucky—
Louisville—Biography.   3. Lifeguards—Kentucky—Louisville—Biography.
4. Children of alcoholics—Kentucky—Louisville—Biography.
5. Lesbians—Kentucky—Louisville—Biography.
6. Louisville (Ky.)—Biography. I. Title.
CT275.M3326A3   2006
797.2'0092—dc22   2005022398

ISBN-13: 978-I-4000-9818-7
ISBN-10: I-4000-9818-I

Printed in the United States of America

Design by Namik Minter

I0 9 8 7 6 5 4 3 2 I

First Edition

for my family
❀ ❀ ❀ ❀ ❀ ❀ ❀ ❀

The cure for anything
is saltwater—sweat,
tears or the sea.

—Isak Dinesen

Lifeguarding

The summer I was twenty-two I perfected my ability to sink. I slipped beneath the pool's surface, exhaled a tower of bubbles, and rode the invisible force that inhabits the bottom of everything. A penny, a body—gravity makes no distinction—heavy, airless objects go down.

Finding silence on the bottom was an illusion. The space there quickly filled with sound, with a hum of intangible currents that started low then built into a darting scream, much like the sizzling sound ocean waves make as they rake over shells and fall away from the shore. It was the sound of agony, of longing, the sound of a wild cry made privately in the dead part of night.

There was something deeply wrong with me, something I couldn't name or fix, something I couldn't come close to defining. I was desperate for stillness, for peace, in need of a buoy or lifeline to grab onto, anything that might steady me, that might pull me from my black swirl.

Sitting on the bottom of the pool helped momentarily, although I wasn't completely still there either. My heart flexed harder and harder against its paltry ration of oxygen. My eyes closed briefly then popped open again. The water pushed against my legs and arms and torso without pause, urging me to merge with it, to join its dizzy mayhem, to dissolve finally into the darkness. So little in life mattered anyway—and here on the bottom of the pool, whatever might have mattered once, faded. All the worries and should-have-dones, the what-ifs and whys, all the meticulous career plans and shameful secrets receded. They slid down a slope that became increasingly steep until only a single point existed, only the nadir of breath.

What about my family?

A surging force burst through me like a geyser. My legs gave a hard shove against the bottom and half a second later my head broke free. My lungs opened to the last bits of oxygen left in the night's humidity. The painted sky was new, everything buffed with distinct and perfect borders: the straightened lounge chairs, the washed deck, the whistle hanging on the corner of the lifeguard desk, my flip-flops beneath it.

The river's odor was everywhere, too. This wasn't unusual for stuffy July evenings in Louisville—it permeated the dampness and mixed with the confused summer scents. Dirt, garbage, pollution, diesel fumes from barges. Only a slim hedge and the two lanes of River Road separated the club pool from the tangled bushes and twisting roots banking into the Ohio River. A number of members kept their boats docked on the river in the summer, which was a special benefit of belonging to the Louisville Boat Club.

I lifted myself out of the pool with a confidence that fell away with the water. A new stain formed instantly on the concrete, its edges bleeding into an irregular pattern. I worked on the borders with my wet big toe, intent on making the curve a uniform one, not jagged and blotchy but smooth, perfect. I pushed at the image in fitful toe stabs, then swept its edge to make it exactly straight, not bumpy.

The blast from a barge startled me away from the stupid game. I glanced around to see if anyone had been watching. The finely brushed tennis courts to the left were empty.

Dusk shaded the pool, fulfilling its promise of delivering softer, if not cooler, air. I grabbed my towel and sat on a lounge chair. This was my favorite time at the club, in the evening after the pool closed, when none of the members were around, when no one could assess how overweight or out of shape I was, or notice that my gait was not ladylike enough.

I wondered what my family was doing, what they'd eaten for dinner, maybe BLTs, then felt guilty about not having thought of them all day, before that moment. The rectangular pool with its wide black stripes stared at me. *You should swim laps.* These days I couldn't make myself swim more than a few. Although the challenge of swimming two full lengths underwater without taking a breath, then seeing the admiring faces of the little kids as they watched, still gave me a little boost of pride.

The sterilized pool, the private clubhouse, the hushed tones that generally lingered in these kinds of places reminded me of Big Spring, the country club that my family belonged to before—well, before we couldn't belong there anymore. When I closed my eyes I could hear the cheering parents, the screaming kids, the crack of the starting gun—so I didn't close my eyes. I wanted to move forward, always forward.

I slid into my flip-flops, unlatched the gate, and took the walkway that went under the road to the river. The Ohio is swift, brown, and deceptively deep. It's wide in some places and enticingly narrow in others. On this particular evening the river was showing its most placid face. The smooth surface offered a misplaced serenity. I knew better than to be deceived by the beauty here. Even good swimmers can drown—in the ocean, in a swimming pool, especially in a river.

There was a fearless man at the club, Mr. Woosley, who hooked a canoe to his ankle every morning and swam across the river, the thought of which brought a strange and secret terror to me. He encouraged me to swim along with him once, since I was such a strong athlete, a lifeguard, a past state champion.

"No thanks," I'd said, making up some excuse to disguise my discomfort. There was just something about the river, about its swallowed history, its submerged logs, its warm then cold currents nipping at you, trying to pull you under. Large boats and barges might barrel through the middle, potentially not seeing the canoe, or a lone swimmer. No one was around on this forgotten evening so I stood on the dock for awhile, staring at the river as if it could give me answers to questions I couldn't articulate.

Miraculously, our family was better—sort of. The vicious arguments and red-eyed dawns had ended. We were grown and alive and still together, except that I was becoming more and more invisible, finally becoming the ghost I had wanted for so long to be.

The water hid the secret of its depths, hid the broken tree stumps and sunken junk, the submerged truths that caused deadly accidents. The uncle I never knew died here, years earlier, in these same invisible currents.

The Ohio is a thief like that; it gives little and takes a lot. I knew that evening that the water would remain deathly silent, that it would hold its knowledge close, that the only way to surface from its depths was to hold on as long as you could and paddle upward, to keep kicking and pulling until you made it, or died trying. Quitting wasn't an option. But what happened when you got tired?

I was tired, not just from working all day but from trudging through the motions of life, from always doing what I was *supposed to do*. On the outside I appeared to fit into the world, but the truth was I didn't. I was increasingly becoming a mismatch, even in my own family.

We have to stick together—we're all we've got.

The lie that was me was getting heavier, wrapping its chains around my ankles—it was pulling me further and further under the surface—and I didn't know what to do.

1974

✻ ✿ ✻ ✿ ✿ ✻ ✿ ✿ ✿ ✻

1

Lifeguard candidates are taught that their
first concern is the safety of others.

American Red Cross Lifeguarding, p. 3

oach stopped us in the middle of swim practice and told us
to go sit on the bleachers. At first I thought he was planning to chew
us out, which would've been out of character—a set of eight hundreds fly-free was more his style of communicating.

Swim practice was never stopped for any reason, other than
lightning, and even then it had to be close enough for Coach to feel
the current on the pier. Our team swam outdoors when the water
was sixty-three degrees, in the first few weeks of May before the
official summer opening of Lakeside, when rumor said they filled
the quarry with river water from the Ohio. We swam when it was
raining, when it was strangely blustery for August, and on red-alert
pollution days, too, when the air was so thick, you could practically
carry it in your hands. Today, plaques of ruffled clouds had turned
the sky a light ash color but no thunder bowled by, no rain fell, there
was no real sign of a summer storm at all.

The twelve lifeguards stood in their chairs and blew their whistles in unison to clear the quarry of all recreational swimmers.
Everyone was looking toward the back part of the lake, except me.
Without my glasses I couldn't see ten feet in front of my face. Water
dripping from my head and bathing suit, I shuffled to the bleachers,

wrapped the towel around my body to hide it, then slipped on my wire-rim glasses. At thirteen, I didn't like being round and curvy, hated that my breasts were getting so big, that I was chunky and the object of teasing from the boys. My older sister, Anne, was the pretty one in the family—slim, auburn haired, broad shouldered.

We all gaped across Granddaddy's pier, past the big raft, which was a large rectangle of metal painted aquamarine blue and anchored to the rocky bottom with thick cables. Kids would swim to it, use it as base in a game of catchers, jump off the sides in splash contests. Swimming underneath it was strictly forbidden, and at first we thought someone must've gotten trapped there.

"What's happening?" I whispered to my sister, already sort of knowing but not wanting to believe it.

"I don't know," she said, without taking her eyes off the deep water. "Something bad."

I pulled my towel tighter against the strange chill. I was glad to be sitting next to her. *We have to stick together—we're all we've got.* She wore her usual solemn expression, brown eyes flat, mouth turned down on the ends. Her freckles appeared darker, more like a tan in the shaded light.

The lifeguards and people who worked in the main office were standing on the small pier at the very back of the lake, near the area called the rocks. With no swimmers, the quarry seemed bigger than usual, its dark waters uncomfortably still and incomprehensibly placid. Two lifeguards kept diving under the water then resurfacing, but there was no evidence of the thrashing and fighting and yelling taught in lifesaving classes. When an ambulance drove up we nodded in speechless agreement that the silent siren wasn't a good sign, even though the red light was flashing.

No words fit when in the presence of death. A different current runs through the air, a fibrous, invisible stream that stops the mealy chatter of the living, exposes the silliness of who likes who and who doesn't—it pulls the life around it to a pause.

The crackling loudspeaker startled us.

"The lake is now closed. Please leave the premises immediately," said the woman's voice.

On the bleachers, we looked at each other briefly, faces stripped for a moment of their usual teenage façades. We weren't sure what we were *supposed to do.* The general rules didn't apply to our swim team; we often had practice when the lake was closed to regular members.

In the deep water, the lifeguards kept doing their textbook surface dives then coming up empty-handed. Coach was standing near the swim team lanes by the phone, talking to a couple of the older girls on the team.

"He said we can stay until our car pools get here, but on the bleachers, no walking over to get a closer look," said one of the girls to the rest of us. We had a clear enough view anyway, like the balcony seats of some Greek tragedy. No one joked, though. Unfolding tragedy is a magnet—we couldn't stop staring.

Then, without warning, the guards pulled a body out of the water, a blinding white, thin limp body; the boy's head was flaccid and bent. Our group gasped in unison, as if a movie was being filmed and we were the extras. Other than that one quick, escaping gasp, there was no sound at all.

They laid him on the pier and the paramedics knelt over him. I knew he was dead—only death could be that still. Some of the older girls started crying. Minutes passed with the men hunched over the body, the orange-cushioned stretcher on the gurney beside them unstrapped and ready. Everyone—the pool manager, the guards, the office people—waited while the resuscitation attempt continued. We were standing by then, too, secretly hoping for the moment when the boy would cough a bit and sit up, when he would reveal his Hollywood Houdini trick and we would be aghast, then relieved, a rage not finding us until later.

As always, great oak and maple trees leaned over the quarry cliffs like curious neighbors, their leaves swollen and heavy, their reflection painting a still life of false middle-class tranquility on the evening water. Had this been a silent movie, then we had definitely reached the point where someone had forgotten their cue, and the action inexplicably stalled. We waited and waited, through interminable minutes, and in that slow-motion moment the reality of the situation started seeping down into my gut—this boy, this rumored guest of a member, had come swimming with his friend on an ordinary summer day, and now he was *dead. You never know what might happen, or when.*

A few teammates came back from talking to Coach, bringing words that flew around the bleachers like a steely gust of wind.

"He's twelve."

"Trapped under a pipe."

"He was down there over five minutes."

"This is so creepy," Anne said to me.

All I could do was nod.

While we'd been finishing our set of two hundreds, all these champion swimmers not a hundred meters from the boy, he was down there writhing and yanking and trying his best to get free. He was dying, right there, in the same water that we were pushing through, singing our individual workout songs, counting the laps before practice would be over, before we could get home and eat supper, watch television and go to bed, just to wake up and play the same game again.

My sister and I waited until the silent ambulance drove along the sidewalk, until we heard it come to life on the street. Then we walked with our friends to the front-entrance gates to sit on the stone wall and wait for our rides.

Cars drove past, completely oblivious to the death that had just occurred in their own neighborhood. I wondered if any of them knew the boy or his family.

Nothing made much sense anymore anyway. Anne and I, and our brother too (whose practice was fortunately at a different time), were doing what we were *supposed to be* doing, we were swimming like hell, being good kids, trying not to cause trouble for anyone, especially for our warring parents. We didn't realize, on that eerie summer afternoon as we left Lakeside, how treacherous the water in our family was getting. We didn't yet recognize the undertow that was dragging our family down, how trapped the five of us were, that we were as pinned as that boy had been under that wretched pipe. Nothing we kids did—nothing anybody did—made a difference, for my parents, for that drowning boy. Nothing.

"Mom," Anne said calmly, when we got home and found Mom in the kitchen. "Something awful happened."

Dish towel draped on her shoulder, her worried green eyes zeroed in on us.

"What? What's the matter?" she said, impatiently.

"A boy drowned at Lakeside," Anne finally said.

"Who?"

"Don't know. Someone's guest."

"*Ahh,*" Mom said. The sound she made was a sort of horrified yelp, her usual reaction to a crisis. Her narrow face would crinkle into a purse of pain and out would come a guttural, aching cry, as if someone had thrust a knife into her stomach. She squinted at us as Anne relayed the brief details, then we all just stood there in the stuffy kitchen, the ghosts gathering around us as they often did when we spoke of death.

"I've got first shower," Anne said, shooting her dark eyes my way, pulling us back to the reality of routine. It never took me as long to wash my hair, since mine was short and thick, cooperative even when ignored. Anne's, on the other hand, was long and prone to tangling, plus, she was older—she always took the first shower.

We didn't tell Dad when he came home later that evening. Drowning wasn't a topic we talked about with him.

Later that night, when I was alone in my room and couldn't fall asleep, I thought about that limp boy, about how devastated his parents must've been, how he'd awoken that morning like normal, having no idea he was going to die that day.

From my bed upstairs, I listened to Mom putting away the pots in the kitchen, could hear the mumble of television voices as they drifted out the den window and floated up to mine. The noise didn't bother me; it mingled with the whirring cicadas. I was in the habit of listening to the house.

Ours was a small, crowded house, where the rooms contracted in the evenings, amplifying sound and pressure and motion. The ghosts of our grandparents and uncle were everywhere, silent mostly, except when the silver tray rattled in the dining room in the middle of the night.

I had perfected the art of knowing everything that was going on—who was in what room, what Dad and Curtie were watching on television, who was talking and whether an argument was about to start. There was the shove of the swollen back door, the faint tap of Mom descending the basement steps, laundry basket in hand, then ascending again. There was the abrupt swish of water when she turned on the dishwasher, the downstairs toilet flushing, the creak of the oven door opening, and the slam of it closing again.

People have distinctive gaits, too, if you listen long enough. Dad's was the heaviest, shuffling and hard. Mom's was a quick, staccato step, muted machine gun fire, the sound of motion itself. Anne's gait was the quietest, a Cherokee Indian tracking a fox in the woods. Hers was the hardest to follow. Curtie's feet thudded in a predictable pattern, sometimes fast in a run, other times slow, always in the same rhythm of determination. And mine? I never thought to listen to my own footsteps.

That night the sky had blackened by the time the dream slapped me awake. It was the falling dream again. I'd taken a wrong step, not over a rock cliff or high-rise balcony, but off the edge of a drained pool. In the dream, I tried and tried to scream, but sound refused me. The bottom of the swimming pool gaped at me, getting bigger and bigger. When I woke up, my heart pulsed in my stomach.

To get oriented, I put on my glasses and focused on the patch of wall in my room that was illuminated by our neighbor's floodlight. The traffic on nearby Chenoweth Lane was silent, no exhaling buses or honking speeders. The birds made no sound, and of course there was no wind. That's when I located the rattling noises in the dining room downstairs. Although I'd heard them before, they didn't fit any recognizable McCall footstep rhythm.

When I was younger and listened to the house like this, I thought burglars were stealing everything we owned, the only tangibles left of our grandparents. The creaking floors signaled stocking-faced men filling black sacks full of mint julep cups and serving trays and those delicate teacups we weren't supposed to touch. They were taking the dark mahogany box of silver cutlery, Mama T's china, the ancient candle snuffer, the antique coffee table with its fragile flap. They were stealing everything.

In the morning, I'd stroll casually through the dining room and open the sticking drawer of the cherry hutch, just to make sure the box of silver was still there, which it always was. The silver tray hadn't been moved either.

At some blurry point, since everything always remained in the same place, I abandoned the burglar theory and began a serious consideration of ghosts and what happens to a person when they die. I wondered if the drowned boy was already a ghost, or an angel, if he was on his way to heaven, if there was such a place.

It wasn't impossible, at least theoretically, that ghosts could be causing a commotion in the dining room. Suppose our grandparents wanted a cigarette and a cocktail, where else would they go but a dining room filled with their own furniture? It seemed as good a rendezvous spot as any, the perfect place to play a round or two of bridge, to tell a few jokes, to reminisce. The liquor cabinet, stocked with Maker's Mark, Jack Daniels, vodka, and scotch, was just a few steps away in the den.

As to my ghost theory, the silver tray was the main clue. It stayed on the serving table in the corner and anytime someone walked through the dining room, you could hear a clear, tinny rattle. That night, I listened to the silver shiver as it often did, felt my heart pulsing in my stomach and knew without a doubt, that something suspicious was going on downstairs.

I didn't venture down the steps to spy on the ghosts, though. Even at thirteen, I was a chicken—the idea of walking through the house in the dark proved too terrifying. I harbored a little girl's fear inside me that ran so deep and so wide, I had to struggle not to drown in it.

Everything changes in the dark anyway, and though I pretended to everyone else that I had no problems or worries, I carried a vague apprehension that, should I come too close to the ghosts, I might be swallowed into their shadows for good.

From the street, nothing about our house suggested it was haunted. It was a basic Cape Cod–style redbrick cottage, with a small second floor. My sister and I each had a bedroom upstairs, separated by a hall and a small bathroom. Downstairs, the front door opened into the living room which led to the dining room. Through the dining room, to the right was the kitchen, which provided the heartbeat of the house. From the other side of the living room, you could turn left into the heartbeat or walk down the short hall to my parents' room on the right, or to Curtie's room on the left. A small bathroom marked the end of the hallway. One year, the enclosed screen porch became our shag-carpeted family den, complete with built-in book and trophy shelves. It made the house, in a way, complete, or at least more balanced.

The architecture lent itself to skirmish warfare. The dining room was the border territory between the den, my father's domain, and the kitchen, which belonged to my mother.

My grandparents' antique furniture was placed throughout the house, with most of it clustered in the neutral territories of the dining and living rooms. The gigantic corner cupboard, the cherry hutch, the deeply stained serving table with the silver tray on top. The pull-down cherry desk, the dining table with its dark shine, the coffee table with its delicate flap. *Don't put your feet on that.*

Still-life photographs and a painting captured all the ghosts but one. Our two grandmothers resided in the living room. A portrait of Grandmother Frances, my father's regal and reserved mother, hung in a gold frame above the fireplace. Mama T, my mother's mother, the one with the great laugh, smiled shyly from a color photograph on the antique desk.

In my parents' room, the photograph on Dad's cherry dresser showed Granddaddy wearing a white shirt, no tie, and dark pants. More thick than fat, he stood at Lakeside with his arms lifted toward the rock cliffs. At first glance he seemed to be standing on water, but he was actually standing on a pier that the photographer, accidentally or not, left out of the shot.

Then there was our other grandfather, the oldest ghost in that he'd been dead the longest, bending down behind my mother when she was a long-haired happy little girl. In the large black and white, they were in a leafy yard and had stopped their raking just long enough to grin at the photographer. This picture was placed on the trophy shelf in the den. I always wondered why Mom didn't keep it on her dresser but figured it was simply too large to fit there.

The last ghost, Uncle Ches, my father's only sibling, wasn't displayed anywhere in the house, and he was mentioned least of all. His name was engraved, though, on a silver bowl that rested on another trophy shelf in the den, just above the liquor cabinet. He'd finished among the top players in the State Amateur golf tournament in 1952 and his prize had been the bowl.

They all died too soon, suddenly and without warning. Heart attacks, cerebral hemorrhage, car accident, drowning. You could never tell when it might be your turn, when death might jump at you from beneath an underwater pipe, put a grip on your heart or a gash in your throat and shut you up for good. *We have to stick together—we're all we've got.*

Morning light helped. When I wandered into the kitchen to eat my bowl of cereal, Mom was making a list of the day's plan.

"Morning," she said brightly, returning quickly to her stenographer pad.

"Morning," I said.

The kitchen always seemed lighter and airier in the first part of the day, as if the storm of night had passed through, leaving a brushed and hopeful feeling in its wake. The focus of daylight kept the ghosts in retreat. It felt like it could be a good day, a Saturday, no afternoon practice.

"He needs to do the yard today," Mom said, as much to herself as to me.

She'd already finished two loads of sheets and towels, vacuumed the downstairs, and put away the dishes by the time Dad emerged from the bathroom in his boxer shorts, newspaper folded under his arm, his whole body smelling of smoke. He was tall and lean and handsome. People always said he looked like John Wayne, although this morning his face was gray and puffy and it was harder to see the resemblance. He poured a cup of coffee and sat down at the round wooden table.

"Are you going to cut the grass today?"

"Yes, *Margaret Anne*, I said I would. Get off my case," he said, not looking up from the paper.

Her jaw tensed as she stared out the kitchen window, her back to him. I was spying on them from the dining room, having cleared out of the kitchen when my father came in. Her finger tapped absently against the edge of the sink. Mom's middle name was efficiency. She liked to plan and predict and be prepared. For years, my father had said he would do something, and then for one reason or another, wouldn't do it. That was happening more and more often, and his unreliability gnawed at her like an ulcer. She rubbed the place in her neck where a shooting pain sometimes climbed. This morning, it was as if this one out-of-her-control item—cutting the grass—had the power to torture her.

"You want me to get Curtie to do it?"

"*Dammit, I said I'll do it.*" Fire left over from the night before spewed from his eyes.

She pursed her lips together hard, a silent debate swinging through her mind. She shook her head, disgusted, and tossed the dish towel on the counter.

"I was just asking," she said, her voice seething.

"No you weren't—and you *know* it."

I backed silently into the center of the living room so my voice would sound more distant. Mama T's expression didn't change as I covered my mouth with my hand.

"What time are we leaving, Mom?" I called.

"About fifteen minutes," she yelled, and it worked. I was on the steps when I heard her going into the basement to empty the dryer.

I hustled upstairs to get ready for practice. The sooner we left, the better.

✴ ❋ ❍ ○ ❋ ❋ ❋ ○ ❋ ❋ ❋ ○ ❍ ○ ❋ ❋ ❍

2

Surface diving enables a lifeguard to
submerge to moderate depths to
rescue or search for a submerged victim.

American Red Cross Lifeguarding, p. 106

That morning it was just Mom and me in the car. Anne swam
with the older kids in Group One on Saturdays and Curtie's practice was later in the day. For some reason, Mom veered from our
usual route to Lakeside, taking Cannon's Lane instead, which
crossed over the expressway then ran alongside the golf course at Big
Spring Country Club.

"Did you miss swimming for them this summer?" She asked this
question offhandedly. As a family, we *never* talked about Big Spring
in terms of bellyaching or complaining about not belonging anymore. Technically, we were still members, we just owed them so
much money that we didn't dare show our faces on the grounds.
None of us knew how to talk about the shame of that.

"Not especially," I said, trying to glimpse the golf course through
the wall of leafy trees that buffered the fairways from the busy road.

"Do you miss playing tennis?" I asked, more to be polite than
out of curiosity.

"Oh, sometimes," she said, her voice trailing into itself. "I miss
seeing my friends."

We rode in silence the rest of the way. The early-Saturday traffic was light. I kept switching the radio, looking for a good song, one that would stay in my head during practice.

The ease that had accompanied my mother and me for most of my life was slowly eroding. The number of people comparing me to her had tapered off, too. I'd grown into a bushy-haired, boyish teenager prone to slouching, while Mom was a perky thirty-nine-year-old with a Carnival Queen smile.

I still hated Dad and loved her—simple as that. But life doesn't stay simple, not when you reach thirteen, or whatever age you are when the first of life's infinite mirages makes your eyes squint.

When I was younger, adults smiled down at me often and commented on how much I looked like my mother. *I'm a carbon copy*, I would say, parroting her words, causing their grins to widen. As "daughter number two," I'd inherited her thick and wavy brown hair, her athlete's body, her curvy legs that tapered at the ankles. She could throw the football the right way, like a boy—so could I. Anne, with her lanky build, red hair, and freckles, was said to be the "milkman's daughter," a distinction I didn't understand for the longest time. Mom was funny, full of animation and verve—everyone at school loved her.

Chenoweth Elementary, where Mom taught fifth and sixth grades, was a place where I heard the most compliments. Since she was a teacher, I became well versed in the behind-the-scenes world of school, including getting to go into the teacher's lounge sometimes. I saw my favorite teacher, Ms. Thompson, laugh in a way she never did in front of the kids, with her head back, eyes closed, deep dimples spreading across her cheeks. I saw the school nearly empty in the afternoons when the janitor buffed the linoleum floors with sweet-smelling polish.

My favorite bonus, though, was helping Mom with her schoolwork. The clean blue scent of mimeographed sheets filled the air in her classroom. In the pre-Xerox 1970s, to make a copy, Mom had to place a delicate sleeve of carbon paper underneath the original math test and above an unlined blank piece of paper—to create three layers. Then she'd trace the numbers on the top page with caution, because everything written on the top sheet could be seen on the receiving sheet—mistakes were irreparable. In the end, she would have two copies—the original and a clear replica—although the pen had never actually touched the bottom page.

When I was old enough, she let me trace the tests, but only sometimes and only if I didn't make any mistakes. I was exceptionally careful, of course, and compliant, as perfect a copy of her as the math and English tests we created for her students. *The only difference between you and me—really—is about twenty-five years.*

Sometimes, if I made an irreversible mistake while copying one of the tests, if I skipped a whole paragraph or accidentally reversed the numbers in the long-division problems, I had to start over completely. This circumstance was to be avoided at all costs because Mom would get irritated. Carbon paper was expensive. Otherwise, she thanked me and sometimes paid me a quarter.

"This is really fun," I said one day while cautiously tracing at the kitchen table. "I might want to be a teacher someday."

"No you don't," Mom said, closing the oven. "You can be anything you want to be."

I kept copying but didn't say anything after that.

For the longest time, the similarities between my mother and me weren't confusing—they made life easier. From her I learned ambition. I learned to plan ahead, way into the future, to recognize opportunities and take advantage of them. Like her, I excelled in school and won awards.

Our greatest clothes struggle occurred when I was four and insisted on wearing my cowgirl outfit—complete with tassels and hat—to a special television event. Exasperated by my stubbornness, she finally acquiesced, only after I agreed to leave my guns in the car.

She was by no means a June Cleaver anyway. She preferred tennis shoes to pumps and, unlike the other mothers, she never minded getting her hair wet when we went swimming. It seemed natural for me to be so much like her—a carbon copy.

Then the day came when I opened my mouth a little too freely.

I was eleven and we were riding down Lexington Road, about to pass Sacred Heart Academy, an all-girls Catholic school. Gold and red and brown leaves lay in bunches beneath enormous old trees on the large grounds that separated the buildings from the road. Secretly, the all-girls school intrigued me, but I wasn't thinking of that right then—I was thinking about my future.

"When I grow up, I want to have a nontraditional family."

"What . . . do you mean by that?" she said, worry crackling in her voice. She pushed the car lighter into the dashboard to heat it up.

"I just mean that . . . I want to work." I watched her hands shake slightly as she lit the cigarette, taking a couple of quick, forceful puffs. Her brown hair was a bit unruly in its waves. "I don't want to just stay home with the kids," I added.

"But you want a husband—you want to get married," she stated, her voice a little higher than usual.

"Yes," I said, not at all certain. "I want to have kids, a husband— I just don't want to be stuck at home." I watched how the cigarette, and my steady voice and my lack of emotion, calmed her.

"Oh," she said. "You just mean you want to work—that's not really nontraditional. . . . I work."

It was a strange conversation, one that didn't flow as easily between us as the hundreds of conversations that preceded it. I knew instantly that something I'd said bothered her. The word *nontraditional* was the stray mark that appeared to fit on the receiving sheet, me, but not on the original, her. It was one of my earliest clues that I wasn't the carbon copy that everyone, including me, thought I was.

Silence increasingly became my ally. It was just easier to listen, especially to my mom, than to risk speaking and inadvertently upsetting her with something I said. I craved the comfort of an imposed design, anyway, and her clear model of how I was *supposed to be*; it was the blank, empty page of being myself that terrified me.

The water at morning practice seemed different after the drowning; it was stained with a dark green sadness, with an inevitability and an apology. Without the other members swimming—the quarry didn't open to everyone else until ten—the water took on a thickness, as if the death left a residue. No one talked much, not unusual for early-Saturday practice, but the mood was more somber than normal. We straggled to the bleachers, dropped our towels and T-shirts, then shuffled to the pier like a flock of obedient, dumb sheep.

I thought of the boy and his family when I dove into the seamless cool water, when I swam lazily down the lanes for warm-up. Under the water, from a distance, the rock area revealed no lingering hint of his presence, no pair of goggles or left-behind shoe. These were stupid thoughts—people don't swim in shoes—and eventually they washed out of my head, especially when Coach gave us our first set and I had to push to keep up the pace.

It was only 1974 but my dream of swimming in the Olympics in Montreal '76 was already fading. It was dissolving like a patch of fog that separates slowly, until the moment comes when the mist vanishes and is replaced by a searing doubt about whether it really existed in the first place.

I never admitted to anyone that my dream was dying. I just sensed a vague, amorphous blob taking over the clean, blue space inside me where I once kept my most private hopes. Deep down I knew I wasn't good enough to swim in the Olympics. And I knew our family was sinking—just because a reality is difficult to accept doesn't make it any less true.

I had no such insight when I was younger and faster, when I fell in love with swimming—before we ever joined the Lakeside team—when my family spent our summer days at the country club.

My parents were happier then, even though they approached life very differently. I learned motion from my mother, inertia from my father. The slower he moved, the more accelerated would be her speed, and vice versa.

Dad's tack, which became most obvious on weekend afternoons when he was home, was to sit so still in his chair in the den that he resembled a piece of furniture, not unlike his mother's prized coffee table. It was a jewel of a table, polished and lovely to look at, though it couldn't withstand the pressure of feet or much weight at all. The table was to be treated with great caution, as if looking at it too long might make it crack.

So Dad sat like a table, watching golf or some old western on television, drinking cans of the discounted beer-of-the-month. Then sometimes, without warning, he'd erupt from the chair, ignited by the invisible match of some inane thing one of us kids did or didn't do.

But that was in the afternoons, and more usual in the past couple of years. When we were younger, weekend mornings held only promise and the excitement that comes with anticipation.

There was a lightness to our house on those golf mornings, to the tune Dad whistled in the shower, to his step as he got ready. His excitement about playing golf lingered in the kitchen and living room like a clean scent, as if he'd been wearing an aftershave lotion. Golf always made him happy—it made him speed up a little.

"See you there later," he said, as he strode confidently out the door.

"Okay," Mom said, glancing his way briefly. She was as focused as any surgeon, head bending down again quickly, eyes narrowed, voice high pitched and commanding. *You need to straighten your rooms. Empty the wastebaskets. Dust the living room and dining room. Turn the TV off!*

As Mom's main assistant and firstborn, Anne was competent by age ten in all aspects of laundry, cooking, and general household commanding. I, at age eight, gave more of an *impression* of helping. In the living room, I tarried at the bookshelves on either side of the fireplace where we kept the set of World Book Encyclopedias, an old T-shirt dust rag in my hand. The antique desk with Mama T's picture had several small drawers, ones I opened gingerly, in hopes of finding some forgotten memento from one of the ghosts—a ring, a pocket watch, a locket. Nothing new ever appeared, but that never deterred my checking. Opening the drawers released a musty scent of cherry wood and history, of past laughter and peaceful sighs. I fingered the same rubber bands, inspected the papers stuck in the center compartment, pushed around the thumbtacks and the pens.

We kept Mama T's slick set of cards in the desk; Curtie and I inherited our love of card playing from her. I wiped my hands then lifted the deck from its holder and ran through a few shuffles. Mom was in the basement and out of range. The cards were stiff, not like the ones Curtie and I played with, which had gotten bent at the corners and spotted by our potato-chip-salty fingers.

Finally, it would be time to go. Anne and Curtie and I wrestled each other to the car, calling the front seat, then deferring to Mom's rotational system. We grumbled and obliged rather than risk being left at home. In the car Mom lit a cigarette, took a deep breath, and shifted the station wagon into reverse. Her slowing down started then.

She was pretty in her terry cover-up, with her wavy brown hair and suntanned face, her eyes greenish and smart behind the large, dark sunglasses.

"What a gorgeous day," she'd say, as we turned onto Chenoweth Lane. "Thanks for all your help." Then we'd start singing or playing

Love Bug or she would tell us a funny story, her urgency from earlier already replaced by humor and ease. We drove through the heart of St. Matthews, past the White Castle and the cow on the roof of Erhler's Ice Cream store, past old maples and oaks on Breckinridge Lane.

The land around Big Spring was called the country, when Dad was a skinned-knee little boy driving to the club with *his* family. Over the decades, buildings and broader roads chopped up the meadows and pastures. Only the large horse farm adjacent to the club's property remained unaltered by the time we were old enough to swim at Big Spring. A white fence surrounded the farm, enclosing dark, muscled horses that grazed in bright green pastures, a world of cars zooming around them.

When we turned into Big Spring a hushed feeling always came over us. The narrow paved road curved gently beneath rows of thick, shapely trees. A delicious scent of fresh, rich grass floated into the opened car windows. Beyond the branches, golfers rode in golf carts or walked with their clubs along brushed green fairways. Sometimes we saw no one playing at all.

From an early age we knew that certain places required children to be good. Places like church or a restaurant or when in the company of adults. Big Spring was one of those places. *Only speak to grown-ups when spoken to. Say "yes, ma'am" and "yes, sir." Don't get into any trouble.*

We knew—my sister and brother and I—that when people looked at us they would think of our parents, and maybe our grandfather, Granddaddy, if they were older and had known him when he was alive. His photograph hung in the clubhouse along with other important club members, many of whom had joined the club when he did, in the 1920s when it was open only to men.

Granddaddy's ghost was outside, too, in the way the air pushed the leaves around, in the roominess of the walkways and the heavy clicking of men's golf spikes as they walked up the back steps to the clubhouse.

The lessons on *how to be* weren't instructed directly. When my sister set up school in our attic, with Curtie and me as her gullible students, we did the usual things kids do. Repeated the ABC's, copied our names, raised our hands with guesses to her sometimes stumping questions. We'd lower our heads and apologize when she impatiently rolled her eyes at our ignorance. She was taller, lankier, smarter, faster. She was two and a half years older than me and she had freckles and hair the color of a chestnut thoroughbred.

The critical information of life we already knew—maybe we were born knowing—such as life has facts to it. Facts like you have to be good, big sisters know everything, fathers play golf, and mothers cook and do laundry—facts like that.

At the pool Curtie and I played our 007 game, which involved elaborate secret rules and imaginary devices. We walked around appearing casual, but really we spied on the ladies in the lounge chairs, eavesdropping on conversations we didn't understand, discovering made-up meanings; then we darted into the pool for cover and to exchange our spy secrets.

Before lunch, Mom wanted to work with Curtie's freestyle, to get him to swim to her in the pool. He was almost four and might be ready to swim in one of the meets this summer.

I swam by myself then, staying under the water as long as I could, diving for a penny. Water changed all the usual rules in life. It slowed everything down. In the underwater world, no one could bother you or correct you or tell you to do something. I liked holding my breath, studying the penny as it floated down, as one side tilted up, turning its brown body shiny in a ray of sun. I experimented with catching it just before it landed, then I dropped it again and tried to hear the sound it made at that last moment, when it hit the bottom and stopped.

The whistles blew and we dawdled at the task of climbing out of the pool for rest period. We ate the peanut butter-and-jelly sandwiches Mom brought from home then sat on the edge of the pool, chins in hands, staring at the placid water. Curtie and I hated rest period; we had no concept of why a lifeguard needed a break—all they did was sit there.

Finally the guard climbed into the chair and in we jumped. During the next rest period, Dad was leaning against the white iron fence, a white towel with a blue stripe on it draped over his shoulder. He was sweaty and pleased, his khaki shorts still clean after playing. Shavings of grass stuck to the edges of his golf shoes.

Curtie and I followed Mom to the fence, to say hello.

"How'd you do?" Mom said.

"Shot a seventy-five," Dad said. When he smiled, his whole face changed: the frown marks between his eyebrows disappeared, he became happy and friendly and not mean. Mom had that rare expression of admiration on her face when she listened to him describe his best shots. She was proud that he was such a good golfer.

At age six, I was something of a hero at Big Spring, at least on summer Sundays during swim meets. I was speedy and already comprehended the importance of winning, of scoring points for our team and making my parents feel proud.

Something happened every second at a swim meet. It wasn't a quiet sport, like golf or tennis, but a busy, noisy one, full of stopping and starting and cheering and clapping. Only when the starter said, "Take your mark" would everyone stop in midgesture, midsentence, as if on a movie set and someone had just yelled "Freeze!" Moments later, the gunshot would release the swimmers, and the whistling and cheers would turn on again.

I loved my turn to race.

"Way to go, Miss Bug," Dad said one day, surprising me. He was standing against the fence with one of the other fathers, grinning in his happy golf way. I'd just won and I could see that he was proud I was his daughter. My dad was handsome—lean with broad shoulders, straight nose, a wide set to the eyes. That day he wore a white golf shirt, khaki shorts, loafers, no socks. The hair on his legs, where his golf socks had been for eighteen holes, was mashed against the band of white skin. I was about as tall as his waist. He introduced me as *Cathy—daughter number two*—to his friend, then he said something that I couldn't hear but that I knew was funny because the other man laughed out loud.

They both held plastic cups with grown-up drinks. When Dad took a sip, the lime peel in his cup stayed pressed against the side; it was shiny green and mushy and I wondered if he would swallow it. I considered asking him if he would eat the lime but decided against it. It wasn't worth risking making his mood turn sour.

From the time I was about three, he had called me Miss Bug. We'd been on vacation in Florida and one day, in exasperation, Mom strapped an orange bubble around my waist since I would fling my body into the deep end of the pool and she'd fret while I haphazardly powered myself to the side. *I couldn't keep up with you.* So they bought the bubble, and to Dad, I resembled a bumblebee.

Big Spring Country Club was a place of relativity, where changes in dress and weight and hairstyle were measured in fractions, a place where everything and everyone was compared. There was a code in that place, a way to be. It was the cultured inside of the shell, where the white pearl itself was polished and served by deferring black men in waiter outfits, and by low-bending black women who managed to keep the clubhouse spotless and fresh without ever being seen.

At six I loved it.

At twelve I hated it.

In those years, before we stopped going, summer was the season when our lives revolved around swimming at Big Spring. At first, there was a comfortable predictability to that routine and to the club itself, to the clothes, the conversations. In the late-1960s, I had only fleeting peripheral awareness of adults paying attention to the war that apparently wasn't a real war, to the impassioned black minister on television, and the angry white sheriffs wearing big hats and swinging black sticks. There were grumblings about "colored people wanting handouts," about "the liberals wanting to just give it all away." The tone of voices signaled what was acceptable and what wasn't. A "long-haired hippie," for instance, was bad. In general, though, the events that would shape our nation so dramatically weren't registering as significant for me or for anyone around me; what mattered most was being the best.

When we were little and it was time to go home, Mom would tell me (or sometimes Anne) to go find Dad in the clubhouse, to tell him we were leaving, even though he had driven his own car. Going inside the building wearing only a bathing suit, no clothes or shoes, was against all the rules but Mom said it was okay *this one time*. She kept the station wagon running in the covered circular drive by the double front door. To me it was a getaway car.

Through the doors the chilly air gave me goose bumps. The clubhouse was a dimly lit place with deep brown chairs and a patterned burgundy carpet that resembled rows of blank stop signs. The scent of clean, rich people things—aged leather, fresh flowers, polished wood—filled the lobby. I looked up to the line of photographs hanging on the wall, men in suits and ties. I squinted at the one I thought was Granddaddy's, the man whose nose was wide and broken like a boxer's, the hair short and white. His face seemed bigger than those of the other men.

Dad wasn't in the dining room when I hurried past it, hopping on my tiptoes, trying not to drip on the carpet. He was in the bar.

He sat on a stool, leaning with his elbows on the wooden overhang, talking to another man, someone I didn't know. Clouds of smoke twisted toward the ceiling and darkened the already dim room. All the chairs were high. A small television showing golf hung in the far corner with the sound turned down. The bartender had some old acne scars on his face and he acted like he didn't see me when I came to the entrance.

"Dad," I called in a loud whisper. I didn't go right to him because I wasn't supposed to be in the bar for several reasons. One: I was a kid. Two: I had a bathing suit on. Three: I was a girl.

He didn't hear me, or if he did, he didn't turn around.

"Dad," I said louder, stepping closer to him. "We're leaving now."

"Oh——" he said, looking down at me from his chair. A moment of confusion narrowed his eyes, as if at first he thought I was somebody else's child.

"Okay," he finally said. "Tell Mom I'll be home in a minute." Which I knew wasn't true but I just nodded and backed away.

He didn't usually sit in the "Men Only" room but I could see the door opened to it, on the back wall, left of the bar. I wondered what I would do if I had to look for him and he was in there, in that strangely foreign place, strictly off-limits for girls—and women. The secret things men did in there by themselves drew my curiosity and anytime I was near the bar, I would take a peek in that door. It was usually open but not always.

"Why do men need a separate room?" I asked Mom when I was back in the getaway car.

"What do you mean?"

"The Men Only room, off the bar."

"Oh," she said, looking left and right before gunning onto Dutchman's Lane. "I don't know—they play cards and things."

Cards! Curtie and I played cards everywhere—sitting on the warm cement during rest period, riding in the back of the station wagon, at home on the floor in the den, or in the living room if Dad was home and in a bad mood. We didn't care if anyone saw us.

"Why do they have to play cards in secret?"

"Well, they play poker, I guess. And they smoke cigars in there, too," she said, in a voice that meant no more questions. Her poolside ease had drained away. I could tell by the way she leaned forward in her seat, gripping the steering wheel tightly. We never sang on the way home from the pool.

I glanced at my sister, but her head was turned. She was silent and stone faced, staring out the window at nothing. I looked out my window for the horses.

3

Depending on whom you ask, a
lifeguard is . . . a teacher who gives
swimming lessons.

American Red Cross Lifeguarding, p. 3

The secret to our swimming success had one name—Lakeside.

For decades, the best swimmers in Louisville, and some of the
best swimmers in the country, had been swimming for Lakeside
Swim Club. Some of those families also belonged to one of the
country clubs. Because the summer country club league was so competitive, because winning meant everything, they allowed year-round
American Athletic Union swimmers to compete against kids who
just swam for a couple of months in the summer. This inequity
meant that the club with the most AAU members would usually win
the City Championship meet. Of the nine country club teams, Big
Spring was one of the powerhouses, along with Audubon and the
Louisville Boat Club.

At age ten, dreams of trophies and Olympic medals sparkled in
Anne's eyes—or at least someone had the idea that she was old
enough to try out for the Lakeside team, to swim year-round. I was
seven and went along to watch because it gave me *something to do*. The
image of handsome Mark Spitz smiling in Mexico City, medals
draped around his neck, played in my mind as we drove through the
park that first time, in September 1968.

After Labor Day, Lakeside emptied the quarry because it was too cold to swim outdoors. They solved the weather challenge by constructing an enormous bubble to cover the twenty-five-yard pool that was also on the premises. The bubble resembled an inflatable spaceship without flashing lights. Like a live, stuffy-nosed alien, it exhaled a guttural whoosh every couple of minutes. I'd never seen anything like this sprawling, soft-sided rubber thing; when I pushed my fingers against the slimy green cover, it caved like a thick-skinned balloon. The vacuum-tight rotating door required a hard shove to move it. The steamy glass blocked the view of the bubble's interior. I could see nothing until the door dumped me into astonishing heat. I took my coat off immediately.

The coach introduced himself. He was wearing a blue T-shirt and shorts. Words echoed like we were in a capsule, or a tunnel, or a cave. The pool was smaller than the one at Big Spring, and rectangular, not shaped like an L. I slipped my thumb in my mouth, turning slightly so Mom couldn't see.

Anne tried to make her freestyle look perfect when she swam across the pool for the coach. He didn't even make her swim the length, just the width.

"What about the little one?" He and Mom studied me. I'd removed my thumb just in time.

"You want *her* to swim?" Mom hesitated. "She's only seven." She pursed her lips for a second, in consideration. I stood up straight.

"I guess it's okay with me," she said, slowly. "Do you have your bathing suit on?"

The chance to go swimming in the winter was like a dream coming true. I raised my shirt. *Of course* I had my bathing suit on.

Mom signed us both up to join the team. The next morning she approached Dad cautiously with the news. They were in the kitchen, and I was spying on them from the hall, peeking around the edge of

the doorway. She was over by the stove, in her nightgown and bare
feet, her brown hair more wavy from sleep. He didn't look so much
like John Wayne, sitting at the table, leaning on his elbows (which
we were never allowed to do), holding his head like it hurt. He
wasn't wearing a shirt.

"It'll be okay, won't it, Curt?"

"I guess so," he said, irritably. I'd missed the first part of the
conversation.

He didn't seem very excited, but he didn't say no, which is what I
was worried about. He poured another cup of coffee and left the
kitchen. I had cleared the hallway before he passed.

It was easy to avoid him, especially in the mornings, because he
didn't look up much. He would walk into the kitchen to sit for a
minute, drinking coffee, reading the paper, until Mom or one of us
would bother him, then he'd huff down the hall to the bathroom.

As a second grader, swimming at Lakeside in the winter meant I
would go to swim practice in the afternoon every day after school,
which meant I'd have *something to do*.

From that day—in 1968—forward, swimming at Lakeside was
the train that scheduled our lives; riding that train became our way
of life, day after day, year after year. It took us to Cincinnati and
Ottawa, to Kansas City and Indianapolis, to Toledo and Nashville
and Myrtle Beach. My brother and sister and I just kept going and
going, toward or away from something, none of us knew what, at
least not until 1974, the summer the boy drowned. By then, we
probably each sensed the brick wall our family train was speeding
toward, sensed in some deep, unspeakable place the inevitable
derailment that, despite the wreckage, might even bring relief.

It was always strange in the hard cold of winter to push through the
foggy door into the bubble's sauna. We threw our bags, stuffed with

towels and hats and a change of clothes if it was really cold, along the edge of the bubble, stripped to our bathing suits, and lined up for practice. Afterward, if the snack bar was open and I had a quarter, I'd buy a Three Musketeers to eat in the car on the way home.

Since we belonged to both Lakeside *and* Big Spring, and since we lived in the "East End," we appeared to be well-to-do but actually our family teetered precariously on the cusp of that upper-middle-class social world. For example, when Curtie began kindergarten in 1968, Mom started teaching school. By doing this, she was pushing the limits of social acceptability. Soon into working, she decided to go to graduate school to earn a master's degree. If she became a principal someday, she would earn more money, then we wouldn't have to rely on Dad. He wasn't as adept at making money—or staying employed—as he was at playing golf. That didn't mean he lounged around the house a lot; it just meant you couldn't count on him.

At that time, the feminist movement wasn't even whispered about—it was a fearful thing happening in those uncomfortably liberal places like New York and California. In the East End of Louisville in the late sixties and early seventies, ladies had their hair done weekly at the salon; black women stood at bus stops in the late afternoon after cleaning the stately homes of those same coifed ladies. Fathers were orthodontists and bank presidents; mothers wore unwrinkled cotton dresses and espadrilles, kept their makeup fresh and their lips smooth with color.

Although born in Danville, Kentucky, Mom grew up in upstate New York. She disliked being cast as "an outsider" by the social cliques of the Louisville-born debutantes, some of whom had been girlfriends to my father at one time or another before my parents' marriage. Among our friends, she was the only mother who worked. Then again, her fierce independence and supreme devotion to her children kept her in motion, her head proudly raised.

• • •

So, once a week, Anne took up the spatula and fed us supper while Mom was at night school. On these U of L nights, Dad was supposed to get home and watch us; sometimes he did, sometimes he didn't. Even when he was home, my sister, age ten, was the little mom, serving "Anne's macaroni stuff" to Curtie and me (and Dad), making us help clean up all the dishes after supper, pots included. She was stricter than Mom. She didn't let us wriggle out of helping.

For years, I tromped downstairs to find Anne standing over the stove in the kitchen, her pale face stern and closed, her hair more red against the background of pale green cabinets. She was a serious person, not prone to laughter or much conversation. She and I rarely fought. Even though she was only two and a half years older than I, the same age difference as between Curtie and me, she was always much more grown-up.

Curtie and I were the siblings who made a game out of everything. We shared a fiercely competitive nature—it made the games more fun—or sometimes we re-created what we'd watched on television. In our "impossible catches" game we reenacted spectacular football plays, using the edge of the street as the sidelines, our driveway and the neighbors' as the goal lines, raising our own voices to mimic the announcer's and those of the roaring crowd.

He and I fought daily and sent game pieces flying. We would be separated in the car or sent to our rooms, only to conspire silently, to sneak expertly beneath their radar so we could deal one more hand of gin rummy.

But Curtie and I never misbehaved on those nights when Mom was at U of L, when Anne was in charge and we were just three kids in the house by ourselves. We were instinctively cautious, never answering the door—not that anyone ever rang the bell—very careful when taking a phone call. Sometimes Dad *was* home, in which case, we'd all retreat to our rooms, or we might watch television—very quietly—until Mom finally got back.

The true magic of Lakeside surfaced in the summer. Even at a slouchy thirteen, a fluttering feeling—an open sky sort of feeling—filled my belly as I walked through the rod-iron entrance gates for the first outdoor practice of the season. Year after year, swimming in the "lake" felt special, at least at summer's beginning.

The sensation had blown through me the first summer I met the real Lakeside—the-rock-quarry-filled-with-green-water Lakeside—in May 1969.

It being summer, the bubble over the regular pool we used in winter was completely gone. That separate pool was now divided into two sections by a green waterproof chain-link fence—the deep end was used only for the diving team. A false bottom was placed in the other half of the pool, converting it into the largest baby pool in the world.

For the summer the swim team moved into the quarry for practice, to the Olympic lanes in the back. Because fifty meters is a long way, we had to try out for the team all over again. They couldn't have any little kids stopping in the middle, hanging on to the lane line crying for their mama. The lake, with its deep, dark water, was scary looking—you had to show you were brave enough to dive right in.

I followed my parents down the steps. On the brown sidewalks bright yellow words warned: Walk. No Diving. Three Feet.

We walked around to the back left, to where the swimming lanes were, to the very place we would be swimming years later, when the boy would get trapped beneath the pipe and drown. Dad had met us from his insurance office, so he was dressed nicely, in starched khaki pants and a light blue button-down shirt. He had removed his tie. His loafers, as usual, were polished to a Marine shine. He knew a lot more about Lakeside than Mom did, since he'd grown up swimming here. He told us about how he and his big brother, Ches, walked to Lakeside from their house, swam all day, not for the team, but just for fun, then how his brother would tease him on the way home. Dad and his friends dove under water to inspect the old trolley cars that were left by the rock company.

Hoisting the miniature trucks out of the quarry after the company abandoned it was deemed too difficult or too expensive, so the company just left them. As a kid, Dad sank to the bottom and swam along the tracks.

"They were kind of scary, those little cars, sort of like ghosts. They were neat, though, sitting there, frozen in time."

"How big were they?" I asked, looking up at my father with a new interest.

"Oh, I don't know. Not like a car. They were pretty good size. Some of them still had rocks in them."

"Rocks?"

"Yeah."

"Where were they, the trolley cars?"

"Back over there," he said, irritably, gesturing toward the far rocks. "They took 'em out a long time ago, so kids wouldn't mess with them," he said, glaring at me briefly. Then he pulled the silver lighter from his pocket. "When are they going to get this show on the road?"

Anne lined up with kids her age to swim the length of the pool. All the parents and other kids watched from the sidewalk, called the ledge, which was at least twelve feet above the water. The lane lines were the longest I'd ever seen, more than twice the length of those at Big Spring. To make the team, I had to swim the entire fifty meters without stopping or holding on. Anne didn't have any trouble.

My group, the eight and under, was next.

Not scared, I told myself as I waited. I told myself over and over that it didn't matter that I couldn't see the bottom; the water was so dark I couldn't be sure there *was* a bottom. You don't have to swim underwater, I told myself, only on top of it. Mom *and* Dad were standing on the ledge watching me.

Do your best.

It was the longest lap of my life. My prize was a ticket on the McCall-Lakeside train.

I couldn't have known then, at age eight, how strange I'd feel five years later. I didn't know how life turns on you, how your own depths can be as dark and green as a moss-bottom quarry, as a cold river, even, how you hop along as a little kid, never suspecting that vines and currents are growing beneath the surface, climbing toward your ankles, preparing to yank you under.

Lakeside presented a whole new, fascinating world, as thrilling to explore as Mars or Jupiter might be. Curtie and I started in the shallow end, which was ten times bigger than the one at Big Spring. It was accessed by long, narrow steps. The water was freezing. It felt every bit as icy as running into the ocean in early April, as if a thousand sharp spikes poked your skin all at once, and your lungs, for an instant, forgot how to breathe.

Rocks and cliffs made the quarry an uneven circle. The giant shallow end extended around the edge of half the circle, the diving boards and deepest water were in the middle, and the swimming lanes and "raft only" area made up the other half of the circle. We flipped on the aluminum fence wire that separated the shallow end from the deep water a few times with the lifeguard looking right at us. He didn't tell us to stop; it was allowed.

Then we tried to touch the bottom in the deeper water, just on the other side of the fence where it was at least eight feet or more. Moss from the bottom felt slimy and soft, not unlike the muddy edge of the river but not as thick. When we surfaced our fingertips were green.

To get to the diving boards you had to walk on the main pier, which was shaped like a T. On the left were the fifty-meter lanes, on the right the diving boards. Kids yelled to one another, *Watch this!* Then there'd be the regular bump of the board, then the splash.

Beyond the top of the T was the "raft only" area, where sunbathers could float on their own rafts in the sun for hours without threat of being splashed by swimmers. A single lane line separated the "raft only" area from a huge expanse of ten-foot water.

In the deep-water area, a raft painted aquamarine—the same one that we would be staring past years later as they pulled that white, motionless boy from the water—was anchored to the bottom with thick wire cables. Curtie and I raced to it, although I gave him a head start because I was older and faster. We climbed onto it then jumped off. We dove underwater, searching for tracks and trolley cars, of course to no avail.

We floated on our backs, looking at the cliffs. Tree branches curved over the edges and fanned out, waving. I gazed at the cloud formations while I floated, but not for very long because I started feeling dizzy.

That first summer, 1969, I came home from Lakeside and often went straight to Dad's dark cherry dresser in their bedroom, to study the picture of Granddaddy. Although he liked Big Spring, he *loved* Lakeside. *Lakeside is like Granddaddy's legacy to you kids,* Mom often said.

Now I understood that in the picture he was standing on the "T" pier at Lakeside, his arms opened to the high rock cliffs, the dark lake water behind him appearing relaxed and wrinkle-free. His smile was a surprisingly gentle one for such a burly man, as if in that moment a grateful thought was humbling him.

For several summers we swam for both teams, Big Spring and Lakeside, although they occupied two vastly different worlds. As a country club, Big Spring gave people a ritzy place to socialize, to play golf and tennis and drink gin and tonics by the pool. As a neighborhood swim club, where no alcohol was ever allowed, Lakeside gave people a place to go swimming, to escape the wretched humidity of July and August. Lakeside also gave young kids like us a place to plant our Olympic dreams.

It led us to a world that existed outside the East End of Louisville. Kids at Lakeside went to any number of different schools, some public, some Catholic, some private. They lived all over town. They wore a variety of clothes; there was no obvious (though unspoken) dress code like at Big Spring. Not everyone at Lakeside was rich; everyone there just loved to swim.

At first, swimming for both teams was really fun. My sister and brother and I were sort of like celebrities because we were so speedy. With each passing summer, though, as the money problems worsened and my parents' war deepened, we spent less and less time at Big Spring, where we appeared to fit in with the other well-to-do families, but secretly, we knew that we didn't.

With the windows open and the wheezing attic fan vainly trying to create the semblance of a breeze, I worried that the neighbors would hear what was going on downstairs, even though at first my parents were trying to keep it down, I guess because it was so late.

"Curt, where were you?" Mom's voice sounded more like a hiss than a whisper. She'd met him in the living room when he'd shuffled through the front door. "I was worried."

"Yeah I bet you've just been crying in your pillow missing me." His voice sounded hard and mean.

"Where did you go?"

"What difference does it make? You're gonna give me a hard time about it, aren't you? Huh?"

Their voices got harsher but more distant as they moved from the living room into the kitchen. On the way, Dad ran into the corner of the pull-down cherry desk.

"Damn this thing!" he said.

It had to be close to midnight. I put my arm over my face. A familiar, loud thought appeared in my head like a banner flying behind an airplane. *Be strong, don't need people.* I didn't know where the words came from or who sent them; they were just there. I repeated them again and again while the fan wheezed on and the remaining night sounds died away.

4

Shallow-water areas that have poor visibility can be searched by having people link arms or hands and wade in line across the area.

American Red Cross Lifeguarding, p. 166

A dreadful lull descended in the couple of weeks between the end of outdoor swim practice and the beginning of the school year. Our family tended to flounder then, in the overstuffed heat of late August, the train off its tracks and unhelpful.

The summer's stale haze was well entrenched by August, resting in the invisible bowl of the Ohio Valley like black water in a smelly ditch. The air was minimally available for breathing but lethal enough to evoke the need for a pollution index to be invented. Red days were the most dangerous. The bleary-eyed sun would rise in a slow, muted way, then be too weak to burn through the blanket of muck that was the sky.

Despite having spent most of the summer either immersed in water or on my way to one pool or another, by August I had completely lost the sound of the ocean. I couldn't retrieve the smell of sea air, the feel of the sand, or that searing reach of the falling afternoon sun.

"Just close your eyes and picture yourself at the beach," Mom said one day on our way home, in those early days when I was in step with her.

"I can't see it."

"Yes you can. Keep them closed—can't you hear it?"

"No, not really."

"Oh, of course you can. *I* can." She turned onto the road that bordered Seneca Park where a Little League team was practicing football. "Now, have you got it?"

"Yes, ma'am," I said, but really I hadn't. The truth was I couldn't picture anything when I closed my eyes, not myself, not the ocean, not the future—there was only blank, unformed darkness.

August was a strange and wily month anyway, notable only for the return of the Kentucky State Fair. The fair presented our first face-to-face encounter with cows and pigs and chickens and sheep. When we were younger, Curtie, Anne, and I feigned interest in the barns— the real attractions were the rides. Privately, I didn't care much for the fair, even when I was a little kid, although I never could've confessed such a secret. August heat and humidity, sticky bodies, crowds of strangers. The old and dirty rides—and the people who turned them on and off—made me nervous. What if the roller coaster flew off the track? What if the Ferris wheel became stuck or tilted and fell?

I liked tossing a penny to see if I could win a glass or shooting at the plastic ducks as they raced across the back of the tent. Mostly, I liked the cotton candy, which always reminded me of a pink afro hairdo, Mod Squad in spring.

One year we never made it to the fair, at least not on the Sunday when we were scheduled to go. The plan was for Mom to wake up early and go to her third job, doing bookkeeping and paperwork for a friend who owned several Burger Chef restaurants, and whose wife was Mom's best friend. Anne, Curtie, and I were to get ourselves up, dressed, and fed because Dad was taking us to the fair.

On Sundays, Napanee Road was usually empty of activity.

From the set of windows in the living room you could watch for cars passing by, watch to see which cars paused at the stop sign in front of our house and which ones cruised right through it. There was a three-way intersection, with our driveway being where the fourth road would ordinarily be. Of course, Sunday mornings meant sparse traffic altogether.

Dressed in our fair clothes—shorts, short-sleeved shirts, and tennis shoes with socks, no sandals because the fair was a dirty place—Anne, Curtie, and I sat in the living room, waiting for Dad. He was supposed to pick us up at nine-thirty so we could get to the fair when it opened at ten. At first we played Around the World, though we petered out quickly, not wanting to be in the middle of a card game when his green Mustang pulled into the driveway.

We didn't know where he had to go that Sunday morning in August. He wasn't playing golf anymore, we didn't have enough money to do anything at Big Spring, although we still belonged because our stellar swimming helped them win another city championship. Every minute spent on the Big Spring grounds was becoming more uncomfortable, wrought with shame and embarrassment. Mom rarely played tennis there with her friends—she worked on Sunday mornings in the Burger Chef office instead.

When Dad hadn't arrived by ten o'clock, the three of us debated about what to do. We stared at the street, at the mowed yard that belonged to the white house on the other side, at the swollen leaves that hung on the lopsided elm by our driveway. Nothing was moving that morning, nothing at all, as if the earth had found a way to stop spinning and this was where we would remain, transfixed, for eternity.

We decided to call Mom. She told us not to worry, that he must be running late, to *sit tight*. We did that literally. We sat in the living room, beneath the watchful eyes of Grandmother Frances and Mama T. Curtie and I moved from the small upholstered couch to the floor to play a card game of Concentration. The pale aqua-colored carpet was worn in a path between the front door and the kitchen but in the middle of the room where we were it was less thin. Anne kept her seat in the antique chair by the bookshelves.

We didn't dare leave the living room to go watch television in the den—not that anything was on except preachers. We didn't want to risk making Dad have to wait a second. We wanted to be out the door as soon as we saw his car pull into the short driveway. Every car coming down the street from the direction of Chenoweth Lane was at first his—we'd step to the window, ready to race out the door, only to slouch at the white van running the stop sign, or the dark red Buick driven by older people dressed for church. They stopped at the sign then proceeded slowly forward.

Mom called once to check on us; we were still in our ready-alert posture. But something cracked between us after that. My sister and brother and I never talked about what was happening in our family—about Dad, who was so prone to grumpiness or outright yelling, about Mom, who was working and worrying so hard her hands sometimes shook, or about that pain in her neck and arm that came more and more often. We never wondered aloud to each other if other families lived this way, with constant concern over what might happen, over who might cry or yell next, over whether we'd have enough money to pay the bills and buy groceries. Or in thinking of the ghosts, of who might die, and when.

But that day, sitting together in the living room for hours like that alone, fear caught hold of us and yanked. Tears quickly took over any conversation we might've started. We convinced ourselves that Dad wasn't coming home, that he'd left us for good. *He's gone.* Anne's freckles merged together as she cried, anguish and fatigue pulling her mouth into a frown. Her shoulders shook even as she put her arms around Curtie and me. We were hugging each other, standing in the middle of the room, crying fragments like "Where is he?" "What happens now?" "Maybe he's never coming back."

That might've been the first time I recognized the hollowed sadness I would come to associate with my sister. She usually kept it hidden beneath a razor-quick temper, the edge of which was best avoided at all costs. Anne always knew more than I—seeing her so upset, and Curtie all crinkled up too, were the reasons for my tears, much more than the thought of Dad never coming home again.

I didn't care about him—no, I *hated* him. But I was crying for my brother and sister, because they cared, because we were the five of us and we were all we had. *We have to stick together—we're all we've got.* For some unknowable reason we needed Dad, or at least, we needed not to lose him.

He never did show up to take us to the fair that day. Mom called at some point and told us she'd come home soon and make us lunch. We shielded her from our collective tears, acting like missing the fair wasn't *that* big of a deal. The sandwiches she made tasted uncommonly good, the perfect balance of extra peanut butter and a thin layer of jelly. She even let us open a new bag of potato chips.

We went on with our day after that. Still, even though we got to go swimming at Lakeside for fun, no team practice, the thick and humid August day progressed slower than most, made longer by the morning's broken hope.

The days kept packing into each other, as if the house actually was shrinking from the growth of our burgeoning adolescent bodies. At sixteen, Anne's ferocity was unstoppable—a match to the flammable liquid that my father couldn't seem to get enough of. And by thirteen, I'd already fallen over that treacherous cliff of puberty. An early bloomer, I'd gotten the bloody shove toward adulthood the year before. Navigating the murky waters of being a teenager made my deep sense of deficiency darken and grow.

Fear still ruled my every decision. Fear of getting in trouble, of displeasing my mother, of being seen as a problem by anyone, fear—already tangled and rooted deeply—of not being *good enough*. I never spoke of that fear. Against its force I bowed my head, I acquiesced, I shut up.

The safest route was to stay bound to my sister's demands, and for my entire life, until I was thirteen, whatever she told me to do, I did. Stone-faced, all-knowing Anne lived the privilege of age; she wore her years like weapons.

Go get my shoes. Move, I'm sitting there. Dry every dish. Clean the shelf in the gerbil cage.

She never physically beat me—she didn't have to—she owned me.

Yet, a day came in our lives when this indentured servitude ended, a day when I startled both of us by being a person with an actual voice.

The moment started like the millions before it. I was walking downstairs from my room since it was time to go somewhere—always time to go somewhere. Anne was slouched in our great-aunt's chair with an open book in her lap. *We're leaving in three minutes.* She and I both recognized that tone of commanding readiness, ringed with hurry, in Mom's voice.

The voice traveled out of the kitchen, through the dining room, into the gaze between my sister and me.

"Go upstairs and get my shoes," Anne said.

Behind her, forgotten books waited on the shelves for attention that never seemed in large supply. To my left, Dad's mom, Frances, watched from the wall, her eyes never fully closing. My sister was named after her—Anne Frances. Supposedly they looked alike. My sister inherited the same high cheekbones that suggested a Native American heritage.

I felt Grandmother watching us, but the attention she offered wasn't the kind I needed. Her steady gaze silently judged my decisions. If she heard all the yelling in the house, her expression never changed. She never helped—she didn't have to—she was dead.

"I said go get my shoes," Anne said again, glaring.

I knew my sister as "the pretty one." I was "the athletic one." Lines get carved in granite when you live as we did, surrounded by still-life pictures of needed dead people, amidst the hot wires of our mother's worry and the volcanic bubbling of our father's anger.

Oxygen was at times in short supply. Outside, the air crowded into the Ohio Valley, packing in tight and close. The late-summer sky looked peaked with fever.

I might've been standing there for minutes—hours—holding my sister's stare.

"No," I said.

"We're leaving in *two* minutes," boomed Mom's voice from her bedroom. Anywhere in the house you could hear my mother's voice, measure its tone, gauge your own pace—we were now in code alert.

Anne's authoritative scowl deepened. Her tough, serious eyes drilled holes straight into my lungs, pulling at the air I was keeping there for myself.

"Don't be stupid. Go get my shoes *right now.*"

My feet refused movement. For the first time in my life I was aware of being uniquely alive, of being a separate person, of being a "me."

"No." My voice jiggled a little. "I—don't have to do everything you say." Something inside tugged hard for me to turn my head, to look down and apologize and race up the stairs to find her tennis shoes before Mom came in the room.

But the voice that hijacked my vocal cords refused to recite the scripted lines. This voice—and my feet—teamed up to ad lib, to change the course of my life forever. At the edge of my vision I glimpsed a movement. Was Grandmother grinning in the portrait— or scowling?

I didn't look because I was still staring at my sister. I started grinning in that giddy way I have when something serious and important is taking place.

"I'm giving you one more chance. Get moving."

"I don't have to," I said with something approaching bona fide defiance.

"Fine," she said with a sudden body jump. In a single giant motion she stood over me, a red tower of glare and disgust. I was taking a step backward.

"See if I *ever* do *anything* for you . . . *ever again!*"

A wind kicked me as she passed by, as if she'd snatched the last straggling molecules of oxygen. I was a defector, a scab, an idiot who gave up her only guide out of the turbulent and unmarked ocean waters. I stood alone in the living room sea, the heightened vibration of anticipation working on my belly. For a single nanosecond of uncommon terror, I didn't know what to do.

"Let's go, we'll be late," Mom was saying as she rushed to her purse that always sat on the chair by the door.

I fell in line behind my little brother, not countering his claim of the front seat. I heard big feet clomping down the steps behind me in bigger shoes. They walked over my shoulders, pushing my independence into the ground like a flicked cigarette butt. I felt her stony face beside me in the backseat of the car. She looked out the window. I felt torn apart inside. I had deepened the scowl on her face. She wouldn't acknowledge my existence when we sat in the car. Mom backed out of the driveway. I would've given Anne the air in my lungs in that moment, just for her to indicate that it was okay, that she wasn't mad at me anymore. Nothing.

I was still in ambivalent disbelief, looking at the bushy green trees lining Chenoweth Lane, at the whitewashed fence, at the cars passing in the other lane, still reliving in my head one of the most important, extraordinary moments of my life. I'd challenged Red-Storm Rising and survived.

I learned to say no to Anne, but saying no to Mom was unthinkable. Anne and I barely talked to each other anyway—it's as if we lived along parallel orbits. She was busy living her teenage life, going to girl club "sorority" meetings, selling doughnuts on Saturday mornings, washing cars with the teenage youth group, listening to blaring music in her room with the door closed. No longer her servant, I didn't exist in her eyes.

But Mom was a different story altogether, she talked to me all the time, and I listened. The four of us had our own schedule, and it never troubled me when Dad wasn't home. There was less yelling and generally more predictable ease. Sometimes Mom's face would crinkle up with worry. She got tired of not knowing where he was or if he'd be home for dinner, or if he was even *alive*, although she didn't *say* that—then she'd brood over what she should do in terms of finding him. He didn't go to the Big Spring clubhouse anymore, since we'd been dropped from their membership—bills still outstanding—so he frequented other, less exclusive bars.

I was nine when Mom came in my room and told me we had to go run an errand. I knew what it was without her saying; there was nothing to do but follow her.

She drove the station wagon hunched forward in her posture of combat—jaw set, anguished squint to her eyes. Smoke from her cigarette tarried around her head, making her face strangely more clear than less so. It was a cold Saturday, late afternoon.

We took the back way to Patrick's, down St. Matthews Avenue, where in the summer a canopy of oak and maple trees shaded the street. But the leaves were mostly dead now, fallen and raked and neatly bagged. Without leaves, the trunks and limbs stood vulnerable and exposed to every staring eye; without leaves the trees might've been dead, too. The usual blankets of unformed clouds crowded into the sky, sealing it against all but the weakest sunlight. Rain wasn't falling, but as usual, its possibility hovered just above the trees.

I gripped the door handle with my nine-year-old fingers as Mom pulled the green Pontiac into the gravel parking lot, next to Dad's green mustang. The car broke the little rocks with its weight. Against my own intentions of feigned nonchalance, I peeked at the door of the one-story building. It looked more like a cave than a bar. Then again, not every bar was as plush as the clubhouse at Big Spring.

"Go in and tell your father to come home."

There was nowhere for me to hide, no Houdini-like trapdoor through which to crawl.

"Go on," she said. "He'll listen to you."

"Yes, ma'am," I said, pushing the obstinate car door hard with my shoulder.

Once inside I couldn't see anything. The place was ten times darker than a movie theater. Offensive odors met me at the entrance. Frightening noises collided above my head. Something moved wildly inside me, like a captured animal pacing and banging the smallness of its cage. My eyes focused on scary, snickering men with stubby beards. Smoke framed their red faces and I thought for an instant about the spooky kind of ghosts.

At first I didn't see my father, since he wasn't sitting on any of the bar stools. But this place had booths like a restaurant and in the back men were playing pool. He was in one of the booths on the right.

I walked up to him but he didn't notice me at first.

"Dad, Mom told me to tell you to come home," I said, trying to speak up.

He turned to me without surprise registering on his face. He was very far away in the way his eyes stayed flat and glassy. He was leaning on his elbows but he didn't seem as big as he did at home.

"Is she outside?"

I nodded.

His mouth turned up on one side and he frowned at the grown-up drink in front of him. It was about half full.

"Tell her I'll be home in a minute," he said, his tone more tired than blustery.

"Yes, sir." I turned around quickly to make my way toward the promise of light that was the front door. It started disappearing, though, in the burning clutch of whiskey. Voices hurled incoherent words into the sea of smoky haze. I dodged them, the best I could, and the stares that crawled all over my body. Coarse laughter rubbed against me as I reached for the door, still holding my breath.

"He said he'll be home in a minute," I said as I closed the car door, careful not to slam it, but shutting it a little harder than usual.

"I'm sorry to make you go in there," she said.

"I know." I looked out the window at the cement wall of sky. "It's okay."

One unspoken benefit of becoming a teenager was that Mom no longer asked me to do that dreariest of favors for her. In a feat of parallel living, and as testimony to the silencing nature of denial, I never knew Anne or Curtie went into Patrick's and they never knew I did—we just each took our turns according to who Mom quietly asked.

Moving into the bubble for practice in September didn't bother me as much as it had when I was little, maybe because by eighth grade, confusion was descending from any number of fronts, and my body was changing more than seemed necessary or even possible.

Because of my speed, I was grouped with kids who were older than me. The older girls, including my sister, didn't treat me like a tag-along, although I kept pretty quiet, really, or I'd goof around in an attempt to be entertaining. I was always aware of my tentative status as the youngest, that at any moment the big kids could roll their eyes at my immaturity and toss me aside like a wet towel. As long as they liked me, as long as I made no fuss or problem, as long as I listened to them, they'd let me hang around.

As the season progressed, the weather (and our mom) mandated that we change clothes after practice. The locker room was a small, dark, musty place. A single wooden bench ran down the center with stall-like dressing areas on either side of it. Stiff, red curtains of cardboard thickness hung on skinny poles, so a person could change in privacy if she wanted to. Most of the older girls took off their bathing suits and crowded into one of the three shower stalls to wash their hair. I could never take my bathing suit off in front of the others or walk around naked like so many of them did. If I had to wash my hair, which I usually didn't because I preferred to wash it at home, I'd leave my bathing suit on.

But in colder weather, Mom made us change out of our wet suits, rather than just throw clothes on over them—*or else you'll catch pneumonia*. Her wrath, rare as it was, could be scalding. The fear of accidentally getting sick, the guilt of inadvertently causing the last crack that would send her to Our Lady of Peace, simply wasn't worth the risk. Mom wasn't a bomb like Dad, she was more of a taut balloon, one wrong edge and smack, she might explode—then disappear.

Sometimes I took my chances against illness anyway, since I hated changing in the locker room that much. If I had to change, I'd step into one of the stalls, turn my back toward the opening, pull my bathing suit straps down, and throw on my bra and shirt. Then I'd do the bottom half. I didn't draw the curtain, because that would elicit teasing.

The time when one of the older girls grabbed my bra and threw it around the locker room was humiliating enough. She had large breasts and shook them from side to side, saying something about my bra fitting her. She didn't mean to be cruel; she'd always been nice to me. I think the older girls were just trying to coax me out of the stall, but I didn't like how big my body was. Even though I wore a bathing suit much of the time, I tried to ignore how big my breasts were getting, how my hips were widening, how my body was shifting itself into fat curves. I laughed good-naturedly while keeping my towel wrapped around my naked body until one of my friends tossed the bra to me. I dressed quickly, rubbed my bushy hair with the towel, put on my hat, grabbed my bag, and hurried out of the bubble, trying not to cry as I walked into the biting, damp air to wait for my ride.

5

When attempting to assist a victim, every
rescuer, even a trained lifeguard, must
maintain a position of safety.

American Red Cross Lifeguarding, p. 113

Being an official teenager didn't change our sleeping arrangements; Mom still slept in the extra twin bed in my room. A couple of years earlier, when Dad starting coming home later and later, she'd wake up, they'd spit darts at each other, she'd cry. It all interfered too much with her being able to get up early and get ready for school. It could be midnight or later and he'd be stumbling around downstairs, the silver tray rattling like a nagging mother, his own mother's portrait deathly silent on the living room wall.

Book in hand, Mom would climb the stairs in her nightgown and get into the other twin bed. We never talked much when she was reading and I was trying to fall asleep. It wasn't right that she was up there in the first place and we both knew it.

The beds in my room were arranged in an L shape, one against the wall, the other beneath the set of double windows. Between the beds stood a floor lamp; its cheap aqua blue metal head resembled the dome of a miniature hairdryer at the salon. It would get hot so quickly that turning it off required dexterous fingers to avoid getting burned. The bulb was painfully bright. It let off that sickly buzzing sound of unharnessed heat, of too much voltage for its small wiring. After a few minutes, a faint burning odor would emanate from its metal dome, the smell similar to when a summer bug lands on a light and gets sizzled.

I hated that light. It intruded into my private darkness, into the time that had once been mine alone. At night when I was ready to sleep and Mom was in the next bed, reading, I would turn my back, face to the wall, and still the light crashed through my thin eyelids, making the interminable day extend. I wanted to sleep, to be oblivious, to be alone.

In the darkness I could hear rain falling against the windows and roof. The constant patter comforted me. The reading light blotted out those sounds somehow, attracting instead my peskiest thoughts—what I should've said, what I should've done. They darted around in my head like a frenzy of biting gnats. The light kept the day endlessly alive, the day I wanted to be gone so the next one would hurry on through, until the one day would come when I would be free.

For awhile, I assumed everyone was like that, that it was normal to want so desperately to get to the future, to be on your own, where freedom was freedom and no further definition was needed.

"Oh, Cathy, you were born twenty-one," my mother's friend said once, when I inquired why they let me sit at the table with them, listening to their talk of grown-up problems, their complaints about their husbands, their worries about their kids. When she said that, I felt proud, taller.

"I wish I was twenty-one," I said in response.

"Oh, no. Don't ever wish your life away."

Shame lowered my head, shame disguised as a smile meant to please. I reached for another cracker and the small knife protruding from the dish of soft cheese. But I shut up after that, kept the counting of days to myself.

When you keep moving, you notice less. Maybe that's why the light at night bothered me so much. I was slowed way down in my skinny bed, interrupted from the dark descent into sleep. Mom wasn't supposed to be sleeping in my room. Parents shared a bedroom with each other and kids had their own rooms, or if they had to share, like on *The Brady Bunch*, then they shared with the other kids in the family.

Not that I could blame Mom for *not* wanting to occupy the same bedroom as Dad. It's just that she wasn't supposed to be sleeping upstairs, in *my* room, even though mine was the only room with two beds, and it was the biggest.

Finally that delicious moment would come, when the light blackened, when sleep descended like a guardian angel and blessed me with a brief route of escape.

Too quickly, though, a noise would jolt the room like an electric current. It took a moment to orient, to recognize the song, or sometimes—often—a blabbering disc jockey. Mom would vault out of bed and disappear into the hall, the darkness there instantly broken by the bathroom light. My sister's door across the hall remained closed.

Mom got up earlier than we did. I'd linger in those dreamy moments of partial darkness, snatching a handful of solitude before the hooks and demands of the day located me. Just as quickly, the solitude slid away like water from a fist. Mom's voice would startle me alert, traveling as it so expertly did from the bathroom to my eardrums at quantum speed.

"Cathy, is it raining?"

"I don't know," I'd mumble, hopping over to the other bed that she'd already made silently in the dark, putting my face against the glass, trying to see if drops were clinging to it. The light from the bathroom turned the window into a mirror, and all I could see was my puffy morning face, the face that looked too much like a boy's.

"I can't tell. They haven't said," I'd say, referring to the radio, backing quickly away from the window mirror. I'd lumber into the bathroom then, while she was putting on her makeup. We did that in our family, too, we shared bathrooms, at the same time.

"Go downstairs and see," she'd order. Not in a mean way, but in her matter-of-fact sergeant way. She was already fully entrenched in her day, planning all the things she had to do, the errands she needed to run after school, which car pool she was driving—whether it was raining or not had to be figured into the mix. It was not a detail she could reliably account for ahead of time, not in Louisville, and my mom needed to know as much as possible what was going to happen and when. It was our job—my brother and sister's and mine—to help her not have to worry so much.

I'd trudge down the steps and open the front door, amazed at how quiet the downstairs was, and the street outside, too. Some mornings there was a softness to the air, as if it was passing through on its way to find a balmy coast somewhere. Other mornings there was a gripping chill, one that took a moment to recognize because it so contrasted with the warm bed I'd just left. Later in the year and rarely, very very rarely, I'd throw my arms open to the sky then race upstairs and report that it was *snowing*.

Many days, though, the monotonous report came in the same. Wet. In the darkness, the blacktop glistened beneath the blurry streetlight like a secret runway. Wishing for something to be different, for someplace new to go, for the opportunity to fly away only made me sad. I'd walk back upstairs, report my weather observation, then sit on the bed—the peppy disc jockey still blabbing—until Mom was finished in the bathroom. Another day of same had begun.

Dad didn't get out of bed in the morning anymore. He came in late and was still asleep when we ate our Rice Krispies and left for school. It's not an exaggeration to say we didn't see much of him. At night, Mom would leave dinner for him if he was late—all he had to do was heat it up. She was a master of fixing suppers on different schedules; since Anne now had the latest swim practice, she didn't get home until eight o'clock at night.

One time, the smell of smoke woke me. I was confused and disoriented in the dark, because I wasn't sure if I was asleep and dreaming or awake and smelling the bedside lamp. I don't know that I even reached for my glasses. Instead, I lay there, listening, my mother breathing roughly in the bed next to mine. She snored, just loudly enough to have bothered me on any other night, to make enough of an irritating sound that falling back to sleep would prove maddening. I didn't feel marred by her snoring on this night; my heart was pounding too wildly.

I listened with the tuned ear of an expert musician. Danger, or the potential of a problem, can do that. I listened for my father's heavy footsteps, to see if he was somewhere downstairs but I heard nothing, not even the rattling silver tray.

The streetlights and the neighbor's floodlight were out, meaning it must've been well past midnight. I listened to the darkness; only the usual house creaks answered—and the undeniable, unavoidable, unmistakable odor of smoke. I wasn't sure what I should do. Maybe I was imagining the whole thing, maybe the ghosts really were sharing a drink and a cigarette in the dining room downstairs.

The smoke odor was too strong to ignore.

"Mom," I said, too softly to be heard. Waking Mom up from sleep was not a good thing to do since sleep was literally the only force that made her motion stop. Leaning off my bed, I could barely reach her without having to get up completely.

"*Mom*," I said again, this time with a more forceful push.

"Huh, what—what is it?" She was irritated with me.

"I smell smoke."

"What!" She glared at me as if I'd done something wrong. "Oh *God*." She was out of the bed in a single jump. Her nightgown puffed behind her like a wind was blowing and in the strange light she could've been a ghost. *"Stay put,"* she yelled as she flew down the stairs.

I sat at my post on the top step, listening. The oven door banged open and Mom started screaming. With that, I was at the kitchen door, standing mostly in the hall, out of the way, but still on alert in case things got out of hand.

Smoke rushed into the small kitchen like circling darts of anger that had no target on which to focus. The smoke appeared strangely indecisive, squirmy even, and thick.

"You could've burned the house down!" She had reached mitted hands into the oven and grabbed the baking sheet with the smoldering black lump on it. Then she dropped it onto the range top. *"What is wrong with you?!"*

My father had stumbled in from the den. He was oddly well dressed, although his white shirt was badly wrinkled and his face was puffy and red.

"I must've fallen asleep," he said.

Mom had switched on the pitiful fan above the range, but it did little to dissipate the smoke. Even though it was freezing outside, she opened the tricky kitchen window, the one that could break your hand if you weren't quick to prop it up with the stick.

"I was just heating up the steak you left for me," he said, sounding less remorseful and more ready to argue.

"Well, *don't*——" she said, strangely, turning just then, seeing me. "You could've killed us, Curt," she said quietly, her voice full of an odd and incredulous wonder. I turned around as she came toward me and raced up the steps.

The next morning the clock radio went off as usual. No rain, just another day. We didn't talk about the night. For the first time I was glad we kept the fire escape ladder under the bed in my room. Until then, a real fire never seemed even a remote possibility. *You never know what might happen, or when.*

• • •

Charged events bubbled up like that—scouting the bar for Dad, smoke filling the kitchen in the middle of the night, Mom's fingers thin and shaking as they counted and recounted the bills in her wallet that were inexplicably disappearing. A crisis would erupt the surface, then everything would turn smooth again, like walking on a wavy fun house floor that suddenly is flat, only you know better than to trust it because at any moment it might start undulating again.

We were on our way through the park when Mom said we weren't going to have much of a Christmas this year. At first I was confused; it was only September.

"It's okay, Mom," I said, reaching for the radio. "We don't need anything." A good song came on and I started singing to it softly.

She kept her focus on the road and didn't say anything else but I could hear her thoughts popping like fresh kindling. Outside the breeze blew erratically through leaves that were starting to crisp up. A field hockey team was doing sprints. I didn't want to think about Christmas; it made me remember what happened last year.

When we were little kids Christmas could be counted on to deliver a certain set of rituals and expectations. It resembled the ocean in that way, something you could count on as always being there. For us, it was also a season of contrasts.

We baked and iced and devoured Christmas cookies, except for the three we left for Santa on Christmas Eve, along with a potato for Rudolph. Like other families, we went to church, squirming with anticipation but trying our best to be good.

We also went together as a family to select a Christmas tree. Every year we dressed in old clothes so the seller would give my parents a better deal, and drove downtown to the Haymarket. We were

supposed to not look rich, which was the same as appearing poor—
even though we'd just driven from the manicured rolling hills of the
East End, past mansions of bricks and columns and candlelights
placed in each of twenty windows.

Brownsboro Road snaked its way into the city of Louisville, but
in the span of less than a mile, the mansions shrunk to cottage
houses, much smaller than ours, then closer to downtown they
turned into skinny, so-called shotgun row houses. These houses had
tiny windows with even tinier red and green lights, if they had lights
at all. Many of the houses displayed no wreaths or Christmas trees
or much that resembled the life we lived on Napanee. As I stared at
the bare houses, most of which seemed too cold and dark to be
homes, I knew the people inside were the real kind of poor.

These tree-buying nights marked the official beginning of the
Christmas season. It was usually fun, since my father was in a chipper
mood and we kids were taking hold of the renewed hope that Christmas promises. He became more of a person and a father then—
helpful and funny. He drove and when we got home, he carried the
tree to the back patio and placed it in a bucket. On the weekend, he'd
set it up in the living room, pour another bourbon, then commence
with the grand challenge of wrapping its branches with lights.

Every year, even when the only words between my parents had
been hisses and bickers—or that icy silence that never lasted
long—Christmas shifted all of us a little. Mom unloaded decorations from the attic (with our help) and Dad placed the lights on
the tree. Sometimes his happy mood would start to bend into frustration, and cuss words would ricochet off the walls. It was a time to
stay away from the living room. Eventually he would call us in, lean
his tall frame behind the tree, and bing! the lights would turn on.

Anne and Curtie and I would smile and coo readily at his
achievement, already moving toward the boxes of ornaments, which

were our job to hang. But invariably my father would glance at my mother—her praise was more important to him than air—and usually she said it looked nice.

These were odd blips of full family unity, these tree-decorating nights, and arguments between my parents rarely erupted into full-gauge warfare. We actually laughed and sang along to Burl Ives and the Ray Conniff Singers. Dad might eventually slip into the den and Mom eventually into the kitchen, but for awhile we were all there, in the living room, if not laughing then at least no one was yelling or crying, seeing a glimpse of the way our family could be, was *supposed to be*.

Anne became the unofficial director when my parents left the room. She instructed Curtie and me on where to place each ornament. If I hung one that was blocking another, she'd be on my mistake immediately. I obliged her and repositioned the glittery red ball or the smiling snowman, often checking back with her to see if where I moved it was okay. There was a right—and perfect—way to do everything, even down to placing ornaments.

While we were all in the living room together, Mom would unwrap "the little man" and my parents would share a moment of memory. They gazed at each other in a rare exchange of affection. For a moment Mom appeared girlish and vulnerable and Dad dropped his mask of false entitlement. The little Christmas man emerging again from his long slumber always pulled their eyes to each other's.

"Remember when we got him?"

"At Camp Lejune."

"That's right."

Dad would hold the little man with a gentle sensitivity, remembering. Then something would close over his face, a thought or a shadow, and he'd hand the man back to Mom and turn away, sometimes walking into the den, or into the kitchen first to make a drink.

Mom would gaze at the decoration, too, the way a mother looks longingly at a newborn baby.

The little man was a plump, fair-skinned elf, with soft yellow hair for a beard, a long nose, and pointy ears. Every Christmas season he stayed in my parents' bathroom on the back of the toilet, so we wouldn't play with him or break him.

On Christmas morning it was always a big moment when Mom opened her present from Dad. He would stand on one foot, then the other, anxious as a boy whose mother is opening his report card. Dad could be boyish, innocent and trusting, hopeful. He smelled of cigarette smoke, shifting as he did, while she unwrapped the big red box with the huge frilly bow. He'd gone to Tweed and Tartan, which was a small, rich-lady boutique in St. Matthews. The box gave away the store.

Oh, Curt, what have you done? Dread mixed with excitement in her voice. Everyone in the room knew we had no money for things from Tweed and Tartan. From the box would be lifted a lovely red coat, or a flimsy silk blouse, or a soft Lanz nightgown. He missed in pleasing her more often than he scored, so eventually, he asked us for gift ideas; we'd always say—*Get her a new nightgown, hers has holes in the elbows,* and he would. Whatever the present (except the nightgowns and sometimes even those), Mom would try to act as if she liked it; usually she didn't—it somehow wasn't right—or else the worry of receiving the bill would come over her. She'd say thank-you and hug him stiffly, but it was not the response he wanted.

Last year, though, when I was twelve, Christmas barely resembled itself. By Christmas Eve, winter had laid bare Louisville's most dismal face. Clouds gathered in clumps in the Ohio Valley, turning the sky to ash. It was a gray day begging for a catharsis, for a hard rain at least, or best of all a big-flaked snowfall. But the clouds refused. The temperature stalled just above freezing, in that space of limbo and nondefinition. The moisture wasn't snow or rain or sleet, it was just something ill defined and ugly. There was nothing compelling about being outside except for the break it offered from being inside.

We hadn't seen Dad all day, which wasn't completely unusual on Christmas Eve day, since he was one of the world's greatest procrastinators. He usually made it to Tweed and Tartan to get Mom's present just before they closed.

Mom said the bars shut their doors at six, so he should be home when we got back from church, but he wasn't. That's when the night started moving in slow motion. The four of us milled around, singing along for awhile with Burl. Curtie and I played hand after hand of gin rummy, switched to crazy eights, then we talked Anne into playing Around the World. It was a strange night indeed if Anne was playing cards with us.

Dad's absence kept getting bigger. Mom said we could open the presents her students had given her from school, so we took our time trying to focus on the gifts and not on the black hole taking over the house. By nine o'clock, Mom called a couple of people to see if Dad had stopped by, or if they'd seen him somewhere. No one could offer much help.

Fear loves a void; it moves in and takes over. The four of us slowly descended into its swirl, not unlike that time when Dad never showed up for the fair, except this felt much bigger. We vacillated between thinking he'd left for good and being terrified that his car was coiled around a tree somewhere. Mom paced and voiced angry threats, then she'd be silent for awhile, sitting on the love seat in the living room, staring at the fire or the decorated tree. Anne and I exchanged silent glances. Grandmother Frances loomed over all of us from the mantel. Mama T had been pushed to the back of the desk to make room for a clump of greens and pinecones. Mom's worry, and the ghosts, amplified the room's silence. I didn't know what *to do*.

"I hear a car," Anne said, quickly. She hurried over to the edge of the curtain. We'd had a few false alarms over the course of the evening. "It's him!" she said, in a voice that made her seem younger than fifteen.

"Okay," Mom said, staying on the small couch, "just act like everything's fine."

The minutes he stayed in the driveway seemed like hours. I dealt the cards so it would look like Curtie and I were acting normal—we wordlessly knew not to play a real hand, to just hold the cards and pretend. From where I sat on the floor I could see the biggest bare spot in the tree. The stockings Mom had knitted for each of us when we were born hung empty on the screen in front of the fire-place. Mine was accidentally longer than the other two, a fact I felt both grateful and guilty about.

There was a moment when everything seemed wildly comical and I felt the urge to burst into a grin. We were the props in a play, the scenery of a cardboard family, picture perfect.

Dad banged gracelessly through the front door.

"Hello," he said, his face bright red and scarred with that defensive expression he so often wore. His eyes were bloodshot. "Sorry I'm late," he said, as if nothing had happened, as if it wasn't ten o'clock on Christmas Eve, and we weren't his wife and kids but more distant relatives awaiting his arrival from out of town.

"Where . . . have you *been?*" Mom said, disregarding her own plan to act like everything was fine.

"I got held up."

"Curt." She shook her head with disbelief or disgust, something. "It's Christmas Eve."

"I know what day it is, *Margaret Anne.* You treat me like I'm a damn *idiot.*"

Mom started to stand, then sat back down on the little plaid couch. Dad was shuffling around the crowded room. His heavy steps made the Christmas tree ornaments shake. Their voices were lightning; we sat still as stones. He pulled a box from beneath his coat and slammed it onto the fragile antique coffee table.

"Tweed and Tartan was closed," he said, acting like that was somehow Mom's fault. It was a box of Whitman Sampler chocolates, similar to one of the school gifts we'd opened a few hours before. That's what he gave Mom for Christmas; her one special gift from him was candy he'd bought at the drugstore down the street. I felt like throwing up but I couldn't move.

Then he stormed out of the door. He never even took off his overcoat.

We stared at each other, the four of us, trying to figure out what was happening, what we were *supposed to do*. We three kids huddled by the window to spy on him, to see which direction he drove away so we could follow him. The streets were empty on Christmas Eve, most people inside their warm homes, sipping drinks and laughing, listening to music, having fun. He was just sitting in the car. Mom was on the couch crying. We alternated posts, hugging her, watching him.

Eventually she figured out that he didn't have anywhere to go; nor did he have any money, and though she was ticked off, underneath we could tell she was relieved. I was simply tired and confused.

On Christmas morning we all acted like nothing had happened. We were appreciative of the presents Mom had scraped together to buy for us, clothes and a new basketball. She tagged each present with "Love, Mom and Dad."

Dad sat quietly in his robe with his legs crossed. His face was pockmarked with gray places, like he'd slept with it mashed between two rocks.

Even if Mom was already there, Christmas was too far in the future for me to think about. There was no telling what might happen between now and then. As the leaves started turning toward their autumnal death, we just kept swimming and swimming, through an ever murkier river of quicksand.

We were leaving Dad in a way, or maybe he was leaving us. *We have to stick together—we're all we've got.* We were five people rowing a tiny lifeboat in the middle of the ocean, no land in sight. Anne, Curtie, and I were doing what we could, paddling and paddling, swimming those laps up and back every day, year after year. Mom was paddling and steering and bailing the water that was seeping into the too small boat. Dad was creating a wake, a drag, falling out, sinking—he was taking on water for all of us, and as a family, we were drowning.

Thoughts of that drowning boy still came to me when I went through the Lakeside gates for practice. I wondered if a moment came when his writhing ceased, when defeat delivered some sort of calm to him. Maybe his thoughts lost their panic and were replaced by a soothing sense of release. Maybe his mind turned blank, like the screen at the end of a movie. It was one of those questions that lacked a certain answer.

6

Two lifeguards may be needed to assist a
very large or nonbuoyant victim.

American Red Cross Lifeguarding, p.142

By 1974, we might've stepped over Dad had he passed out on
the living room floor, which he never did. He was our proverbial ele-
phant, though. As such, he preferred being home when we were
gone and being away (or asleep) when we were home.

It meant that the four of us could spin on our own train-schedule
track, whooshing in and out of the station without *routine* delays.
Occasionally, during these smooth-tracked days, Mom would invite
a born-twenty-one opinion from me—a comment or idea I might
have that pertained to the predicament that was our life.

Most often, it worked best between us when Mom talked and I
listened. She'd be putting on makeup or folding clothes or browning
hamburger. I'd sit on the closed toilet seat in the bathroom upstairs,
listening to her ideas about what to do about Dad, or how we were
going to pay the electric bill or if Lakeside would let us pay our
team dues a few weeks late.

One Saturday afternoon Mom came upstairs to talk with me. It was
unusual that she wasn't carrying a basket of clothes or anything in
her slender, veined hands.

Through the open windows cooler autumn air danced into the

room. It was a day of low humidity, one of those beautiful days that could erase the leftover muck of summer. Central air-conditioning existed in the realm of bigger houses located across Brownsboro Road, among the family dreams that perpetually turned as black as unpolished silver. When autumn arrived, though, all complaints of sweating in bed at night died away, at least for another year.

I sat up as Mom came in the room; her demeanor was that quiet, serious kind. This didn't feel like more of our usual running conversation but something bigger, more deliberate, I could tell by the uncertainty shaping itself around her eyes. *The only difference between you and me is about twenty-five years.* I was thirteen; she was thirty-nine.

"I need to talk to you," she said, sitting down on the other bed. I dismissed being in some kind of trouble because I would've already heard about it. Still, I felt a moment of awkwardness, since I was on the bed underneath the window, the one she slept in at night, and she was sitting on the bed by the wall, where I usually slept. She always napped downstairs, though, so I knew she didn't want me to move, I just wasn't sure if I should or not.

"Okay."

The waves in her hair gave her a rumpled, tired appearance. She was very thin and with her eyes narrowed, the anguish and worry were unmistakable. I noticed a familiar fist in my belly.

"I've been thinking a lot about this. What would you think . . ." She gazed out the window for a blank moment, then blinked. Her eyes were such a light brown they could seem green, especially in afternoon light like this.

"What would you think—if I—divorced you father?"

Outside the breeze became as motionless as death. The breeze might've been in my imagination all along. This was a moment, *the* moment, when I was supposed to know the right thing to say. Her face was unguarded in a way that scared me, as if underneath the worry lines and determined frowns, she was just a girl herself, just as confused by the world, just as longing and misplaced in her own life. *The only difference between you and me is about twenty-five years.*

"I think we'd be fine without him."

Her eyes and mouth squinted as if startled. They were red rimmed, like she'd been crying, but that could've been left over from the night before.

"You deserve to be happy, Mom."

She turned away, toward that faraway place that sometimes turned her head, as if she could hear a song in the distance or some-one whistling while they were coming up the walk. It was the kind of talk she needed to have with one of the ghosts, but all she had was me and my sister; my brother was too young to understand such things.

"He's just not coming home until so late; he hasn't made any money. He's so cross and angry all the time. He's lying to me. I just can't count on him for anything."

"You don't have to convince me, Mom—I hate him."

"No, you don't," she said, in a way that made me fear I had burst her momentum. It was true, though, I *did* hate him—his selfishness, his completely unfair and misplaced authority, his laziness, his act-ing like a big shot when he wasn't. He was grumpy and imposing and he baited you into an argument—everyone except me, because I never took his bait; I chose silence instead.

"Mom, why *wouldn't* you divorce him?"

"I've just never wanted to"—tears made her eyes shiny—"I've just never wanted to take your father away from you kids."

The room suddenly felt intensely stuffy with silence and ghosts and the black cliffs that the unknown always brings. Outside the yellowing leaves still hung motionless. That princely northern breeze had turned and run away. Only white weight filled the place where air was supposed to be.

"It's not the same thing," the born-twenty-one sage in me said, as if I was an unaffected observer, the narrator in a Greek tragedy. "Your father died. Ours just doesn't care."

"Yes he *does care*," she said. "There's just something wrong with him, and I don't know what it is."

"Well, you won't be taking our father away—he has something to do with it, too, Mom."

She'd fallen into herself again and I wasn't certain she was hearing me. A car screeched its brakes on Chenoweth Lane but otherwise the outdoors was choked empty of sound.

"It'll be okay, Mom," I said, getting up to hug her. "We'll get along fine, you'll see."

Days and weeks piled up after that; the topic of divorce was not mentioned again or revisited. The simpler days of first grade were long gone, too, those days when I experimented with mashing my index finger and thumb together with glue. There always came an absurdly terrifying instant when I envisioned a tour to the principal's office, to the kitchen table at home with my parents staring down at me, then to the doctor's office for the scalpel. A fraction of a moment when I thought I'd done something irreparable, when I couldn't free my finger and thumb from their bondage to each other. Then, in a rush of determination, or if Mrs. Albright was walking past my desk, I'd release my stuck fingers and relish the surge of power such a gesture gave me.

By eighth grade, self-imposed glue was the least of my concerns. Everything, everywhere, was breaking apart. Courts deemed our public school system unfair to black kids, which meant that a plan to desegregate the schools had to be devised. A scary pain was shooting through Mom's neck more and more often, sometimes climbing down her shoulder and left arm, reminding us of how suddenly her parents had died. I was crumbling beneath the pressure of trying to be perfect. And Dad was exceedingly cross—though thankfully more scarce—except on Sundays, when no one had anywhere to go, when the pressure of the world converged into the cramped space of our house.

Artfully separated since morning, despite the small square footage of the house, the battlefield compressed in the cocktail/dinner preparation hour, when Mom stepped into the den to retrieve the bottle of bourbon from the cabinet underneath the bookshelf or when Dad stepped into the kitchen to pour himself another drink. He guzzled beer in the afternoon, bourbon in the evening.

Her request/command for him to start the grill could be a verbal torch. I might appear at the top of the step as if called, a burning spike of nausea poking at my belly. I'd sit on the step and wait, a self-appointed patrol. At the first smack of heated voices I'd casually appear in the kitchen to ask Dad about the football game, or to divert the brimming argument in some other disguised way.

You—stay out of this.

I'd back into the dining room, then hover near the antique cherry desk in the living room, silent as a spy. But sometimes my distracting tactics worked. Dad would glance toward the television, remembering the game. We'd resume our places in the den—the skirmish thwarted, at least for the moment.

Because I lacked courage, I relied on spy tactics—eavesdropping, anticipation, diversion, silence. I never could've been a firefighter—although I could've studied the wind patterns, flying above the blaze in a plane, calculating an estimate as to the direction the blaze would likely take.

My usually quiet, sometimes sulky sister could walk straight into fire. She stayed to herself much of the time, in her room listening to music or sitting in the living room reading a book—not wishing to be disturbed. But she had red hair, which confirmed that her temper could match the intensity of any flame, including my father's.

"Don't lean back in the chair."

Slam.

"Didn't mean to." Anne didn't look up. Her lips went thin, making the splash of freckles between her lips and nose more obvious.

We were sitting at the small wooden table in the kitchen, making an attempt to resemble the family we were *supposed to be*. It happened the same every week, every spring, summer, and fall, like a rerun played over and over.

Dad burned chicken on the grill, although we said it was good, that we liked it that way. To the tarred chicken, Mom added our favorite peas, the tiny ones from the silver can, and baked "all rotten" potatoes. We held hands while Dad murmured the blessing. Last week we made it through supper without a scene, like other families did—like performing a dress rehearsal without a glitch. Some nights, though, like this one, it became clear that we weren't going to make it.

"Watch the attitude, young lady."

"What about yours?" Anne's defiant eyes flashed contempt.

"What did you say?!" He leaned forward, shrinking the space over the table, staring at her with his combative Marine Corps eyes. "Look at me when I'm talking to you, young lady. What did you just say?!"

The kitchen walls started creeping toward one another, ready to crush us into one compressed glob of McCall flesh and guts. They were moving in slowly, mashing us into each other, making us stick closer and closer together. I didn't dare breathe.

"Nothing," Anne said with a bite on the g, lifting her head.

"WHAT?!"

"Nothing!" she said again, staring straight into his eyes.

"Don't talk to ME in that tone!" His face was red, his chair already pushed away from the table. My stomach twisted on itself. I stared across the table at my little brother, who made a face at me. No, Curtie, not now.

"What're you doing, BOY?"

"Leave him out of it," my sister yelled, from the middle of the collapsing kitchen. She was crouched like a wrestler, thin though, no match for the steaming tower of my father.

"That'll be enough out of you!" When Dad took a step toward her, she took off. He followed her out of the kitchen through the living room to the steps leading upstairs. Their voices flew through the house like black exhaust.

"Curt!" Mom's voice had a distinctive shrill to it whenever she tried to divert his attention, when she tried to control him and make him be quiet.

"I'm talking about respect, here, *dammit!*"

The anger streaked through every corner in the house, a flame hungry for flesh or furniture or something to burn. I just wanted to get upstairs, to slip past the combustible words of this strange planet. All this yelling never helped anything; it was a futile waste of energy and air.

Anne had stormed up to her room, screaming the whole way. My father went as far as the steps but he didn't follow her up. I waited in the corner of the dining room, near the bulky corner cupboard. When Dad stormed into the kitchen, the silver tray on the serving table rattled. The ghosts were never any help in these explosions; it's as if they picked these moments to be unforgivably absent. I wanted to be like them, to be a ghost, to move through the house without anyone ever seeing me.

I thought there was a lull, that I could sneak upstairs unseen, but somehow I screwed up, I miscalculated. I made it to only the third step.

"Where do you think you're going?"

I was standing nearly eye level with him, only the white bars of the banister separating us. Behind him I could see the portrait of his mother, Grandmother Frances, gazing at me with her passive, sorrowful eyes.

I answered with silence. I felt caught behind the bars, like an animal in a zoo, caught like in a dream, when you're falling and you need to scream but no sound will come out. I wanted to disintegrate into the air molecules between the white wood spindles, to be invisible, to blend into the thinning fabric of my great-aunt's chair. I wanted to be in another room, in another house, on another planet, but I'd just fallen into a pool of crushed ice. Every part of me was frozen—emotionless—except my heart that beat against the inside of my chest like a hot fist.

"Something wrong with your ears?"

"I . . . have to get ready for tomorrow."

"I won't take any lip out of any of you—you understand that?"

"Yes, sir."

He fumed at me a moment longer, clumsy with an enemy that refused to engage directly, one that practiced guerrilla warfare instead of face-to-face combat. He chewed the inside of his cheek for a second, still staring. He was twenty-five years older than me; this was all such a waste.

Why do you do this? Any thoughts I had remained unspoken. I had no voice then, no sense that words could belong to me—saying things got people in trouble—silence made the trouble stop. Eventually, he huffed out of the living room and into the den. I hurried upstairs and knocked on my sister's door. I could hear that she was crying.

"Go away" was all she said.

Sunday wasn't the only explosion day, just the most popular. Two or three times a year, for example, on a Saturday afternoon, Mom would plant herself unannounced in the border territory of the dining room, frustrated tears and words gushing from her pained face. Grabbing her head she'd say she was about to go crazy, that we needed to give her some help or she'd end up at Our Lady of Peace—and we couldn't afford that.

During these eruptions, my brother and I would bolt upright on the floor, or stand, unsure in that instant of what we could do to make her better. Dad usually had the good sense to turn off the television. My sister was upstairs in her room or off doing some sorority car wash. She wasn't accused in these wrathful outbursts because she already helped more than her share. Anne simply knew what needed to be done around the house and did it, she didn't have to be told and told like Curtie and me.

Dad turned into a parent in those moments after Mom's tirade. *You heard your mother, get off your duff and pull your weight around here.* Curtie and I would buzz into motion, dividing up the chores—he'd go to the wastebaskets, I'd grab the dust rag and head for the living room. The television would stay off for a few minutes, but my father wouldn't do any house chores, although he might go outside for a few minutes. It wouldn't be long before he'd be back in the den again, sitting in his chair, a fresh beer beside him, the second half of the ball game starting. Mom might've set Curtie and me to the project of washing the front windows, inside and out.

For the longest time I believed the irony was lost on my father, that he actually didn't realize the inequity of the situation, how unfair it was for him to tell us what to do when he didn't do *anything*—and that's what Mom was mad about in the *first* place.

The more usual weekday scenario, especially when we were younger, would be for Curtie and I to be lying on the brown-and-gold shag carpet in the den. We distinguished the days of the week by the television schedule, which we memorized and quizzed each other on as if studying for a spelling test. *Leave It to Beaver*, Monday through Friday at five. *The Patty Duke Show*. *Hogan's Heroes*, every evening at seven-thirty. *My Three Sons*.

We had to keep quiet if Dad was home because his presence in the den activated the battleground. From his chair, Dad could eavesdrop on conversations taking place in the kitchen. He could hear my mother complaining about him to my sister or me, if I'd been summoned away from the television to keep Mom company. Often, she'd be in the kitchen alone, making lists of what she had to do the next day, cooking dinner, folding clothes—everything in a hurry because there was always so much to do.

On the weekends in the den, we'd be glued to the football games. From the den, I could monitor the pace of Mom's movements, ready to jump up and help if I heard her banging the oven door or shrieking if something was boiling over. Too often, though, I'd get overly involved with the Vikings or the Giants and forget to stay alert. Curtie and I would debate quietly whether they should go for it on fourth and two or play it safe and kick the field goal. We were careful not to make too much noise, since our John Wayne look-alike father was sitting right there, reading the paper, smoking a cigarette, drinking a beer, eavesdropping on Mom. No ticking was audible, but he was a bomb, nonetheless.

Get in there and give your mother some help. The mute statue in the chair would roar into life, not into movement, just into exploding sound. In that instant I'd realize I hadn't been paying attention, that I'd been lost in examining how the quarterback dodged the rush. Curtie, still motionless on the floor beside me, didn't flinch. He didn't have to help. He was a boy.

I never really did much in the kitchen, other than to give my reeling and fiercely independent mother some company. Gasping at the size of the tiny oven, or lamenting the limited counterspace, she preferred doing things—everything—herself.

I preferred not attempting the things that needed to be done because the edge of her criticism stayed sharper than the knives in the butcher block. I somehow learned there was one right way to do everything—except I never knew what it was. Simple tasks, like chopping vegetables, for example.

What're you doing? For heaven sake—here, like this, or never mind, I'll do it. Just sit there and keep me company.

I learned an inertia of my own—not to pick up a knife to chop something, not to stand near the stove to stir something. My sister, "the pretty one," was also "the cook." The most basic cooking activities held banal mystery to me, and the distinct probability of failing in some way. I simply avoided ever trying—ever.

Instead, I'd haphazardly set the table, listening intently to my mother's complaints about my father. *He never lifts a finger. I don't know if he's tired or was just born lazy. Lazy* was the worst possible thing in the world a person could be. I shouldn't have been lazing in the den watching television at all.

I never understood why she allowed Dad to sit there, why she raced around doing everything, including serving his dinner, and then complained about it.

Still, it was there in the kitchen where Mom and I would have our conversations, when she would talk and I would listen. We goofed around sometimes, and laughed. She'd do her camel walk for me where she made her arms seem longer and noodlelike, her knees pointing out, the expression on her face that of a mischievous little girl. I'd start laughing, then she'd get infected, until Curtie, or sometimes Dad would appear in the doorway and say something like, "What're you two doing in here?"

"Oh, nothing," one of us would say, still giggling.

Often, Mom told me stories about her past; through her words our grandparents came to gigantic life. When she talked, you could feel the ghosts huddle into the small kitchen.

Her father had been a doer, a true Renaissance sort of man, and according to Mom, he was as close to perfect as a person could get. *He called me his shadow because when I was little I'd sit outside the bathroom door waiting for him. He taught me to drive when I was thirteen. He and I talked about my becoming a doctor, about my going to college somewhere like Smith.*

He enjoyed hunting and fishing and traveling and would send them postcards from the train trips he took once or twice a year to the West Coast. He always returned with gifts and great adventure stories, like the time he was taking a picture from the train window, only to be greeted upon arrival by FBI agents, who confiscated the film. He'd inadvertently photographed a plant busy making bomb components or something else for the war effort. For awhile there, Mom had concocted a growing theory that her father was an under-cover spy and when she heard about the government agents taking his film, she took that as proof.

When Mom talked of her father, she would slow way down, gaz-ing for a time out the window above the sink. She was looking back, to a place I couldn't go to or see. In those motionless moments, a hap-piness and a sadness, too, would emerge from beneath her unfocused gaze, her tense jaw would soften—it was so rare to see my mother become still. She'd sometimes start crying, not major sobs but pained, wretched tears that had been circulating in the cold depths of her grief and had just now found a current to ride to the surface.

I'm sorry, Mom, I might say, or something equally lame, feeling bad that my questions had made her cry.

No, it's okay, she'd say, putting a dish towel to her face, or excusing herself for a minute to go to the bathroom. I'd dry a pot or two, waiting for her to return, which she always did, fresh faced, her mood lighter, and with renewed resolve to find every stray crumb on the counter and wipe it clean.

Sometimes, after doing the dishes, we'd take a walk around the neighborhood, just to get out of the house. We might end up sitting on the front stoop afterward, if she was telling me a new story, or an old one that she felt compelled to tell again.

On one of those nights Mom told me what happened to Mama T. She was in Louisville visiting for the weekend, which was an hour or so away from Danville, Kentucky, where she lived with her sister. It was June 1960. *Before you were even thought about.*

Anne was almost two. She and our parents lived in a small house on a dead end street not too far from Lakeside. *I hated that house,* Mom said more than once. That Saturday afternoon in June Mama T developed a sudden horrible pain in her side. Not one to complain, she went to lie down but it was clear by her writhing that something was terribly wrong. Eventually she agreed to have my mother call the doctor, who came to the house and decided Mama T was having "an ulcer attack." He gave her a hypodermic shot and instructions that "she should be quiet."

After the doctor left Mama T's pain worsened. My parents decided that Dad would take her to the hospital; Mom would stay home with Anne. *I'll never forget. Your father picked her up in his arms. She was so small, wrapped in this white blanket with tiny roses on it. He just carried her to the car and the man across the street drove them to the hospital.*

Tests confirmed Mama T's pain was from a heart attack—but she seemed to be feeling better once in the hospital bed. She even made sure she had money to buy a Coca-Cola before Dad left. It was almost midnight. He came home so that Mom could go to the hospital to be with her mother, but as he arrived for the switch, the phone rang and the nurse told Mom that Mama T had died. She was fifty-nine.

It was as if someone took a gun and shot the sun right out of the sky.

Mom and I had been sitting on the front stoop as she talked. Around us, the evening had quieted way down, as if the birds could sense the presence of old-growth pain, as if they'd been stroked into silence by the ghosts. Her gaze was blurry, her greenish eyes full of tears.

Not long after that I became pregnant. I was convinced that when I went to the hospital to have you I was going to die—everyone I knew who went to that hospital died. I said good-bye to Anne thinking I'd never see her again. And then you were born and then I understood. The Lord takes away but he gives, too. You were such a gift.

At twenty-five years old, Mom didn't have any parents left. It must've been terrifying for her to risk loving us. Then again, what choice did she have?

We have to stick together—we're all we've got.

Those were quiet moments with Mom and relatively rare—she didn't stop for long at any one time, not even for the ghosts. So most of our conversations were snippets actually, paragraphs and story clips, then it would be time to get ready for the next day. She'd take a bath, lay out what she was going to wear to school, make sure all her schoolwork was graded and sitting in the small tote bag she kept in the living room by the front door, next to her purse.

Eventually, by the time I was thirteen, I spent less time watching football and more time upstairs in my room, ostensibly to do homework but really just to breathe in the quiet there. I liked my room, with its slanted ceilings and two large windows on the wall opposite the bedroom door. For years I had a Peanuts poster on the back of my door. Lucy was sitting in her doctor's booth, listening to Charlie Brown: "The Doctor is In."

That fall of 1974, Anne, the family maverick at sixteen, found someplace to go on Sunday nights, which shifted our entrenched burned-chicken ritual that had marked so many years. She stepped further away from our glued-together family by joining the Presbyterian church, so she could go to youth-group events with her boyfriend.

This represented a significant return to formalized church. We had been dressed in appliquéd dresses and patent leather shoes—kneesocks and seersucker shorts for Curtie—worn little white gloves and long faces when we were very young children, filing in like prisoners to the Baptist church of Dad's childhood, but eventually, with the arrival of the year-round swimming train, the habit of family churchgoing fell easily away.

Curtie and Anne and I replaced it rather creatively with our own reenactment of *Jesus Christ Superstar*, upstairs in Anne's room on Sunday mornings, each of us singing multiple parts, although usually Curtie was King Herod, Anne was Jesus, and I was almost always Judas. My favorite Judas song: *It seems to me a strange thing mystifying . . .*

We sang this play often enough that each of us knew all the parts and all the songs—they became backup material for swim practices when the radio offered no suitable alternatives. The play and its songs harnessed the constant noise in our heads, giving us each a model, a way you were *supposed to be. Jesus is cool.*

This Broadway on Napanee had pretty much dissolved by the time Anne was sixteen and making plans with her boyfriend and the youth group on Sunday evenings. The church was a lovely redbrick building with a new steeple, located on the rich-people side of Brownsboro Road. We drove past it all the time on our way to the bank, or to Taylor Drugstore, which sold bourbon and whiskey and wine to the East End, in addition to candy and toothpaste and gum.

Typical of our stick-together approach, youth group on Sunday evenings would give Curtie and me *something to do* too, so we signed up to join the church, which meant we had to take a Confirmation class, even though we were embarrassingly older than the other kids in the group.

For the final project, I made up a poem and wrote it on yellow construction paper, using my most careful writing. In the fellowship hall that afternoon, when everyone's "project" was on display for the curious among the congregation, a man I didn't know told me he really liked my prayer, that he thought it was beautiful. I could see he was being serious, not sarcastic—that he had actually *liked* it. I didn't know how to respond, except of course to shrug and act like it was nothing special and, of course, to say thank-you.

I had a private journal at the time that held no words of my own, other than the few prayer/poems I'd written. Its pages held quotations from other people, sayings I noticed in the newspaper or read on a poster or a card somewhere. There was one sermon's message that also made it to the blank pages of my journal.

The preacher spoke one morning on the perfection of Jesus, how Jesus always knew the right thing to do. From the raised, freshly painted pulpit, the soft-spoken white-haired man outlined seven ways to know if what you are doing is morally right. I scribbled down the seven guides in the corners of a pledge envelope when I was sitting in the sanctuary that morning, convinced that this man was telling us right then and there the secret to life—how to be *perfect*.

Jesus employed experience, common sense, sportsmanship, and foresight in taking each of his perfect steps. He also took into account the influence of his actions and matched it to the ideal of a "model person." None of this made much sense to me, although as I was listening I felt I qualified well enough, that I already tried to do all those things. I was a good sport, I thought ahead about the consequences of things and used the little bit of common sense I possessed. I tried not to bother anyone—except my brother, he didn't count—and to not make any trouble.

It was the final guideline, offered by the tall, stooped man with the somber voice, that exposed me as a doomed failure—any *right* action or deed should be able to be made *public*. If what you're doing can't be known publicly, then what you're doing is wrong, imperfect, morally suspect, *sinful.*

Those words would stalk me for the next eleven years.

7

A lifeguard must have the knowledge
and ability to rescue someone in trouble.

American Red Cross Lifeguarding, p.6

The best way to help my mother, even more than sitting in the kitchen to keep her company, had always been to not cause her any problems, to make her feel proud to be our mother. This wasn't too difficult during my preteenage, carbon-copy years. When people complimented us, when we earned good grades and won awards, Mom would smile and her face would relax briefly.

One Friday after school when I was ten, I was supposed to go on an out-of-town weekend swimming trip. My bag was packed and sitting by the front door when Mom wheeled the big Pontiac into the driveway and honked.

"We have to go by the bank," she said, as I climbed into the front seat, careful not to slam the door. Worry had worked its way into the skin above her eyes. It was changing her—making her speak faster, allowing her only short, shallow breaths. In those kinds of moments especially, I tried to help her by being extra calm and I certainly didn't say anything about our being late.

I was supposed to take thirty-five dollars as my share of the room expenses and meals on the trip. That morning she didn't have thirty-five dollars, not in her purse, not in her checking account, not anywhere. She'd just told me that she would figure something out.

When she'd finished tutoring after school, miraculously, the kid's mother wrote her a check for exactly thirty-five dollars. At the drive-through window at Liberty Bank, Mom forced a lightness to her chat with the teller. I said "thank-you" when the woman sent a couple of dum-dum suckers through the chute. Mom handed the blue-and-white bank envelope to me. The weight of the bills was surprisingly heavy.

"Count it to make sure it's right," she said, as she maneuvered the big wagon through the drugstore parking lot, to the stoplight on Brownsboro Road.

"Are you sure?" I knew she didn't have any other money. It wasn't a payday Friday.

"It'll be okay. I'm working for Burger Chef on Sunday; I'll get paid then." She was zooming down Chenoweth Lane, intent on getting me to Lakeside so I could catch my ride to Cincinnati. My sister was riding with someone else and had already been picked up by her car pool. Curtie wasn't going on the trip; he'd gone home after school with one of his friends to play until Mom could pick him up.

I packed the precious envelope of money carefully in the zipper pocket of the bag that was resting on my legs. I was wearing my team warm-up suit, made of a navy stretchy material with red stripes down the side. On the back of my jacket was written *Lakeside* in script. To the world, and to my mom, I looked like a champion.

We learned not to tug on Mom's arm and beg her to buy us something. At the grocery store—the Gateway—she'd stare at the few bills in her wallet, as if they'd just performed a magic trick of shrinking, then vanishing. Her hair was sometimes bloused up in a strange way, especially if she'd gotten it "done" recently. Lipstick and makeup made my mom appear different than who she really was, and she wore them only sporadically, and less so as the years trudged on.

In the store, I watched her lips move silently as she calculated what the total bill would be, then recount her cash to see if she'd have enough. Sometimes she'd slip a box of cereal off the checkout belt and whisper for me or Curtie to take it back to the shelf.

Other times we'd drive through the window at Liberty Bank, and the tense way she chatted with the teller and the meticulous way she placed the envelope of money in her purse—these gestures and a thousand voiced worries—told the story of our family: we did not have enough . . . money.

That is, not enough to buy the clothes we were supposed to wear or move to the bigger house we were supposed to live in. There was less and less money, given that the lapses between my father's jobs were getting longer and longer—a river of shame filled the void. We never went hungry like the starving children in India, never even came close, although at privately desperate times she had to choose between buying hot dogs and toothpaste—because she didn't have the money for both.

Still, we were white middle-class Americans, living in a house that could be mortgaged over and over again. She paid the bills with her teacher salary (*borrowing from Peter to pay Paul*) and we didn't embarrass her by asking for things when we were in a store.

Just by looking at us, we seemed to belong in the East End. Our preppie clothes, good manners, and all-American smiles gave us the appearance of ease and privilege worn by the other families. And like them, we traveled south every year for spring break.

What was less easily recognized was how common it was for teachers like my mom to look toward spring break as a beacon of hope that could pull them through the bleak, relentless gray of a Louisville winter. But the invisible thing that separated us from other families and teachers was the depth of our need: to us, spending one week in Florida a year had become a lifeline to our survival.

This past spring, when I turned thirteen, we stayed home.

Always before, and especially in the last few years, we'd gone to the beach *on a wing and a prayer*. We would count and recount the money Mom had saved all year, add in Curtie's grass-cutting money, the savings Anne had in the bank, and anything I had earned.

Last year, when I was twelve, after tallying our means and coming up a couple hundred dollars short, the four of us had a family meeting in the living room, by the piano. At fifteen, Anne's hair was long and a bit straggly. She'd quit taking piano lessons a few years previously, and there was no money or time for Curtie or me to take lessons.

Our debate was whether to sell the piano and go to Florida or save the money and stay home. We *should've* saved the money. When we voted, it was unanimous—we sold. Dad didn't vote because he wasn't chipping in or going.

Like so many other things, retreating to Ormond Beach—our self-designated family Mecca—hadn't always been wrought with angst and complication. In the early sixties, when we started taking the annual Florida vacation, we were just like other up-and-coming families. In those sunny years of relative ease, my father basked in the vacation play as much as the rest of us.

My parents always shared a love of the ocean—the waves, the water, the bodysurfing. In the ocean together they laughed and shook their heads, admired the waves each one rode, bobbed over the breakers with the effortless synchronicity of a pair of pelicans.

In the 1950s, Daytona Beach played host to frolicking college kids. Groups of students from everywhere, including Centre College in Danville, tracked the interstate highways to the sun and surf. They stayed at beachfront establishments with Hollywood names like the Castaway Motel. *Look, the Driftwood is still there.*

These coral-and-blue cardboardlike motels evoked giggles from my brother and sister and me as we peered out the backseat windows on my parents' annual "sentimental journey." The spring migration that had commenced in college resumed when we were little children, although with parenthood, my parents moved up the beach to the more family-centered strip known as Ormond Beach.

One night during our week vacation, we'd leave the beach early enough in the afternoon to shower, have aloe cream rubbed onto our scorched backs by Mom, then put on clean shirts that stuck to our skin. We'd lace the new tennis shoes we'd bought for the trip and try not to make a fuss while we waited for Dad to be ready to go.

From the car we'd see lobster red college kids hanging off balconies. Music, familiar and strange, blared from passing cars. Lights flashed on some of the bigger hotels—like the Hawaiian Inn— promising live music and happy-hour two-for-ones. Mom and Dad would joke and start telling stories about the time when so-and-so, a Beta, tried to steal Mom away from Dad.

Their words revealed whole worlds my parents had once inhabited that could never include us. We kept quiet in the backseat, our eyes staring at the glitzy high-rise lights flashing neon green and pink and blue. That my parents had memories of enjoying each other comforted me. There was a delicate air in the car on those evenings, something special and sacred and important.

Mom and Dad talked to each other and laughed. They both forgot we kids existed. For those precious minutes of driving down the Daytona strip, and then later on, as they walked hand-in-hand on the boardwalk, the universe of my family ordered itself properly.

Dad didn't pout or steam because Mom paid more attention to Curtie. Mom didn't complain to me or Anne about Dad not making enough money. I didn't try to deflect or anticipate or offset their potential arguments; nor did I needle my brother into making a scene. Anne didn't get mouthy with Dad, speaking the words Mom thought but for some reason dared not say to him.

We were our best family on those magical Florida evenings.

Once a year none of our usual dance steps applied. No one danced at all, we simply lived, breathing in the salty Atlantic air, crinkling our sunburned shoulders, trying our hardest to make a hole-in-one at putt-putt. The ocean, so big and colorful and consistent, with its ushering in and out of waves, freed each of us from our roles. The ocean made anything possible; it gave us the night off.

It didn't last, of course. The magic of those nights faded in later years. The boardwalk fell into the dangerous motley hands of "hippies" and "druggies." We'd still drive down the beach, gawking, but never getting out of the car. It wasn't the same by then anyway because we were four, not five. We'd left Dad at home.

Our Florida ritual changed the spring I turned nine, when we went to Ormond for the first time without him. This was a significant shift for my parents, for my Mom really. Dad had just started another new job. Since it wouldn't be right for him to ask for a week off, we went without him. Taking the trip by ourselves didn't scare me; Mom could move the world if she needed to.

We didn't talk about Dad not going as Mom packed the car that Thursday night. Our plan was to jump in right after school on Friday. Curtie, Anne, and I rotated sitting in the front seat, serving as Mom's copilot. By the time we were out of Louisville, on I-65 South toward Nashville, thoughts of my father were nonexistent, at least for me. If my brother and sister were thinking of him, they didn't say. It was easier to travel without his sharp, angry moods and her seething criticism of him, without the razor-edge arguments that sparked up between them.

In Nashville, we picked up I-75, through "Chagganooga," as my brother called it, and on through Atlanta. It was dark by then. We were extra quiet because Mom would get nervous driving in so many lanes of traffic, through the interminable construction and alongside cars that drove extremely fast.

We spent the night in Perry, Georgia, in one of those dots on the map at a Day's Inn. We were back in the car by six a.m., heading south to Lake City, where we took I-10 east toward Jacksonville. *If everybody had an ocean, across the USA. Then everybody'd be surfing, like Cali-forn-I-A.*

We were speed monsters at the "pit stops." We knew better than to ask Mom for anything more than a Coke. We timed ourselves and it was always a frustration when the line to the bathroom was a long one. By Jacksonville, the warm, moist Florida air started working on us, massaging our necks and shoulders, blowing hope into our nostrils along with that airy scent of oranges. We debated whether to take I-95 all the way to Ormond or exit early at Flagler Beach and drive alongside the ocean.

Mom laughed and talked and planned. Her grip loosened on the steering wheel and her shoulders relaxed, her sporty good looks and spunk coming alive. If the driving made her tired, it didn't show. Going to Florida made my mother happier than anything in the world.

When we pulled into the Ormond Biltmore, hours earlier than check-in time, we flew out of the car, since we'd already changed into our bathing suits in the car. Anne, Curtie, and I walked quickly past the pool (no running allowed), then onto the sidewalk that separated four sets of shuffleboard courts, down the steps onto the beach, then sprinted into the Atlantic. It stung, it was so cold; we didn't care. We just screamed straight into the waves.

"They're huge," I yelled, bobbing over the top of a wave.

Anne threw back her head and let out an exuberant wail. She was clownish the way she flailed herself into a crest and I laughed.

"Wait up," Curtie yelled, just as he disappeared in the foam of a wave he'd been trying to jump. The roar was tremendous. I floated back toward him.

"C'mon," I yelled, glancing quickly toward the breakers, pretending to be a seasoned mariner in a heaving sea. He was sturdy

and strong and impish when I reached him, so I knew he was fine—
we'd just gotten a head start on him and he always hated that.

The Ormond Biltmore was a small, cozy home-away-from-
home motel, built in a semicircle with a kidney-shaped pool in the
middle. Beyond the pool area, a rug of Bermuda grass separated the
motel rooms from the beach. There was a ledge of about ten feet or
so, which made the view from the grass even wider than if you were
standing on the beach itself.

I was standing there, with my towel wrapped around my shoulders, gazing at the ocean, wanting to swallow it with my eyes and my
ears and my nose. I'd missed it so much!

"C'mon," Anne said, walking up behind me. "Mom said it's
time to go unpack the car and go to the store."

I followed my sister to the car then to 2B, which was a roomy
two-bedroom model, with a small kitchen and living room. The
couch unfolded into a bed. The carpet was a purplish speckled
indoor/outdoor type and the furniture was wood veneer and sturdy.
The television worked, although we rarely turned it on, except in the
mornings when my brother watched it before we went down to the
beach, while Mom was painting our faces with zinc oxide.

She called us her three Indians, although Anne had to wear long
sleeves, and sometimes pants, when she went swimming because her
fair skin burned fast. Curtie and I turned tan without much problem.

We were four people very accustomed to routine. As a family—
minus my father—we shifted easily into a beach rhythm. Mom
packed her beach bag and down we walked, past the pool, which
offered little appeal with the ocean waves inviting us to come play.

The wide, flat beach allowed room for every thought, every
dream, every wish. Worries evaporated in the friendly sun. Our main
financial splurge of the week was to rent rafts from Bob, a guy who
showed up with an old truck painted navy with bright orange letters. He rented everything—chairs, rafts, cabanas, umbrellas.

Mom was clever when she negotiated a price with tan, twinkle-eyed Bob. She waited him out, knowing by the sly way he inquired about her husband that he was admiring her legs. She was trying to cut a deal for renting three rafts, because otherwise we could afford only two. Curtie and I gazed longingly at the rafts, until Bob finally gave in.

Large and cumbersome, the rafts had thick rubber edges that scratched up our legs when we rode the waves. We didn't care. Despite Bob's encouragement, we didn't rent a cabana—too expensive—and Mom had packed her own sand chair from Kentucky.

On Sunday, our first full beach day, Anne and Curtie were already in the ocean. I was about to go in myself.

Mom leaned her head back in the lounge chair and sighed in the deepest way. The ocean air and the sun rubbed the lines off her face. A peace relaxed the muscles around her mouth and she smiled in a way that showed how pretty she was.

"I know we can't afford this," she said, "but it's a lot cheaper than Our Lady of Peace." She laughed, face still directed to the sun, her eyes closed. I laughed and agreed with her. I'd heard her say that many times before.

"What is Our Lady of Peace anyway?"

She pulled her face from the sun and squinted at me. "It's a psychiatric hospital—where people go when they crack up," she said.

"Oh," I said, grabbing my raft. "I'm going in now."

"Okay. Keep an eye on your brother."

Packing a whole year of childhood into one week made the days pass way too quickly. They advanced in fast motion, an unstoppable tide that rose and rose until that dreaded, inevitable moment when it was time to pack our bags. On the last morning I would stand at the edge of the waves and close my eyes. I'd concentrate completely on the sound, on the rush of their surging exhale, the hiss of the retreating inhale. Shhhh. Hsss. Shhhh. Hsss. Shhh. Hsss. My breath matched their breath. I kept my eyes closed as the water wrapped its invitation around my ankles, nearly pulling me over by the fourth or fifth wave. Still I focused on the sound, on that unmistakable rhythm. I wanted it to sink into me so I would remember it, not let its distinctive chant fade, like it had every year before. This time I wanted to take it with me and keep it. This was my friend ocean's way of talking to me, of reminding me it was always here, no matter what might happen. I wanted to get better at listening so I could still hear it when I was so far away in Kentucky.

My tears mixed with the saltwater as I bent down in my yearly ritual to kiss the ocean good-bye. That was the hardest day of the year, the day we drove away from the ocean, a giant mountain of time ahead of us.

There was no way I could close my eyes and hear the ocean now; it had been too long since I'd seen it. When I tried picturing the ocean, all I could see was dark blank nothingness.

It was strange the way it turned out, though, that this had been the first year, 1974, we'd stayed home for spring break. Then again, maybe what happened was meant to be a signal, a flare sent from the ghosts that our world really was spinning out of control.

Louisville sits in the border zone between the Midwest and the South. From a weather perspective, it resembles Ohio and Indiana, except that the Ohio Valley possessively keeps its clouds tucked in, keeping winter temperatures in Louisville from falling to the magic numbers that bring periodic fresh offerings of snow to those other places. In spring, too, Louisville takes on more notable characteristics of its western neighbors, hosting wildly erratic storms that can change the sky into extraordinary colors: sweet mossy green, topaz and silver gray, even charcoal black at three in the afternoon.

Socially southern in its preppie dress and the import placed on lineage, in its pattern of disapproval expressed with politely smiling faces, down to the last drop of bourbon in its charmed mint juleps, Louisville will never be wholly southern. It can never escape the ambivalence of its border state identity—Civil War aside. The spring weather won't permit it.

And it was one of those midwestern-but-want-to-be-southern days—April 3, 1974—when early grass brought with it a transient hope that life would right itself, that the tipped axis of winter was correcting toward the promises of a second-chance spring.

On that day after school, girls from Anne's sorority club started arriving at our house for their meeting. They were all dressed to varying degrees in pink and green and yellow blouses and blue and green and white skirts, complemented by their ribbon belts with gold belt buckles shaped in shells and bears and tulips. Their brown or blond hair was pulled back and held in place with invisible bobby pins and color-coordinated bows.

I'd turned thirteen two weeks earlier but I wasn't old enough to belong to Dasmine—members had to be in high school; I was only in seventh grade. Anne, a tenth grader, was the president—which translated into boxes of unsold Krispie Kreme doughnuts filling our freezer every Saturday morning. Surprisingly, she agreed to my request to assist with the meeting. I could welcome people as they arrived and replace bowls of pretzels and Bugle Boys, a special treat Mom bought just for the occasion. (We ate them too fast for her to buy them on a regular basis just for the three of us—too expensive.)

By this time in our lives it was an extremely rare event for Curtie or Anne or me to invite any friends to our house. We would traipse through front and back doors of our friends' big houses. Any gatherings at our house occurred outside on the sidewalk, where a kickball game could be organized or a plan made to caravan our bikes to Bonnie Woods's or Taylor's.

So this meeting at our house was an unusual situation from the beginning. The girl who was supposed to host the club canceled, which left my ultraresponsible presidential sister to fill in the gap, to have the meeting at our house, much to the shock of my mother and brother and me. She'd said it wouldn't take very long, that they just had to make some invitations or something.

They never ended up having an official construction-paper event that day, although twelve or fifteen girls were chatting excitedly for a few minutes in our house. I was busily trying to respond to each of them, to make them feel comfortable, to pull their discerning glances away from the worn living room carpet and the house that was too small. I never noticed when the rain began to stop, when the sky transformed itself into that infamous and disquieting green.

Mom and Anne noticed, though, because they told me to take the girls into the basement. From the worried expression on Mom's face I didn't argue, although I had to think quickly about a whole new set of apologies and explanations for the state of our basement. It was a dusty, messy place, which I was reminded of when I saw lips curl downward and slim bottoms sit on the outermost edge of the few old wooden chairs down there.

"NOW ," came the bellow from my mother, who was running down the steps with Curtie. I didn't think to wonder about Anne— I was more pressed with the fact that we'd never had this many people to our house before, much less invited them into the basement!

And then it hit. The small basement windows revealed a suddenly colorless and utterly black outdoors, as if a curtain had been yanked closed on this little experiment known as Earth, shut momentarily for repairs or simply for the gods to readjust the positions of their pawns. Everyone got very quiet. Outside there was an eerie void in place of the usual sounds. The pressured stillness silenced all bird songs, all car horns, all racing sirens, all coughing buses. Nothing could be heard except a distant rumble that didn't sound like thunder.

Later, my sister would describe the sound as that of a freight train running over the roof of our house—she knew because she was still standing in the living room, planted face-to-face with the monster, too caught by awe to take herself downstairs for her own safety. She could stare down *anything*.

In a matter of three minutes or less, it—whatever *it* was—was over. The black curtain lifted and through the dirty basement windows the bright light of a returning sun shone through. As I ascended the gray-planked stairs of the basement I wondered absurdly if we would emerge into Munchkin-land. Of course not, although the kitchen clock had stopped at 4:44, as if to remind us never to forget that minute.

Our haunted house was completely intact, dusted and straightened better than usual because of the occasion of having visitors. The antiques were all unblemished—the hutch and the desk and the coffee table in the living room with its weak flap. Even the kitchen window that could chop your arm off if you didn't prop it up hadn't shattered or even fallen closed.

Outside, the houses on our street stood as always, except for a neighbor's shed that had been lifted off the ground and pushed into a tree. Leaves strewn across the streets and yards resembled clothes on the floor of a messy kid's room, like mine, but overall there wasn't much to see—at least not on our street.

With the power and phone lines dead, we couldn't figure out how to contact the parents of all these girls, but somehow, over the next thirty minutes or so, they disbursed. By then, reports on transistor radios confirmed that Louisville had been hit by a tornado. Broken traffic lights and telephone poles closed many streets. We didn't know where Dad was or if he was okay.

On bikes with Mom, we rode through the disheveled but intact streets of our small neighborhood with increasing curiosity. Mom started shrieking when we rode up the walk to Chenoweth Elementary (where she taught and where Curtie was in the fifth grade). The very gymnasium where my sister, four years earlier, had worn a pink dress and sang "The Age of Aquarius" with her class during graduation from sixth grade was now a pile of bricks and plaster.

Some of the windows in the cafeteria were blown out. It wasn't clear if the kids would be able to return to school, although the rest of the building appeared undamaged.

It wasn't until we ducked under the crisscrossed cables hanging over Brownsboro Road and entered the rich neighborhood that we glimpsed firsthand what war might be like. People we knew and didn't know were in the streets crying, or standing agape at their crumpled multistory houses. Mattresses, shattered glass, dining room tables, candlesticks, toilet seats, paper, trash cans, books. Piles of twisted, disembodied, unrecognizable objects lay scattered beside rooms completely intact, save for the front face of the house that had been torn away.

We spent the afternoon avoiding sparking wires, climbing over felled trees, staring into the mangled rooms of shattered mansions, secretly marveling at the exactitude of the storm. One house could be completely wrecked, as if a missile had been dropped squarely on its roof, while the house right next door stood completely intact and unharmed.

It was a drunken path the tornado took, throwing itself this way and that, grabbing at victims haphazardly and with a seemingly unquenchable thirst. It unearthed hundred-year-old trees, ripped shingles from their glue, pushed cars around telephone poles. It pulverized everything in its path—showing no favor to anyone or anything—its randomness absolute.

When the supply of pressure that compelled it to keep spinning its destruction gave out, it diminished. That's one of the oddest aspects of tornadoes: as deadly as they can be, there comes a moment when they simply stop, when they are unrecognizable as a destructive force, when they take on the motion of common wind.

Nowhere is it blacker than in a city without lights. Mom didn't sleep in my room that night and neither did I. It was just the five of us and we had to stick together. Of course that included Dad, who had come home that day about five-thirty, relieved, as we were, that each of us was uninjured. He remained vague about the specifics of his whereabouts at 4:44 in the afternoon, a sign he'd been leaning his elbows on a bar somewhere.

That night Mom and Dad slept in their room. Anne and I shared the bunk beds in Curtie's room across the hall from my parents, and Curtie slept on cushions on the floor next to the bunk beds. The dark-stained night amplified the constant thrum of the helicopters overhead, piloted by National Guardsmen who'd arrived from somewhere to enforce the curfew and keep burglars and looters off the streets.

Before going to bed at eight o'clock, because it was too dark to do anything else, we'd spent the evening a bit bleary eyed and shocked, silently aghast at the oddity of our good fortune. One of my friends couldn't even sleep in her own house that night because it didn't have a roof on it.

We boiled water on the grill for hot dogs and endured Dad's irritable barks about the resistant charcoal, unconvincing in his attempt to disguise his discomfort with having all of us dependent on him for a meal. We couldn't have starved, not with the special Bugle Boys uneaten and the jar of peanut butter in the hall closet, but reality gets distorted by a crisis. We couldn't eat our normal dinner in our usual, train-scheduled way, and that translated into belly growls and unspoken fears of what might happen next. *You never know what might happen, or when.* Curtie and Anne and I didn't say much in that pitch-black bedroom that night, and none of us slept much, either.

Months after the audacious shock of the tornado, after power lines were lifted off roads and reattached to leaning poles, after glass shards were scraped off pavement and pieces of T-shirts and nightgowns were ripped down from trees, even after houses were rebuilt to even grander designs, you could still measure the exact path the tornado took. On the ride through Seneca Park, to and from Lakeside, broken and uprooted trees—or simply an absence of them—lay just yards to the right or left of old maples and oaks still standing perfectly erect and unscathed.

The early and mid-seventies were strangely marked times anyway: bell-bottoms and disco fever, the resignation of an American president and Archie Bunker in the den every Saturday night. Perhaps a community, a country even, doesn't so much heal as go on, moving as it has to, slowly or quickly, toward a renewed source of energy, relying on routine, on the familiar motion of simply putting one foot in front of the other.

Families don't always work that way but, theoretically, anything is possible. In the East End of Louisville, the sixties and seventies were not yet marked by frequent divorce or other social trends such as adolescent psychiatric units and talk shows discussing the most private of psychological and emotional struggles. They were times of deepened whispers, when an *alcoholic* was the unshaven bum under the bridge, when bankruptcy carried with it the scorn of a scarlet mark, and when being *strange* referred to a short-haired marine lookalike who reportedly carried a contagion dangerous to young girls.

8

My parents shared the peculiarity of both having brothers who were seven years their senior. In the life of childhood, seven years means separate worlds: schools, friends, interests or lack thereof. My parents were children during the forties—while they collected ration slips to purchase a prized piece of bubble gum, their brothers marched through adolescence toward the widening war and its call to service.

Both brothers were lovely golfers, both won silver bowls and varsity letters on their college golf teams. Both men married slim wives who gave birth to pairs of sons. Both were accustomed to the blazing privileges afforded firstborn sons of their social class and southern roots.

And even though there must have been many differences, the most distinctive between the two young twenty-six-year-olds remained the most obvious—one lived and one died. The survivor, the uncle I knew, belonged to my mother. He and his wife and three kids lived in a large house in a neighborhood a few miles from ours.

Every few weeks we visited them, usually according to the same routine. Mom would be talking to my aunt, who would invite her over to have a drink. My brother and sister and I would go, or sometimes it was just Curtie and me. Mom always wanted at least one of us to go with her, even though once we were there she sat in the den, or later on their converted porch, and chatted over bourbon and water while we kids tried to muster up something to do. They had a gigantic pool table in the basement, and sometimes, when we were old enough, we were allowed to spend our time down there.

Theirs was a safe, roomy, clean-scented house with the kind of thick creamy carpet that was fun to walk on in your bare feet. What wasn't as visible were the lines that marked when we could visit and when we couldn't, what was appropriate to talk about and what wasn't, what was proper behavior and what would be considered tacky or gauche. In the early years of my life I spent the night often with my cousin, but when swimming began to involve greater traveling, when she and I developed more diverging interests, I stopped going over there as much. She spent the night with me only rarely.

They were our only family, though, so we kept going over with Mom to visit on those stilted afternoons when she'd stop to share a cocktail. We went to their house for Thanksgiving or Christmas dinner since theirs was bigger and more plush than ours.

Our aunt and uncle did enter our house on infrequent occasions, not routinely and not usually to stay long enough for a relaxed cocktail. Yet, as unexpected as it was, that's precisely what happened one afternoon that fall when the phone rang. They'd been at their friends' house in one of the most affluent neighborhoods across Brownsboro Road and wondered if it would suit us for them to drop by on their way home. My mother, thrilled to be included in their social plans, automatically said yes.

Things were a rotten mess in our house. The famous conversation she'd had with me about divorcing Dad seemed to have never happened. The summer Olympics would be in Montreal and despite the airy dreams I'd had at age ten, I would not be swimming in them.

I was tired of swimming, tired of waking up at five a.m. three days a week to catch a ride with a mute though polite boy to go to swim practice before school and then to swim again after school. It was an insane way to live—and the insanity, or something, was slowing me down in the water. Half the time I felt like I was sinking rather than swimming, weighted down like a waterlogged whale, injured by the swipe of a propeller, but still digging, still pushing, never giving up.

Yes, talk of divorce had subsided, swallowed perhaps by the ever-increasing pace of our now intensely teenage lives, or perhaps just covered over by the sheer impracticality of it. Dad couldn't have afforded to live elsewhere.

Anne was staying away from the house, working at the Gateway or spending time at her boyfriend's house. I was thirteen, full grown, abhorrently confused, and burdened by perfection's constant demands, by trying to be good at everything I did but never being good enough.

That strange evening when my uncle called we'd just gotten home from watching my brother's football practice. We'd endured the horrific sight of my father arriving at the park wearing dark sunglasses despite the late hour. He wore a short-sleeved white T-shirt and some old pair of shorts, the same loafers he always wore and as usual, no socks. Other fathers arrived to watch practice still dressed in ties and starched shirts, blue or white or occasionally extra preppie pink or yellow. Not our dad. The dark, square glasses made him look suspicious, and I kept my distance.

It wasn't until we were home and he'd gone into my parents' room and fallen face-first on the bed, his legs sticking off the side like those of a corpse, that I realized he was drunk. Drunk! I'd never completely understood the meaning of that word before that moment. I stood in the doorway staring at him, his face mashed into the bed, his breathing mixed with a ragged-edged snoring that resembled the labored sound of an old woman who'd lost her balance and her ability to right herself. I was standing there when the phone rang. I recognized from Mom's tone of voice who she was talking to, imagined accurately the other half of the conversation, and wasn't surprised when she hung up the phone and yelled, *They'll be here in five minutes!*

My father didn't move, not a head turn, not an eyelid raised, not an ankle twitch—nothing. I backed into the hallway, pulled by the swirl of my mother's rising panic. In the kitchen she handed me a rag and told me to dust the living room, that there wasn't time to use furniture polish. I sprayed a little anyway to make the room smell fresher. Mom accelerated into Tasmanian mode so rapidly that every molecule of space in the house was in motion—every one except for those in the absolute inertia achieved by my father's drunken state.

I raced through the living and dining rooms with harsh eyes, stuffing clutter into closets and drawers even as their car pulled into the driveway. Before I could ask the question, I watched Mom close the bedroom door at the end of the hall.

The embarrassment felt hot as it poured over my skin, the lie transparent and shameful. *He isn't feeling well so he is taking a nap,* came the flimsy explanation. In the living room, they sat with the same reluctance I'd seen in the faces of the sorority girls in our basement, the same hesitation to lean back, to stretch their legs and really relax. Our house was too small, our upholstery too worn. I sat near the hallway, in the hard-back captain's chair, able to hear his snoring faintly from the living room, on guard in case one of our visitors had to use the bathroom.

If they walked down the short hall to the downstairs bathroom, they would hear him in the room snoring; a deaf person would've heard him. But maybe they would just think he was sick, just sleeping extra soundly, especially if I was rummaging in the hall closet while they were in the bathroom. Maybe the extra noise would disguise the reality; maybe if they saw me when they opened the bathroom door, they'd think I had to go, too, so they'd hurry through the hall and back into the living room. Maybe they would want only one drink. They never stayed long during these rare visits—*maybe they wouldn't know.*

Not long after that visit Dad walked into the kitchen with a bloody slice above his left eye. The blood had collected in a ridge that might've resembled a third eyebrow had it not been accompanied by brown and purple bruising. I'd already noticed that his car was not in the driveway.

He'd run out of gas the night before, so he'd gotten a ride home. He was vague about the details of who gave him the ride and what time he finally made it home and where his car was now. I could tell he was lying from the way his eyebrows lifted slightly on the end (my brother did the same thing), by the way his eyes scanned the floor, his head tilted downward. Plus, how would that explain his cut?

Somehow the truth began eking out of him. My father was a hopelessly honest man. He paid for his lies with a leaden guilt I had yet to recognize or understand. He'd gotten tired and accidentally driven off Brownsboro Road, hitting a telephone pole in the process. His favorite car of all time, the green Mustang, was totaled. He didn't have to mention the small detail that he'd been drunk.

When a cop drove up to see what happened, Dad showed the cop the Commanding Officers Club card that he carried in his wallet. The policeman told him to be more careful next time and gave him a ride home. Once again my dad dodged a ticket, the embarrassing kind that gets reported in the newspaper.

Mom and Dad stared at each other while a chilly shudder coursed through the kitchen. It was eerie, that moment, the kind of moment that lasts for several minutes, that flips time inside out, that makes you notice the puppet strings attached to your back, that makes you aware of how vulnerable to fate and death a person is at every moment of their life. *You never know what might happen, or when.*

What was even more strange was that Mom didn't start nagging Dad, and he didn't start getting defensive. They didn't launch into the same choreographed argument: her lamenting worry upon worry; him offering excuse upon excuse. When the chilly shadow of their mutual past approached, they always quieted down, as if they lived many days pretending such a shadow fades with time, only to be reminded that death never goes away, and of the vexing circumstance that they were both still alive.

My dad's father, "Granddaddy," made a name for himself in Louisville, first as an All-State high school football player, a distinction he earned his junior and senior years at Male High School. From a young age he commanded attention from others on and off the playing field. He liked being known, being involved in the development of such projects as the founding of Lakeside, the opening of Big Spring, the establishment of large, leafy parks for everyone in the city to enjoy. A man's man from the outset, Granddaddy was a local force, a dedicated city alderman. He could also be as stubborn as the Ohio Valley humidity in summer.

In the early sixties, gatherings of decision-making white men was the social rule. Plans and decisions and ideas mingled with the scent of good bourbon and fine cigars. Civic leaders and networking businessmen regularly met for "stag" functions—it was the way the world worked. Dad and Granddaddy both belonged to the Commanding Officers Club of Louisville, both carried the card of membership in their wallets, both were undoubtedly released from speeding tickets, or other infractions, because they belonged to the club.

One night, in July 1962, they drove separate cars to the meeting, as usual. They lived in different parts of town. Granddaddy lived over near Lakeside; Dad lived in the East End, on Napanee, with Mom and Anne and me. Curtie wasn't born yet. The meeting took place in south Louisville, a good drive for each of them, out where the interstate got twisted and confusing. After the gathering, after the cigar smoking and bourbon drinking, Dad told Granddaddy he looked tired and asked if he wanted a ride home.

"No, I'll be fine," came the graveled, irritated response. Granddaddy was a huge man, his hands alone were the size of a bear's paws. No one told him what to do—ever.

On that dark, hazy night he got turned around on the interstate, driving south, away from the city. He fell asleep at the wheel and his car hit an embankment. He was a serving alderman at the time, so news of Ches McCall's one-car accident was reported throughout the following few days on the radio. Had the man not been so physically strong, he likely wouldn't have survived the accident, or so the doctor told my dazed father and mother.

But he never regained consciousness: the local football legend and popular civic leader died like the others, like his wife and son before him, suddenly and in the month of July. Granddaddy was the last ghost to ascend. My parents were twenty-seven years old.

I remember I had one black dress. I only ever wore it to funerals. I hated that dress. After Granddaddy's funeral I threw it away.

Sometime that winter after Granddaddy died, Mom became pregnant. She was using birth control meticulously when she became pregnant with me and with my brother—so much for being in control. A few months into her third go-around with having a baby, her doctor told her that because of some problem with her ovary, he doubted that she'd be able to carry this baby, to prepare for what might happen.

Her private response to the news was to have a one-sided conversation with God, where she clenched her jaw with iron-clad determination and told Him flat out: *I will* have this baby!

The months rocked along as bumpily as expected, given that Anne would be five in August, when the baby was due, and I was a wandering two-and-a-half-year-old. We swam in the pool at Big Spring; Dad played golf in the club championship and on most weekends. They still had some financial cushion from the small inheritance Mom had received after the death of Mama T.

The slow leak caused by Dad's already flourishing alcoholism was obscured by the bourbon-drinking culture of country club life. The undertow of grief was mitigated for awhile by their two adorable daughters and one more baby on the way. The nine months ended, though, with Mom once again saying a fearful good-bye to us, then to Dad, as the hospital orderlies wheeled her through the double doors of the Baptist Hospital.

The early sixties in Louisville resembled the fifties in the fearful manner in which childbirth was approached. Presumably well-trained and well-meaning male obstetricians nodded to anesthesiologists, who performed their miracles while the delivering mother "slept." When she woke up, a newborn wrapped in blankets and wearing a little hat was presented to her. *The doctor and Dad were crying. "Oh, Curt, you got your boy." I was crying not because he was a boy but because he was born.*

I always watched, years later, as she wrapped her arms around Curtie's back, and they marched down the hall for his bedtime ritual, she singing softly: *On the day that you were born the angels got together and decided to create a dream come true. . . .*

He would grin and sway in step with her tune, and sometimes I'd sing along, too, as they made their way down the hall. She'd tuck him in and close the door, not all the way, but enough so noises wouldn't disturb his sleep.

He was everyone's gift, mine too.

As we got older, Mom would sometimes tell us the story of her theory about how God—and life and death—work. *I always felt like you three were sent straight from heaven.* Grandmother Frances sent Anne to be born, which explained why Anne looked so much like her. When Mama T got to heaven, she worked it out with God to override Mom's birth control and send me. Later, Granddaddy special-ordered Curtie.

We were everything to Mom. Her determination to never take our father away ran as deeply as her resolve to give us three kids everything we might possibly need—almost.

9

Occasionally, near-drowning situations occur
that involve two or more victims. Often
the victims clutch each other in their panic.

American Red Cross Lifeguarding, p. 150

A rupture always happened on an ordinary afternoon, in those breathless minutes of transition between school and swim practice, after dropping books in bedrooms and before the time we needed to leave to get to the bank, then to the other kids' houses to pick them up to get to practice on time. On a day that was humming, keeping to the tight train schedule without significant delay, you could never tell when the phone's ring would pop a nail in the track and create yet another derailment.

"Who's Mom talking to?" I said to Curtie, who was watching television in the den, munching on a stack of graham crackers.

"How should I know?" He was eleven; I was thirteen. We were inching our way into that phase in our lives when we would despise being in the same room with each other.

"Yes, yes of course, I'll come over right away," Mom said. As she hung up the phone I could see her face already starting to squish up.

"*OH GOD*," she screamed, running into the den, across the orange-and-brown shag carpet, to the small desk where they kept *the checkbook*, where Mom would sit sometimes at night and fidget and fret over which bills to pay and which to leave past due.

She always elicited pride at making a dollar stretch a little further, at keeping her records so accurate that her balance could dip below ten dollars, or below one dollar, and still she never bounced a check. But now the bank had called and reported that not one but five of the last checks she'd written had bounced. Bacon's and LG&E, the phone company, even the Gateway (everyone in town would know) had received checks stamped with that reddest of marks—insufficient funds.

With Mom screaming in the den, crying and yelling, her eyes squinting and her shoulders caving in, Curtie turned off the television. He looked at me to see if I could make sense out of what was going on, to see what we needed to do. We silently agreed that Mom might be *really* cracking up this time.

"That dirty rat!" she said, her tears drying into a scowl of unmatched rage. I didn't have the guts to ask if I should call Eddie and Ellen, to see if they could get another ride to practice, since I wasn't sure if we were still going to swimming or not. Staring at the checkbook as she was, it seemed she'd forgotten about the train and it needing to be on time.

"He's been taking checks from the back and not writing them down! I'm going to *kill* him!" Just then she looked up at Curtie and me. Curtie was holding a paper towel with graham cracker crumbs on it. I had my beach towel on my shoulder and my goggles in my hand.

"Am I still going to practice?"

"Oh, *God*, what time is it?" She glanced around in a disoriented manner, like she wasn't sure she'd ever seen carpet as ugly, or children as needy. Then, just as steam races through the train's steel pipes setting its massive wheels in motion, a renewed focus surged through her. "Of course we're going! I'll take you to practice, then I have to go over to the bank to get this straightened out. Curtie, you come with me."

He just stood there blinking, the modified plan sinking slowly into his always deliberate thoughts.

"Okay," he said, never one to mind skipping practice, giving me a squint when Mom's back was turned.

In the next instant we were in the car, listening as Mom blasted Dad nonstop for the three minutes it took to get to Ellen's house, then we were quiet, because we *never* discussed our family problems *with anyone*.

As we drove through St. Matthews, behind the pet store, on our way to Eddie's house, I noticed a knot in my stomach, the kind that made it hard to take a deep breath.

Life inside our house was like one of those creepy haunted houses at the fair, where you round a corner and see yourself distorted into a short fat blob or you get caught in a multisided corner of mirrors and no matter how hard you try, you can't find your way out.

It was crazy; it was all getting to be so crazy. I turned the radio knob looking for a good song for practice, one that I could sing while I swam. The best ones had an upbeat rhythm and interesting lyrics to keep me company. In the thirty minutes we were in the car, riding through the park, past the wide spaces of a golf course still marked by tornado-ravaged trees, past grass that was smattered with curling dead leaves, no good songs came on the radio. Some days were like that—no good songs at all.

That night and the next one they argued again, about the money and the nagging, about the lying and the spending. The nights and days blurred in that final week; we were spinning faster and faster and faster, like a car that keeps accelerating, its driver ignoring how sharp the approaching curves really are. Or maybe a better image is the tilt-a-wheel at the fair, where you go round and round, spinning until your brain and guts threaten to spill out of you. That's what that week was like—being on a tilt-a-wheel and not being able to get off.

Mom and Dad were in the kitchen, yelling at each other, their voices so loud I worried the neighbors could hear them.

He stood near the table by the phone, his Marine shoulders pushed forward, his face red and clenched. He spit words like they were knives, cutting anything they touched. She cried and glared at him, her back to the corner where the counters met.

I observed them from the border territory, peering around the door-frame corner, the ghosts huddling behind me, as if *they* needed protection. My heart hit against me like a fist, like it wanted to escape the prison of my chest. It beat down into my stomach and up into my throat. The only thing that leaked out of me was a sense of being safe; it slunk out beneath the back door.

All of a sudden, Mom lunged toward the table, grabbing the short, heavy tumbler full of bourbon.

"I can't take it anymore!" She screamed, heaving the glass into the sink with the arm of a Major League pitcher. Glass and ice sprayed everywhere when it hit the stainless steel.

"I *won't* take it," she yelled again, running out of the kitchen.

Dad stood motionless, not yelling, not following her, just staring at the empty kitchen doorway, momentarily stunned. I ducked into the corner so he wouldn't turn around and catch me spying. That Curtie could continue watching television without looking up was completely unbelievable to me.

"I'm going out for awhile," Mom said, as she passed by the kitchen, keys in her hand. She said nothing to me, nor did she look at Dad or give him a chance to reply. I scooted into the den and pretended to watch television, although it was hard through the tears.

As a family, we'd learned to tiptoe after horrible eruptions like this. Always before, Dad would get nicer, more conciliatory and full of promises. Mom would get drawn into his intentions, into wanting so much to believe what he said. Not this time.

We tiptoed like always, except Dad stayed away until late at night, and I don't think they said many words to each other at all.

A few days later, Mom and I were at the park one evening, watching Curtie's Little League football practice. Orange-and-yellow October leaves drifted to the ground, carrying that musty scent of autumn. There was motion everywhere: little kids squealing down the slide or begging to be pushed higher on the swings. Joggers, walkers, a girls' field hockey team.

A small crowd of mothers and fathers gathered on the sidelines to watch their miniature Vikings and Giants. The boys were an army of munchkins, with clean helmets and oversized shoulders, their skinny, dirty legs poking out the lower ends of their pants. When they tackled each other, their pads clicked more than smacked. The crows cawing in the trees made more racket. Still, they were fun to watch.

Dad didn't show, not a surprise. We were a broken record standing there in the harvest air, a broken record still going around and around. The tilt-a-wheel was slipping off its axle.

Dad wasn't home when we got there; nor was Anne. She worked at the Gateway until seven. We'd been in the house only ten minutes or so when the nail-popping phone rang, when Mom froze in the kitchen like she was staring down the barrel of a gun.

"I understand," she finally said. "Yes. Yes, I see. Thank you for calling." She hung up the phone in a quiet, mechanical way. "That was the man from Plum Run," she said, her voice a monotone. "Your father's been fired."

Her calm marked the moment. None of the usual signs emerged, no shrieking cries, crinkling face, pursed lips turning white. She walked into the dining room, her face to the ceiling, and stood that way with her eyes closed, not saying anything. I didn't know what she was doing, couldn't tell what she was *going to do*.

The air frequency changes in the midst of a crisis, like the para-

lyzed stillness that inhabits trees and animals in the moments before
a tornado appears. Time doesn't so much stop as it changes speed;
everything becomes crystallized and sharp, and slows way down.

"He's here," I called, from my self-appointed post at the living
room window.

Mom jumped into motion then, hauling through the living
room with her determined general's walk, the one where she leaned
forward, face tensed and tilted down—the posture you never
wanted her to have when she was approaching you.

She met him in the front yard. Curtie and I slouched on the
front stoop, quietly picking at the tiny boxwood leaves in the bush
by the railing. We didn't want to miss the most significant moment
of our lives, the moment when my parents would decide to divorce.

"You won't believe what happened," Dad said, trying to be light,
shifting from foot to foot. He was handsome in his blue button-
down and khakis, a weather-beaten John Wayne in a tie, his shirt
still relatively unwrinkled. "They fired *everyone* today."

"Oh, Curt."

Mom had changed into slacks and a shirt after school. Anyone
driving by would've assumed that *he* was the one who had worked all
day, making money for the family, not her. Still strangely calm, she
stood with her hands on her slim hips, green eyes narrowed, hair
wavy with a few rumples of gray. He was much taller than she, even
when he stood as he did now, with his shoulders drooping and his
head hanging low.

"Curt—we love you . . . but we can't carry you anymore."

Curtie and I stared at each other without breathing; we stopped
picking leaves. Any sort of movement seemed like too much. Maybe
it was for my parents, too, because something was definitely different. Dad didn't holler and threaten and get red in the face. Mom
didn't cry and lash out at him. They didn't yell at all—they just
stood there in the front yard, as if frozen on a movie set, the script

lost, neither one knowing what they were *supposed to do* next. My family *never* stopped its motion, ever.

It felt like a hundred years as we stood there, watching them looking at each other, neither seeming aware of anyone or anything else, just the world they inhabited—had shared together for so many years. Dad stood hunched and defeated. He reminded me of an injured tiger skulking in the corner of its cage, the normally proud head fallen, the brown eyes full of sorrow.

Mom said something to him that I couldn't hear and he answered with the faintest nod. He was thirty-nine years old but he looked like he didn't have any idea what he was *supposed to do*.

Then there was movement—Mom walking toward us.

"You kids go watch TV or something; your father and I need to talk."

"Are you okay, Mom?" I said, as we followed her through the door. Dad was getting cigarettes from his car.

"I'm fine," she said, in that tone that meant no more discussion.

Curtie and I obeyed her direction and slipped into the den, although we kept the volume on the set turned down. Curtie sat cross-legged on the floor, three feet in front of the tube while I tip-toed into the edge of the border-territory dining room, in between Dad's den and Mom's kitchen.

He slouched in the kitchen chair closest to the phone, and for once, neither of them poured a drink.

"Curt, why don't you call Charlie."

Charlie? I didn't know this Charlie person and I usually knew *everything* that was going on.

Dad just sat there, his back slumped forward, his long legs stretched out, loafers still on. Mom was going through the phone book, asking what road Charlie lived on.

"That's probably it," Dad said to the second choice.

On the phone, Dad was quiet, using a serious tone I didn't recognize. He sounded more grown-up, in the true sense of the word, not in his usual fake, put-on sort of way.

While on the phone, with its long extension cord, people in my family usually meandered into the dining room to gaze through the living room windows, to *watch the world go by*. I was standing on the step leading from the dining room to the den, eavesdropping, while he talked. When his back was turned, I scooted into the kitchen.

"Mom, what's going on?"

"You're father's making a phone call—just go in there and be quiet."

I hated it when I miss-timed a situation like that, when I was being too nosey and got called down for it. I did as I was told, as if I was nine instead of almost fourteen. I still stayed within earshot, which was more difficult than usual because they weren't yelling at each other.

"Here, his wife wants to talk to you." There was the slightest quiver in Dad's voice.

"No, it's okay, we can come over there," Mom said into the phone.

She hung up and there was more motion in the kitchen, the jingle of keys, Dad walking through the hall to their bedroom, then Mom standing on the step in the dining room.

Until now, Curtie hadn't glanced away from the television, not to ask for supper, not to ask for a snack, not to ask for anything.

"We have to go somewhere," she said.

"Where?" I said, still uncertain if this was the way a divorce happened. I should've known, but I didn't.

"We're going . . . to talk to some friends for a little while." She half-turned. "There's 'Anne's macaroni stuff' in the fridge; you just have to heat it up."

"Okay," I said, not sure how to do that.

"Or Anne'll be home soon; she can fix supper—just tell her where we've gone."

"Okay," I said, unfamiliar with this calm, resigned side of Mom, and with feeling on the outside of what was really happening. "Mom?" I stepped toward her and lowered my head so Curtie wouldn't hear me. "Who is Charlie?"

"He's a man we know—who's an alcoholic—who doesn't drink anymore."

My father had always been a beautiful swimmer. Wide shoulders, powerful arms, he pulled himself through the water with a strong sweeping stroke. Sometimes, in the early Big Spring days, on those stuffy July Sundays when fathers from both teams had gulped enough gin and tonics to turn their cheeks red and make their chests puff out, there would be an extra event added to the swim meet, a relay race pitting four men from our country club against four men from the other side. On occasion, my father swam for the Big Spring "team." Filled with excitement and pride, and a rising fear of possible embarrassment, I'd stand with my brother and sister on the edge of the pool and cheer.

We'd giggle at their belly flop racing dives and at the way some of the men seemed to wrestle with the water rather than glide through it. Secretly, I'd be surprised every time—surprised and proud—as my father slid through the water hardly making a splash. He was strong, he didn't flap like some of the other men, or kick his feet in a frenetic rhythm out of sync with his stroke. He plowed through the water, steady as a barge or a tugboat at full tilt. His head cut the surface without a ripple. His hands dug and paddled as if they were suddenly webbed and ten inches in diameter. Sometimes he'd win; sometimes, lose—it never mattered. All the kids, including us, would jump in the pool after the race, and the jubilant after-meet chaos would begin.

• • •

Had I been remembering his swimming ability, I might not have been so surprised with the events that followed Dad's being fired from Plum Run. For years we'd been paddling, hopelessly, the five of us in a too small lifeboat, or rather the four of us inside and Dad slowly falling off the side, still hanging on but creating an ever-worsening drag on the whole vessel. When Mom finally cut the rope that was connecting Dad to our sinking little boat, we probably all figured he would just sink away. Instead, he swam.

My parents didn't divorce or separate. In fact, they came home a couple of hours later, on that Friday night in 1974, together—not arguing, not crying, but *talking*. Something was definitely different, as I lingered in the kitchen, filling my bowl with a second helping of ice cream while they spoke in low, intimate voices at the table. Something was moving beneath a surface that otherwise appeared absolutely unchanged.

It would be months before I'd begin to recognize the tidal shift that was happening in our family, and years before, well, before the underwater volcano still brewing in our family would explode.

Up until that point, and a year beyond it really, I'd thought every family problem was Dad's fault—everyone did, including him, although he never owned up to his inadequacy outright; he hid his guilt beneath his blustery scowl. He'd turn his head often in disgust, and for years I'd misplaced that disgust, thinking it was us he was disappointed in, not himself. He was the culprit, the one who would be blamed if their marriage—and our family—finally broke apart. *We have to stick together—we're all we've got.*

When I turned fourteen, I was still the perfect daughter. Good grades, responsible, compliant, never had any problems—I was "born twenty-one," in the eyes of my mother and of the world, one of those kids who seemed to have it all together. My sister and brother were the same way, although both of them showed their tempers more directly, making their back talk an untamed animal in need of constant monitoring. I used the "silent treatment" throughout, becoming a glacier in the face of anyone's fire.

I didn't know then that when a glacier melts, it sends out a thunderous cry, a kind of shrieking that echoes against mountain ridges, that swirls into the bowls of canyons. The sound lasts longer than ordinary thunder and is made more surreal by its invisibility, especially against the perfect blue of a clear sky. At fourteen, as I trudged through my days wearing the perfect disguise, no one in the family would've believed (including me) that *I* would turn out to be the culprit, the one responsible for testing the family with a potentially fatal crack. If our family was to shatter, it would be at the words and actions of the least suspected of all—me.

1983

✦ ✦ ✦ ✦ ✦ ✦ ✦ ✦ ✦ ✦

10

*You must be aware of your strengths and
weaknesses in relation to the victim and the
environment when making a body-contact rescue.*

American Red Cross Lifeguarding, p. 142

I n the natural sequence of life in the East End in the early 1980s,
college graduation was followed by marriage and/or employment
by either a prestigious or family company, or admission into a pro-
fessional school, preferably medical or law. Not everyone returned
to a future in Louisville, although a good number of graduates did.
For all my dreams of college offering an escape from the town, and
despite my reliance on a tautly planned future, destiny's neat trick
was to take me right back to where I'd started.

There's only so much planning you can do, only so many ways to
fool yourself into believing that fate doesn't hold the trump cards.

After plotting from age fifteen to be "a doctor" I was now a college alum on a waiting list for acceptance to medical school, my
future at its all-time most blank. My first job out of college was the
same as my last job in high school: lifeguard at the Louisville Boat
Club.

This was the summer of my sinking, when I regularly sat on the
bottom of the pool after hours, unable to cross into the blackness
that pulled on me yet unable to burst into life either. I lived in no-
man's-land, in that vacuous space between teenager and grown-up.
I'd gained and lost and gained weight at school; at the club I felt

whalelike around the slim, tanned mothers of two and three. It takes a barge full of denial to chug around a swimming pool in a tank suit and not think about how you look. Instead, I sat in the chair and twirled a whistle around two fingers, first to the right, then to the left.

The oversized prescription sunglasses that I wore left me with a headache by the end of the day. I still coached, as an assistant, but the glory days for the club had passed—or at least my singular passion for leading them to another City Championship was gone. This place, this league, this summer team had been so vitally important to me just a few years earlier—now it was hopelessly small time, even with its affluence. There was a wider world out there and no place for me in it.

"That's a warning, Matthew. One more time and you're sitting!" I yelled. It was a busy Saturday, the humidity ferocious and the wind lost to the north. It was the kind of day where even the coiffed mothers dipped into the shallow end because to sit outside for too long made you cranky.

The precious little kids I'd coached for the past several summers were now prank-pulling teenyboppers. Their bodies and gestures, their curiosity and entitlement—their foreignness—had been special delivered and absorbed without my ever recognizing it.

I could no longer sing and play imaginary games with them as we'd done when they were six and eight and nine. Now their interests lay solely with each other. They moved in packs rather than as single units. The boys were a tribe, the girls were a tribe, and they were constantly mixing via ad hoc chicken fights (not allowed) or via snapping butts with their towels (also not allowed). I didn't know them anymore, not really, even though I'd taught many of them to swim, had carried their light, wet bodies on my back and shoulders at one time or another. Worst of all, though, as I sat in that unforgiving heat watching them, they made me remember what I'd tried so hard to forget.

• • •

As a teenager I was still swimming on a fierce schedule. Tired, dragging, feeling heavy. Morning brought a certain kind of dread with it, one that developed into a strong westerly current against which I had to push. A silent predawn ride to the chilly water, laps to swim before school, then a stinky, complicated bus trip into the dismal streets of downtown.

This was my life in ninth grade. It was a confusing time in the city, 1975, given that for the first time a mass of convoluted bus routes carried black children to the suburbs, including the East End, and white kids—like myself—down Brownsboro Road, to Zorn Avenue, onto the interstate then off, past the stockyards and into the parking lot of Meyzeek Junior High School.

This was the year things shifted. A cold murk started accumulating inside me like that foamy, brown scum that collects in the pocket of a river cove, a place where the water doesn't flow as cleanly, where junk and disgust gather and stay.

Every morning at Meyzeek those of us who arrived on early buses waited for several minutes in a glass-enclosed foyer until the first bell rang. The small space smelled of old linoleum and beaten air, of orange juice burps and the shavings of whittled pencils. With my hair still damp from swim practice and smelling of chlorine, I shifted my backpack from one shoulder to the other and kept my eyes away from everyone else's. None of my classmates rode these buses so I didn't know the kids standing in the foyer well enough to have a conversation with them. We weren't supposed to talk anyway, as we stood there like corralled animals awaiting our walk up the stockyard plank.

Outside, the gray asphalt merged so convincingly with the low, swollen clouds that it was difficult to discern one from the other. One November morning, as I stared out the window at the unending sea of gray, I became aware of the dread in my belly, how it so perfectly matched the gray wall of parking-lot sky. I stared at the cement ground, the cement sky, at the prison walls that kept me locked inside this stuffy city, confined to the cage of this school, sentenced to a life—inside me—without parole.

I knew for certain at that moment that something was terribly wrong with me, something I couldn't name or define; it was like a deadly mat of tangled weeds spreading underneath the surface of my smile, cold fingers coming up from the depths of my interior. I couldn't let *anyone* know—not ever—because if they ever knew the *real* me, they would hate me, they would despise and laugh at me, they would know—finally—what a fake I really was.

After a couple of minutes of staring, a new thought floated into my head like steam off a warm river when it meets the cold crack of dawn air. *I can always kill myself.* This was a decisively new thought. Its clarity and absolute privacy didn't frighten me—they brought a strange sort of soothing companionship. Here, finally, was an optional plan, an escape channel, a way to drift instead of having to swim.

When the bell rang, the thoughts disappeared. Motion always helped. We shuffled into the halls like sleepy cattle. I nodded to students and teachers. They reoriented me to myself—my outer, more comfortable self—as did the metallic smell of my locker, the bright shock of blue as I lifted the math folder from my backpack, the neat enough handwriting on the lined notebook paper—college rule, of course, always college rule.

"Good morning, Madame President," Mr. Johnson said, bowing his stout frame as I walked into geometry.

"Morning," I said brightly, giving him a little salute, which made him grin. I'd been elected Student Council president earlier in the year and he still called me that sometimes.

"And to you, Miss Veep," he said, which turned me around.

Kelly was my best friend. She lived in Ballard's school district so this would be the only year we were in school together.

"Hey," I said, glad to see her after the weekend. The bell then blasted through the walls—that school had the longest, most irritating bells—and all conversation between us, between anyone, ceased. His rule was you had to be in your seat before the bell ended or you started the class with one demerit. I swung into my desk and concentrated on how to pass a note to Kelly without getting caught.

I *liked* school and I was good at it. The more confusing part of me—the girl who was unsure about certain things—was always deeply camouflaged at school. The me the world saw—friends, teachers, parents, coaches—had a quick, genuine smile and a mature, easygoing manner.

"You have a good countenance," Ms. Barret told me sometime later.

"Thanks" I said, sensing a compliment. "What's that?"

"Look it up," she said, laughing.

I was as much a paradox at fifteen as I was in the lifeguard chair at twenty-two. Like the surface of a summer ocean, I appeared calm, inviting, playful. But underneath—where no one could see—there were hollowed craters and dark, dangerous caves that harbored a treacherous undertow. So long as I stayed away from that tug, or so I thought, I could make everything okay. Life is so much easier when you keep it in your head, when no other people are involved. Reality is what gets in the way.

That ninth-grade spring limber daffodils and brave grass popped up from the dead brown earth. The air carried brand-new light, making the gray recede. It also delivered a bona fide miracle to our family—two miracles really.

Dad celebrated one year of living without taking a drink. It was like living with a new person in our house, one who thoughtfully tracked the deeper running streams of life like me.

One Sunday afternoon I was upstairs writing a few lines of a never-to-be-shown poem, staring out the window, thinking about something Dad had said earlier. He and I had fallen into talking regularly, *really* talking, and when I emerged from my room there he was again, at the bottom of the steps, a battered yellow legal pad in his hand.

"Did you understand what I meant earlier?" he said. I could see the beginning of a bald spot in the center of his head. The skin on his face that once furrowed so often in a scowl now relaxed into an expression of honesty when he looked up. Baiting spite didn't flash in his eyes. He leaned his John Wayne frame against the banister in a casual, even self-conscious, way.

"I *do* believe there is a power greater than myself, a Higher Power. For me that's God—but for some people it might be something else," he said.

"Like what?" I asked, intrigued by this curious stranger, the one who kept presenting himself, wanting to start another conversation. Not an argument. Not a list of commands. *A conversation.*

"Well, like the group. They say you can believe in the power of the group."

"That's like God, too, don't you think?" I descended the steps as lightly as I could.

"What do you mean?"

"Well—I believe that all things are connected, I mean all living things. Nature, people—everything. What connects them is, well, like a spiritual current—or something—the same thing that connects the group."

He studied me as I spoke. I watched him watch me, saw him consider the words I'd said, saw him respect them and stretch them to see how well they fit.

"Okay—I see what you mean."

We stood in the living room, the serene gaze of his mother's portrait cascading into the space, and talked about life and the universe and God. Mom's footsteps tapped on the wooden basement stairs as she carried laundry; they beat like a drum in the distance. He wanted to talk, to share the things he was discovering about life and himself. I liked talking about the meanings of things—plus, I was a good listener.

In an uncommon arrangement of timing, my father and I were both fifteen and waking up to the world at the same time. I read *Walden*, he read "The Big Book." He made notes on his readings and was bursting to share them. Mom, still living at a machine-gun pace, had very little patience to listen to his philosophizing.

Always the practical planner, the lead general of the family, the one who had led us through hell without losing a single soldier, she still wanted him to make more money so we wouldn't have to worry all the time. She wanted to be invited to parties and feel comfortable hosting them; she wanted him to have a job she could be proud of. Basically, she still wanted him to be different.

But he *was* different. He no longer yelled or baited or huffed out of the room with a red face. He wanted to *help*, to actually participate; he wanted to take over writing the bills and balancing the checkbook—a suggestion she didn't exactly trust or welcome.

He still came home late because he went to "attitude meetings," but he was up and showered early every morning, no more sore head hanging in his hands at the kitchen table. The day he came home with a job—cleaning a church—Mom was both relieved and embarrassed; it wasn't the kind of job suitable to Big Spring fathers, not that we ever went near the place anymore, anyway. Still, she could see he was trying, that he'd quit drinking and was now trying to learn how to live as an adult. He had to make peace with the ghosts, too.

• • •

The summer Dad was sixteen he worked for the Parks and Recreation Department, a job that assigned him any number of tasks. His brother, Ches, still lived at home, with plans to start medical school in the fall at the University of Louisville, his ambition to be a surgeon.

That particular Saturday morning, in the choking heat of July, there was strain between Dad and his mother. He'd smarted off to her the night before—something that was rare for him to do— although perhaps not so unusual for a teenager his age. So in the morning he decided to walk to the upper diamond at Cherokee Park, since it wasn't far from their house. He had a Little League game to umpire.

When he got home he learned that his mother had buckled from the pain of a brain-splitting headache and she'd been taken to the hospital. His father and brother said she had to stay but that she'd be coming home soon, that there wasn't any reason to go back to the hospital that evening.

Ches Sr. and Jr. visited her the next two days, when Dad was at work, and by the evening they reported optimistically that the next day she'd be coming home.

"We'll go tomorrow," his father said, his voice delivering the authority of a gavel.

That Tuesday Dad was working at the Parks warehouse, a good ways from home, when he received a call to go immediately to St. Anthony's hospital downtown. When he arrived she was dead. Cerebral hemorrhage. She was fifty.

Life kind of went to hell in a handbasket after that.

The bellow of a boat horn soared up from the river. Rest period sent the teenyboppers into the snack bar and little kids to play a game of tag outside the fence. A couple of mothers waded in the shallow end with their babies but otherwise the pool was still. I jumped into the deep end and swam a couple of snail-paced laps.

"Can I race you?" Michael said, swinging on the ladder.

"I don't know, you're getting pretty fast," I said. He was a skinny eight-year-old with two oversized front teeth and an enormous smile. "Maybe another day."

"Betcha can't swim underwater—two laps like Rick can."

"Whatcha betting?" I said, winking. Then I took a breath and pushed off. The silence under the surface massaged and quieted me. I took strong breaststroke pulls and powerful frog kicks. At the wall I turned without lifting up. By midway down the second length I felt my heart beating harder and fixed my eyes on the wall.

"Ahhh," I said, reaching the edge.

He grinned like I'd just flown to the moon and back. Ah, the thrills of summer.

Mine wasn't shaping up to be anything as flashy as Anne or Curtie's. She was now living in Lexington, researching genealogies on a horse farm, putting a life together for herself. And Curtie, midway through college, was spending the summer in the North Carolina mountains teaching little campers how to sail and swim and make their beds in the morning.

My parents didn't say much about my future, or lack thereof, sensing that I didn't want to talk about it. They were silently hoping as much as I was that another miracle would drop into our family sphere. Dad marking a year of solid sobriety had been the first of that incredible year when I turned fifteen, but it hadn't been the most magical.

By the spring of 1976 hope was everywhere. The city had survived its first year of desegregation without splintering into race riots and was now readying for its signature event, the Kentucky Derby. American flags appeared on front porches as the nation geared up for both a presidential election and a bicentennial bash. The breeze blew freedom all around, especially in our neighborhood.

This breeze bore no resemblance to the tornado or to anything other than the gentle wave of an old friend. Everywhere the dogwood branches were bumpy with buds. The laughing breeze came in bursts through the windows in the den, sailing over the silver bowl in the middle of the dining room table. It whisked past the cherry hutch into the living room toward the front screen door. It brushed your cheek like a finger, like a whisper, as if the ghosts knew before we did of the next great fortune coming our way. Then again, of course they knew—the importance of education was passed through generations of my family as steadily as broad shoulders and wide-set eyes.

In the layered world of social prestige in the affluent East End, the question wasn't *are* you going to college but *where*. More important than having a bigger house, an enviable bank account, or membership to a smooth-lawned country club was going to "a good school." It was the last front on which my mother could compete with the social world she missed, the world she'd grown up in.

By age fourteen, she and her father had already discussed where she might go to college. Living in upstate New York, the logical places were the top schools in the Northeast. Smith. Vasser. Radcliffe. She was smart, ambitious, well liked. Her father was an undeclared feminist in the way he raised his daughter to seize opportunities, to study hard, to seek an interest in the world around her. In 1947, he told her she could be anything in the world she wanted to be.

William West was a man of contrasts, a devoted family man who also harbored a call to adventure. He traveled the country by train, sending postcards from such places as San Francisco and Milwaukee. In those long years of war rations and gas lines after the Great Depression, he advanced as an executive for the much revered company of Beechnut. Rising to vice president, the young man had a blazing future ahead of him. He walked the streets of New York City with the authority granted only to the most worldly, taking his daughter on the train to shop for Christmas or to see a Broadway show. His kids owned the finest ski equipment, rifles for duck hunting, the latest in saddle shoe fashions.

Originally from the humble town of Hopkinsville, Kentucky, he found his way to Washington and Lee, that preeminent southern school for men, but the excessive drinking among his fellow students bothered him, so after a year he transferred to Centre College, the respected private college not far from his home. It was there that he fell in love with "T" Fox, the fun-loving and soon-to-be Carnival Queen—and she with him. These were the fairy tale days of the 1920s, when the Charleston was in and the waltz was out. A time when you could count on the security of custom, when convention rolled out its wide red carpet for those Southerners fortunate enough to have white skin and social position.

But it's always the twisting curves in the road that you can't see coming, the hard turns when the pavement gives way to gravel or to a rocky cliff. My mother's dreams of going to Smith, of being a doctor, of exploring the world, died in the woods that cold day in October 1950 when her father went hunting and never came home. Massive heart attack. No warning. He was forty-five; she was fifteen.

All the words over all the years, all the achievements by her children, all the longing and the tears, could never fill the gash his death created. Money always short, her marriage disappointing and in tatters, the only dreams she had left lay squarely on the shoulders of her three kids. Good grades were an unspoken requirement in our childhood. Her own example set a fixed standard for us—she'd not gone to Smith or Vasser but to Centre on a full academic scholarship with a stipend for living expenses.

Where the McCall kids went to college mattered—a lot.

• • •

When Anne applied to schools in the fall, things were still confusing for our family. Dad hadn't been drinking for a few months, which was good, but he hadn't gotten his job at the church yet, which meant he brought home no paycheck. There was no such thing in our household as a college savings account.

Anne wanted to go to Centre, like her parents and grandparents before her. Mom didn't like the idea. *You don't want to go there, it's too small.* There wasn't a lot of arguing—my mother spoke with a certainty that could make you doubt the color of the sky you were seeing with your own eyes. *Why would you want to go there?*

So-and-so got accepted to Duke—if they took her, maybe they'll take you.

By spring Dad was working—and he didn't have vacation time—so he couldn't go on our annual pilgrimage to the holy land of Ormond Beach during spring break. Anne left him with specific instructions: if she received any mail from colleges, he was to open it right away and call.

We were in that postbeach, predinner showering period on April 15 when the phone rang. Anne was still on the beach with her friends.

"Hello?" Mom said, relaxed and starting to get tan. I was sitting on the couch with my feet on an indestructible coffee table, enjoying the feel of cool lotion on my prickly skin.

"What?" she said. I turned at the alarm in her voice. Then she started laughing.

"There's no way she can go," she said, absently wiping lunch crumbs from the little kitchen table.

"You're kidding," she said, giving me the thumbs-up. "Okay. Oh, we're doing fine. I love you too. Bye."

"What?" I said, my arms raised. By now I was standing in the middle of the room. Curtie appeared with his head and face still wet from the shower. His shoulders were pink.

"She got in," Mom said, in a daze. She shook her head as if to wake up. "Go find Anne. She got into Duke—and they gave her a scholarship!"

We whooped and high-fived and then Curtie and I ran down to the beach with the miracle news.

We rode Anne's Duke wave all the way to the end of the school year, until the grand bicentennial summer began like all the less decorated before it, with Lakeside swim practice in the morning and afternoon. Except unbeknownst to anyone, including me, a secret being had taken up residence inside me by then, one that hid out in those dark inner caverns. From time to time it would send up bubbles of energy that seized my voice box and sent words of *its* choice into the world. This intangible stream explained why sometimes people looked at me as if I was wise—like my father did that day—as if I maybe knew more than they'd given me credit for knowing, which of course I didn't because this *being* wasn't really *me*, not in any knowable sense.

Louisville wore a pretty face that day in mid-June. The scent of magnolias and honeysuckle gave a loose, easy feeling to the air as Mom drove Curtie and me across town. She turned onto Lakeside Drive, hoping to get a good parking place, when this voice appeared in the back of my mouth and pushed my lips into a paradoxical smile. At times that called for sadness or seriousness or something approaching reverence, the stupidest smile would plant itself on my face.

"Mom," the voice said, with nary a conscious intention from me.

"Yes?"

"I think I want to quit." That particular smile widened; it was a smile of incredulity, of release, a smile of a thousand birds taking flight.

"What?"

"I want to quit swimming."

She stopped at the stop sign and looked at me.

"I want to quit, too," Curtie said from the backseat, my ally to the death.

"There's a space in front," I said, pointing.

Mom gunned around the corner to the spot, turned the engine off, and sat there, as if she could feel the weight of our mighty train coming to a surprising and much-needed halt. We could all feel it in the way we just sat there in the car, not saying anything, the breeze as buoyant as an ocean scent washing over us through the open windows.

"Well," she said, still stunned. Her tan was deepening to light copper and there were lines around her eyes from squinting and laughing and worrying. "Go on to practice. We'll talk about it with your father when we get home."

There was a lightness to my gait as I hopped on the stone wall on my way to the entrance. Everything appeared altered. I noticed all the people swimming at Lakeside just for the fun of it, kids jumping off the diving boards, Moms and their toddlers in the baby pool, or sitting on the long narrow steps leading to the shallow end.

Our family had been cracking apart two summers earlier when Anne turned sixteen and quietly dropped off the team and into the after-school workforce. Like about making good grades, there was an unspoken understanding among us kids that when we were old enough, which was sixteen in the state of Kentucky, we would get a real job. If we could contribute to the household finances, maybe Mom wouldn't have to work three jobs.

Mom never told Anne to quit the team and get a job; she just did. We had a paper route and Curtie, age ten, started the grass-cutting business that would one day buy him a car. When Anne turned sixteen she applied to be a cashier at the Gateway—she was tired of swimming anyway.

• • •

The waters, though, had now changed dramatically. Anne was going to Duke in the fall, and Dad, solidly sober, was reliably employed. One result of this great tidal shift was that I was experiencing the thrilling luxury of *having a choice.*

Before that day I'd never considered choosing to swim; it was just something we did. We swam like hell, swam as if we were crossing the ocean. We swam to stay afloat, to stay alive. Day in and day out, we stayed in motion, following the train schedule of workouts and weekend meets and car pools and naps between practices. We did what we were *supposed to do*—we swam.

"Well—it's your life," my parents said that evening. They asked me a few questions but really they were accepting of my decision, and Curtie's too. Football practice would begin for him in August anyway.

The rest of the summer promised to be different from all the others before it, a carefree childhood packed into two months. Because she was now a principal, Mom worked in the summer. That meant that for the first time Curtie and I were free agents, able to hang around the house unsupervised, to do whatever we wanted.

After we spent a week watching television, devouring bags of potato chips and chocolate chip cookies, Mom returned from work one day and announced that she had signed us up for group tennis lessons at the park. He and I liked the plan since we were already bored by having nothing *to do.*

As little kids we'd taken a tennis clinic at Big Spring, where the most fun thing to do was hit the ball as hard as you could over the fence to see if you could land it in the pool. Of course that meant getting kicked off the court, unless you could do it without the pro seeing you.

These public lessons at Crescent Hill would be different, of course, open to anyone. Plus, we wouldn't be dependent on a car pool, once we convinced Mom to let us ride our bikes—four or five miles, mostly on sidewalks. In the most practical ways, then, we really were free.

"Wait up," Curtie yelled as he approached on his yellow ten-speed.

I coasted to a halt in front of the car wash, just this side of the railroad tracks. At eight-thirty in the morning the grease from the White Castle grill smelled like wet rust.

"I got caught when that bus turned," he said, stopping. A rim of sweat glistened at the edge of his forehead. He would be thirteen in a month or so and although his feet were getting bigger, his hopeful expression was the same one he wore when he was five.

"We should ride through the parking lot then cross at the light on Frankfurt," I said.

"Okay," he said, adjusting the tennis racquet on his shoulder.

We stayed on the sidewalk on Frankfurt Avenue, which was pretty smooth except for the gravel leading into the nursery, and the various slants where tree roots were pushing it up. Our trek took us past the Vogue theater on the left and the green fields of the Masonic Home orphanage on the right. During a break in traffic we crossed in the middle of the street, over the railroad tracks again, to the park entrance. Fully leafed oak trees threw a canopy of shade along the short road. It was late June with green busting out everywhere. A tractor rumbled along the golf course beyond the fence, sending the scent of grass clippings our way.

"That wasn't too bad," I said to Curtie as we both silently sized up the other kids. Neither of us knew anyone. Kids, eleven through fifteen, some black, most white, lounged or bounced balls against their racquets. In such social circumstances especially, McCall kids stuck together.

"Is this okay?" Curtie said, about to drop his bag on the court, inside the fence. He spoke in that quiet way we had, so no one else would hear.

"Let's put them over here," I said, not wanting anyone to get into our lunch by mistake or intent. It was just about to start; we'd need to leave a little earlier tomorrow so we'd have more time.

"Okay everybody, good morning. I want everyone twelve and under on courts one and two—over there. The rest of you line up over here."

"See you at break," I said and winked.

"Okay," Curtie said, walking with his head up, his steps with their signature deliberateness.

Time evaporated as we ran around the court, chasing the ball, sprinting when we could, loafing when we got tired. I felt free, sprung from the shackling schedule of the past couple of years. Just to run around, to be sweating and whacking the ball, to be laughing and cutting up; it was fun, more fun than I'd had in a long time.

There was no way to know, in those easy summer days at the park, how drastically life would change for me in the coming months. Just because you can't see a tidal wave in the distance doesn't mean it isn't there.

11

One sticky day in August we loaded the big green Pontiac wagon to take Anne to Duke. We left a few days before she was scheduled to arrive on campus so Mom and Dad could enjoy a sentimental journey through Camp Lejune on the North Carolina coast.

"Remember when we used to go to the movies on Friday nights?" Dad said, driving.

"Sure," Mom said, turning around to talk to us. "One night we got there late and none of the lounge chairs in the back were available—that's where we'd been sitting all summer. Then they made an announcement that those seats were for field officers only." Her eyes lifted in an impish expression.

"What were you?" Curtie said.

"Second lieutenant," Dad said.

"So what happened? Did you get in trouble?" I said.

Mom and Dad laughed. "Nothing happened—we just didn't sit there after that."

Curtie and I rolled our eyes at each other.

"Your go," he said.

We were playing gin in the backseat. The car was exceptionally cramped, given Anne's trunk and all our bags. Anne was leaning against the window, her legs taking up more than her third of the seat, so I was balancing the pick-up and discard piles on my thigh.

"You kids put those cards away, we're here," Dad said, sounding more like the father on *My Three Sons* than at any other moment in my life. We instinctively straightened our posture when we saw the uniformed marine standing at the gate. Some of the cards slid between my legs. We were dead silent while Dad spoke with him.

"I used to love it when they saluted as I drove by," Mom said, as we drove away.

"Why'd they salute *you*?" Curtie said.

"Well—they saluted the car," Dad said.

"Did you make special trips just so they'd do it?" I said, wisecracking.

"Of course not," Mom said, turning around with a mock frown and a surprising wink. "Not too often," she said glancing over at Dad who laughed.

My parents hadn't been in this good of a mood since we'd driven the strip at Daytona Beach, seven or eight years earlier. Like then, they were full of stories and nostalgia, like the time Dad left at four o'clock in the morning for maneuvers. When he got home after dark his face was black from mud and camouflage.

"That first night he nearly scared me to death," she said.

The stories excited us and kept us looking out the window, hoping to glimpse a tank or an armored truck, even a jeep. Mostly we saw pine trees.

"I thought I could find . . ." Dad was saying, turning down yet another road lined with pine forest. Curtie and I dealt another hand. Anne closed her eyes again and tried to fall back to sleep.

Finally, we left the base and came upon a bridge to Topsail Island.

"It's beautiful," Anne said, sitting up, her hair mussed from sleeping.

"I want to play putt-putt," Curtie said.

"Let's find where we're going first," Dad said. "What's the name of the place?"

More familiar with the swept, overly developed beaches of Ormond and Daytona, at first we didn't quite know what to make of the clapboard houses and occasional two-story motels, much less these things called dunes.

The hotel was a dud; at least it didn't measure up to the Ormond Biltmore, but nothing ever would. The same ocean called to us, though, and we charged in just like when we were little. The waves felt bigger than the ones in Florida. Mom and Dad joined us soon after; they were both expert bodysurfers. We laughed and compared rides. Then we all rode the same wave and dedicated it to Anne.

After that I glanced at her a little more closely. It was beginning to dawn on me that she really wasn't coming home with us. So far it just felt like we were on vacation.

Until the day we drove onto campus. Even Curtie and I were held breathless by that first gothic view of the Duke Chapel.

"Oh wow," Mom said. The rest of us just stared.

What an astonishing, awesome, intimidating place! Anne didn't say a lot as we all traipsed around campus, trying not to look like the undercultured country club dropouts that we were. Then the moment came when we had to drive away, when our tight-knit family universe, as knotted up as it was, had to untangle a bit and extend a little farther into the world. *We have to stick together—we're all we've got.*

"I love you," Anne said bravely as she hugged me, dry eyed.

"I love you, too," I said, hugging her back, suddenly more curious about what she was going *to do.* "Good luck."

She stood on the landing area on the side of the East Campus dorm, blotches of wet spots staining the yellow bricks of the building behind her. Her long hair curled a little in the drizzle and there was a familiar sadness in her eyes. The rain that had started some-time in the morning was still falling in an obstinate drip by the time we drove away.

Mom cried and cried and cried. Curtie and I teased her in our typical manner of minimizing anything of seriousness. Dad drove the car, steady and calm and patient.

It's like I'm losing my right arm.

We arrived at the roadside hotel after a hot, tearful day of driving and piled out of the wagon, which still seemed full even without Anne and her trunk. Appreciative of the air-conditioning and the space, Curtie, Dad, and I plopped on the beds and flipped on a preseason football game. Dad was stretched out, glad to be out of the car.

Mom came into the room, her face lined and puffy. "Curt, can I see you for a minute?"

They exchanged a gaze of knowing, her revealing that vulnera-bility she so closely guarded, him offering his emotional steadiness to her. She never nagged him in these rare times—when she needed him outright—nor did he gripe about his help being requested. At fifteen, I was putting together that this interaction between them had less to do with his sobriety and everything to do with history, with what they'd been through on this planet—together. They could seem to hate each other one minute then be there for each other the next. Underneath everything—all the anger and resent-ment and longing and deaths—underneath it all, they were best friends.

A heavy exhale escaped as he sat up and slid into his loafers. Mom still stood in the door frame, waiting. After they left I went to the window and peeked at them from the edge of the curtain. She was crying harder and he held her as she shook. They were back in their world that could never fully include us, where someone you love and need goes away, leaving your heart cracked. Except Anne hadn't died, she'd gotten a scholarship to Duke. Mom was so proud of her; it had never occurred to me that it would be hard for her to have Anne—or any of us—go away to school even though that's what she wanted for us, desperately.

I turned around and hopped on the bed before they got back to the room.

"What's the score?" Dad said as he came in behind Mom.

"Twenty-one fourteen Packers," Curtie said, his face squished between his hands as he lay on his stomach on the bed.

"Anybody mind if I take a shower?" Mom said.

I don't think any of us looked up or answered. After a few seconds she gathered her things and went into the bathroom.

Excitement faded to reality when we returned to the house without Anne. We were now outnumbered: four people to five ghosts, although with Dad becoming more of a real person, the teams seemed closer to even. Still, dead people reach a perfection the rest of us can only dream about. The mistakes they made while alive are quickly forgotten; what endures is the trademark laugh, the bear-claw handshake, the celebrity smile.

In the wake of Dad's sobriety, the floors in our house turned from the fun house variety to normal. The attic floors still creaked, though, and our grandmothers kept watch on all the coming and going from the living room. Without the train schedule of swim practice, our individual activities spun with less synchrony. Curtie sweated most evenings in the park learning to be a middle linebacker. I spent most evenings at Lakeside, of all places, since I'd said yes when the coach offered me a job coaching the eight and under team.

My interest in school started slipping a little, as did my enthusiasm for much of anything. I didn't notice at first the sludge feeling taking hold inside. My focus had locked on one thing: basketball tryouts.

• • •

In the gym I wore a poker face of ease as I scrutinized the girls from last year's team. They flew down the court—dribbling, blocking out, popping twenty-footers. My stomach fluttered at how good they were. They were all excellent athletes like me, or better. They were tall, fast, strong, and . . . physical. I grabbed one of the balls from the rack and tossed it gently between my hands, waiting for my turn.

It was a sunny day but cool outside. Inside, the gym felt hot and smelled of fresh sweat. Afternoon sun threw blocks of light on the wood floor from high rectangular windows. The coach, a woman about my height with black bangs cut straight across her forehead, wore sweat pants, an orange short-sleeve shirt, and a whistle around her neck. Something about her unnerved me.

"Here," yelled Yvonne, a seemingly fearless player who darted and sprinted faster than anyone I'd ever seen. She made a great move and laid the ball up, eliciting a few claps, to which she answered with a cocky strut.

There was so much to take in, more than I could figure out. Being there charged me up despite the spikes of intimidation in my belly. It helped when we started scrimmaging, although I felt slow and awkward; the moves that worked against Curtie at our neighbor's basket weren't fooling any of these girls. Some of them could read me cold.

I made the first cut but the second week got harder. We scrimmaged more, although I could never tell how—or if—I was measuring up.

"Nice move," Yvonne said to me once.

"Thanks," I said, half-smiling, not revealing how much it meant.

On the last day, after we ran "suicides," which meant running up and back and up and back slapping this line then the next one, Coach said she had a few announcements.

"By tomorrow after school I'll have the team posted. You all have done a good job, but we're limited to the number we can carry on the team."

She was all business. Her soft-spoken voice didn't match the toughness of her countenance. She could get your attention with that whistle, though.

"Games are Tuesday and Friday nights. Away games we meet here and ride the bus together. Got that?"

People nodded although I knew this wouldn't include me. I wasn't good enough to make the team.

The next day I hurried down the hall to the gym to find Coach during lunch. When I saw her talking to a girl near a hall bulletin board, I got nervous but I pushed the feeling down with a deep breath.

I stepped closer when the girl walked away.

"Excuse me?" I said, my voice flimsy at first.

"Yes. Cathy, right?" She turned to face me directly. She didn't seem as tall standing this close to me.

"Yes ma'am."

She just stood there looking at me, her eyes small. She wore no makeup.

"I needed to tell you that I have a job on Friday evenings so—I have to drop out of tryouts."

Her eyes narrowed.

"What kind of job?" she asked.

I explained about the coaching, that I didn't usually get home until eight, the same time the games started. She suggested that something might be able to be worked out. That secret being inside me seized my voice.

"Well, I—I need to work," I said in a way that invited no compromise, "so I guess I better just withdraw." I was doing this to avoid suffering the rejection of not being good enough—that much about myself I did know.

"That's too bad," she said, her small eyes looking through me. "You probably would've made the team."

My heart fell like a lead weight going straight to the bottom of the ocean. There was nothing I could say to undo my stupidity. *Nothing*. My disappointment was so huge I couldn't even *think* about it.

The next afternoon I told Mom I couldn't play on the team because the games conflicted with my Lakeside job. She was in the kitchen, still dressed from school in khaki skirt and a blue-striped button-down shirt. I wore my standard Levi's, an Izod shirt—I'd taken my pullover sweater off when I'd come in the house—and a ribbon belt with gold turtle buckles.

"Is that same woman still over there coaching?" she asked, straining to sound casual. She knew most of the teachers from the four years Anne spent at Waggener.

"Uh, huh."

Mom turned toward the kitchen sink but her intention was unmistakable. "It's just as well," she said, opening the dishwasher. "I always thought she might be a little 'weird.'"

I frowned behind her back and started to ask what she meant but didn't. Deep down I sort of knew.

"What's for dinner?" I opened the refrigerator.

"Pot roast and beautiful people peas."

"Great," I said, perusing the shelves for a snack. I gave up and went to the hall closet in search of crackers. Mom was saying something about Anne having found a ride home for Thanksgiving. I was just relieved that I didn't have to confess to actually quitting tryouts.

"I almost forgot," Mom said. "Elizabeth called. There's a Dasmine meeting tomorrow night at her house at seven."

"Okay, thanks."

"Will you need a ride?" she asked as I slathered a third cracker with peanut butter. I'd put the other two on a paper towel to take upstairs.

"No, I'll get someone to pick me up."

• • •

Dasmine was the high school sorority that many of the future debutantes of Louisville belonged to. Its male counterpart, Atheneum, boasted many of these girls' fathers on its alumni list, including mine. The "who-you-know" networking that began early in life stretched for generations in some East End families.

Belonging to Dasmine was fun enough, although I never had a desire to follow in my sister's footsteps to be president. In high school I hovered on the edges of a few social crowds, Dasmine being just one of them. I knew people from school, from swimming, from the year I was bussed to Meyzeek. And I still knew a lot of girls in the East End simply from having grown up in adjacent neighborhoods and going to Chenoweth Elementary with them. Everyone who went to Chenoweth—which was a good chunk of the affluent East End—knew Mom. She was a favorite teacher.

Geography and other, less visible forces kept me on the outer edges of the Dasmine/debutante crowd. The girls who didn't go to private school went to Ballard because they lived on the wealthier side of Brownsboro Road. Our house was in the Waggener district.

I was more of a tomboy than Sarah and Elizabeth and Lori and Lynn anyway, although most of them were good field hockey players. Being a swimmer excused my tomboyish athleticism—Title IX had yet to rewrite women's sports but the crest of its wave was building.

In the mid-1970s, girls could be athletic so long as they didn't take it too far—meaning act too much like a boy or in some other way cause people to think you might be "weird." To be "strange," or "that way" or "a lezzie" was an unmentionable taboo with an unfathomable fate.

I learned instinctively from voice intonations and averted eyes what was acceptable and what wasn't. At age fifteen I'd never heard

the word homosexuality spoken, nor did I have any conscious concept of what it meant. Such questions were unthinkable, both in
conversation and in my own mind.

That evening after supper, before finishing my math homework, I
went into Anne's bedroom for a minute. Mom kept it dusted and
vacuumed, the bed always made with the same cotton bedspread.
The wallpaper with its tiny flowers still appeared surprisingly fresh
despite its age. The antique cannonball bed post felt smooth. The
flap on the tiny wooden desk opened without a squeak and the
antique rocker now held a good-sized teddy bear. In the closet there
was an empty space, just a few hangers dangling, then some coats
and other bulky stuff that Mom had put there.

I was beginning to understand how little I knew about my sister.
Now that I finally wanted to talk to her about, well, about life, she
was gone. It was like we'd always lived on different latitudes, she in
the hot South, me in the dark North. We'd met in our travels, rarely,
like the time I was in second grade and was assigned the task of
writing complete sentences on index cards—my first foray into
writing creatively. Unsure of my product, I read them to Anne, who
was sitting at the desk in our room upstairs.

We shared a bedroom at the time, despite the fact that my
messiness was really bugging her. She was a young fifth-grade Felix;
I was Oscar—we even put a piece of tape down the middle of the
room so that my mess wouldn't extend into her orderly world. Our
parents finally broke down and shifted us into different rooms out
of concern for their oldest daughter's mental well-being.

After I read her my sentences, she grimaced at me as if encoun-
tering a terrible stench, disbelieving that her prize attic pupil from a
few years earlier could be so trite and simplistic. Any Hemingway
influence to my writing died on that day, in the quake of her horror:

Can't you do any better than that? Can't you make them a little longer? After second grade, I never showed her or my mother *anything* I wrote—ever.

Now I couldn't even if I wanted to because Anne was gone. That I couldn't call up memories of being *with* her bothered me. We had so rarely played cards together or done anything just the two of us, without Curtie. We didn't share girl things—like curling our hair or painting our fingernails—she wasn't a tomboy like me but she wasn't prissy, either. She was just older, somehow, and always reading or doing something else when Curtie and I played together. He and I looked so much alike when we were little that strangers sometimes asked if we were twins. Plus, we liked all the same things—football, cards, basketball, riding bikes, kickball—everything.

Anne had always been there, though, somewhere near, even when she was stone-faced or had her door closed, Led Zeppelin leaking from underneath it. Tonight the room was eerie with quiet.

I backed out of her room and quickly flicked on the light in mine.

"You sure you don't mind switching on Saturday?" Rick said.

The voice shook me out of my reverie. A lifeguard stand is not a good place for daydreaming, not on a stifling July afternoon with a pool full of kids.

"No, no, not at all," I said.

"Even though you're closing tonight, too?"

I had to think for a second to remember it was Thursday.

"Really, it's okay. Not a problem."

"Hey, great," he said. "Thanks."

I was cordial to the other lifeguards at the Boat Club, all early-college guys who liked partying by night and being Joe Cool by day. It was a scene I was familiar with, just not one that I ever quite fit into, not easily anyway. There were no sororities in town for career-less college graduates, but that wasn't it, not really.

My past in Louisville held a single skeleton, the one person I wanted to call but didn't dare. I couldn't go back, *not anymore*. That entire experience needed to be stuffed in a metal box marked "unacceptable" and tossed in the brown churning waters of the past.

The angle of the sun suggested it wouldn't be much longer before dusk would send people home, then I could drop down to the bottom and not have to think anymore.

12

Simple assists, such as reaching, throwing, and wading, are the safest ways to help a person in difficulty without exposing yourself to unnecessary dangers.

American Red Cross Lifeguarding, p. 113

The sludge inside me deepened during that first winter when Anne was gone. It stuck to my innards like an obstinate adhesive, one that no one could see but that I could feel with every breath.

Dad walked into the living room in his jeans and plain sweatshirt.

"Ready to go?"

Curtie and I followed him to his new car—an ancient Volkswagen Bug that chugged down the road like a fat man with emphysema. It was my turn to sit up front, a spot we no longer coveted or fought over.

"Watch out," Dad said as we bumped over the tracks next to the White Castle.

"Whoa—" I said, lifting my feet as a few sparks flew. The floorboard had a couple of rust holes in it, which made the pavement all too visible.

"Gives a whole new meaning to fancy footwork," Dad said, grinning, reaching up to rub a bigger circle in the condensation on the windshield. He'd named the car Lurch.

"Okay. Here we go," he said as it huffed to its top speed of thirty miles an hour. Riding in Lurch was like getting on some rickety roller coaster at the fair. We joked on the way to school just about every day.

Dad's wit seeded our laughter. He'd been employed continuously for almost a year, which made rifts between him and Mom far fewer. He liked the church and the quiet, solitary work of scrubbing toilets and sweeping floors. It gave him time to read and reflect, a place to gather himself, to be.

Curtie and I behaved in a civil manner in the mornings when we were with Dad, which was the only time of the day we did; otherwise we avoided each other or argued viciously. Something had happened to make our lifelong alliance disintegrate; the most obvious explanation was puberty—as in his—although it's not a match without two people in the ring.

One Sunday evening I crept into his room as quietly as I could, pulled the squeaky drawer open as slowly as possible, and scanned which of his alligator shirts were clean and therefore available for hijack.

"Get out of my room!" He stood at the door, fuming. He was almost my height, growing taller at a dangerous pace.

"Cool it. I'm just getting a shirt."

"MO—OM!"

We glared at each other, warriors occupying opposite sides of the battle-zone border.

"*What?*" Mom's voice fired from the kitchen, down the hall and into the space between us, tracking the invisible line over which we were fighting. Her rapid footsteps followed quickly.

"I hate you," Curtie said, his voice a raspy whisper, just low enough so Mom couldn't hear. He had me trapped, was standing his ground, an eyewitness intent on preserving the events of the crime. Truth was he *had* caught me red-handed.

"What's the problem here?" Mom, known also as the Little

General, was all business with the work of Sunday night, the work of preparing for not just the next day, but for the next week, month, and year. Her tone told us she didn't appreciate this kind of hassle.

"I was just getting a shirt for schoo-ol."

"Watch the tone, young lady," Mom said, rubbing on her neck as she often did these days. She was no longer my abiding ally, not always, not when placed in between Curtie and me. Still pressed with money worries, she strove to maintain a neutral, Switzerland status when it came to Curtie and me. Pulled between us, she usually split—or maybe favored him a bit more, since he was her only son *and* her baby.

"It's *my shirt,*" Curt said, pouting, having leaned just a little to allow Mom to step into the room. "And she didn't ask." He was as tall now as she was, his hair brown and almost shabby, his body becoming oddly lanky after a boyhood of being compact and muscular.

She glanced between us for a second, pursing her lips in efficient, problem-solving thought. "Can she wear it this time—if she promises not to take shirts from your drawer again?"

He sighed heavily, his long face falling into a disgusted frown. "All right," he said, his voice seething, although I don't think Mom noticed.

I took the turquoise shirt, my favorite, and walked toward the door, where he straightened up for a second to stare at me, a silent reminder to both of us that the physical superiority between us was shifting and would remain this way for the rest of our lives.

"Thanks," I said, half-smiling, trying to keep the mocking from my voice. Had he ever decided to, Curtie could've pummeled me, thrown me in the bushes, and left me whimpering. I wasn't exactly a twig but his football player shoulders were widening, his oak stump legs were growing; every part of him was lengthening into the tower we all knew he would be one day.

Later I was up in my room loading my backpack for school.

"*Cathy,*" Mom called.

"Yes, ma'am," I said. We had a habit of having conversations from different rooms, which required loud and persistent speaking—what people in other families might describe as shouting.

"Come here a minute," said the unusually quiet voice at the bottom of the steps.

I peered out of my room. "Yes, ma'am," I said again, descending the steps slowly, sensing something out of the ordinary.

"He doesn't like you wearing his shirts because, well, he says you stretch them out—in the chest—and his friends tease him about it."

I pulled my lips inside my mouth, trying desperately to hold back the tears that were suddenly pressing up from inside me—her words stung like a bee, even though she was being sweet and gentle and not meaning to embarrass me.

"Okay," I managed to say, without her noticing my shame. When she walked away, I climbed the steps and carefully closed the door to my bedroom before I dove onto the bed, burying my face. The sobs spewed from me, stuffing up my nose, wetting my face and skin and pillow. The mantra that came to me every time I cried like this played over and over in my mind: *Be strong, don't need people.*

I needed to talk to her but just couldn't. I couldn't tell her that I hated how big and round and womanly my body was. I couldn't help it if I stretched out his shirts. I avoided the whole fashion question by wearing Levi's jeans, a button-down or polo shirt, and Top-Siders to school—every day, and a pullover sweater when it was cold. Predictable, comfortable, not-attention-getting, or so I believed.

Terrible thoughts rushed forth as they so often did when I cried, just crashed right through the flimsy flood walls in my mind, through the tattered shield of being strong. *I can always kill myself. Maybe it would be better if I was dead. What about my family?*

When my sobs stuttered to an end, I heard a creak in the floor, like someone walking on the loose boards in the attic, which was just off my room. The house did that from time to time, rearranged its posture or revealed the footsteps of one of the ghosts. I wondered what really happens when a person dies, what it would be like, if there's really nothing there—which seemed impossible given that the ghosts *were* here but weren't.

I sat on my bed with my Biology book and slogged through the end of my homework. Outside, a cold darkness blotted everything out, as if life was simply a light and someone pulled the plug. I leaned against the window, which felt cool to the tip of my nose, and looked at nothing.

Not long after that, in the amazing way fate grants you wings and vaults you into the air, I was sitting in Algebra II class trying to pay attention. A few open windows let the mid-March wind filter through the classroom; in one week I would turn sixteen.

The loudspeaker jolted us out of our dulled state. The principal announced the name of a senior who'd won an award and would she please come to the office. The next thing I knew, that secret being inside me was pulling me out of my chair and propelling me to ask the teacher if I could go to the bathroom—being a good student the teachers let me do what I wanted. I was hustling down the stairs and moving straight for the main hallway when I saw the senior— when I saw *her*—walking toward me.

I took a breath to focus, to appear casual and cool.

"Hey, congratulations on your award," I said, stopping as she approached. She was taller than me and wore a yellow button-down shirt and jeans. Her blond hair was thin, of medium length, her eyes brown and big. In one hand she held an envelope.

She cocked her head as if trying to remember my name, realizing eventually that she'd never seen me before. We shared an awkward moment standing there in the middle of the hall.

"Thank you," she finally said, a bit formally.

"Sure," I said.

And that was it—except of course that wasn't it, not at all.

I looked for her everywhere. In the mornings before school I scanned the parking lot until I figured out which car was hers—a little blue Datsun. Then I'd finagle a way to be "coincidentally" walking near her in the hall. In the afternoons I'd hang near the gym before the bus came, hoping to get a glimpse of her or maybe even to say hello.

"I see you everywhere," she said one day, her eyebrows pulling toward one another. What she was thinking I couldn't tell.

I smiled and shrugged my shoulders. "Yeah, kind of amazing, isn't it?" Right then my bus drove up. "See you tomorrow—maybe."

"Okay," she said, smiling. That smile made it easy to ignore the stinky bus ride and the wild, taunting kids who sat in the backseat. I just looked out the window and all I could see was that smile on her face.

Dad had gotten a "real job"—back in the insurance business—so he no longer gave us a ride to school. Now that it was light enough in the mornings I had the brilliant idea of riding my bike to school—the thought of which opened up all kinds of possibilities in my suddenly buzzing little brain.

"Are you sure it's not too far?" Mom said, studying my face a little more closely than usual.

"Pretty sure. It's not as far as Crescent Hill." I explained the route I'd take through connected neighborhoods, which would avoid the major roads. I pulled three graham crackers from the box, trying to appear nonchalant. "Plus, if I make the tennis team then I'll have a way home after practice."

"True," Mom said, the eternal pragmatist. "Okay, give it a try."
"Thanks," I said.

In the hierarchy of high school, seniors were under no obligation to
notice or speak to freshmen or sophomores, but she started standing longer by her car, me on my bike, us using conversation to try
and find our way through whatever was pulling us toward each
other—or pulling me toward her, I should say. She was getting
ready to graduate and go to college in August.

I had no conscious idea of what I was doing or why—I just
knew *I had to do it*, had to talk to her, had to get to know her. I would
never have used the word *crush* to describe this . . . this force inside
me because, well, Donna was a girl, and so was I. Girls weren't
allowed to *like* each other, not like *that*. But I couldn't let myself think
about that; I couldn't think about much of anything except when I'd
get to talk to her again.

"Are you really on the tennis team?" I said one day, standing
with one leg on each side of my bike. She was leaning against her
car, cool and relaxed.

"Sure am. Why?"

A grin spread across my face against my will to keep it in check.
"What?"

"I was thinking about trying out," I said, watching her nod start
slowly.

"That'll be great," she said, both of us venturing closer into
something we couldn't name. "Really great."

I practically flew home on my bike. Literally—whistling,
singing—I don't think the tires touched the ground. I rode by new
grass sprouting and tree buds fattening up, propelled by the energy
that comes when there's someone special to think about, someone
to look for in the hall, someone to dress for and act cool around.

• • •

One day, between the end of school and the beginning of tennis practice, Donna and I went to visit Mrs. Hill, the Biology teacher. We hurried up the stairs laughing. The scent of linoleum polish was more obvious now that the halls were mostly empty. We talked about the petri dish experiments our classes had performed in the stairwell, trying to isolate the bacteria we lived with every day. We talked about everything and nothing, our unnamed fascination being as much with being physically near each other as with anything else.

Mrs. Hill, a tiny woman with large, smart eyes and finely painted fingernails, always wore a generous spray of perfume. Still in the classroom doing paperwork, she had the reputation of being one of the best—and hardest—teachers in the school. She'd written a recommendation to Duke for Anne, who had been one of her all-time favorite students.

"Well, hello, Donna. I haven't seen you in the longest time. How are you?" Mrs. Hill said.

"Doing well, thanks," Donna said, casually crossing one arm over the other.

I shifted from one foot to the other. "I think I left my folder in here," I said, suddenly needing a purpose for being there. I knew there was no lost folder but an inexplicable energy raced through me, something that had a motor of its own.

Then Mrs. Hill, the small feisty woman who'd been teaching me all year—and who knew my sister and mom so well—looked straight at me.

"It's good to see you smiling, dear."

I didn't quite understand what she meant.

Then she turned to Donna, nodding once in my direction. "Whatever you're doing, I can see it's helping our friend here."

My face exploded into double red, a million thoughts firing off at once. One: she'd noticed my *sludge*. How many days that winter had I dragged into her class, trying to care about my homework and my grade but still not being able to muster the energy to make more than an unremarkable B effort? Mrs. Hill and I both knew I could do better—and yet, through that creeping sophomore winter I didn't, or couldn't, or wouldn't.

The deeper red came from Reason Number Two: she'd noticed and acknowledged Donna's importance to me, something I couldn't allow myself to do in the privacy of my own head!

"Thanks," I said, absurdly. "We better get to practice."

"Okay, girls—have fun."

I could feel her wise, thoughtful eyes follow our exit. Neither of us risked speech for fear there might be someone around the corner. We could read each other's minds though: *What did she mean by that?* We didn't dare answer ourselves or each other, not then anyway.

By the luck of sheer demographics, Donna's house wasn't very far from my own, within easy biking distance. Even though I could drive, I didn't have a car, nor did I need one as long as I had my ten-speed. I rode over on weekends or after school, when we didn't have tennis practice. We shot baskets and took walks, just anything to be together. On tennis days I'd catch the bus to school so I could get a ride home with her.

One afternoon after practice we were heading down Hubbard's Lane when we passed a field of long grass moving in waves against the breeze.

"That's neat," I said.

"Beautiful," she said.

The tone of her voice turned my head. We were stopped at a light, looking into each other's eyes. My left leg started bouncing a little. An invisible magnet connected us across the small space of the car, yet I wanted something to happen, something *more*.

The light changed and she kept driving, but soon after she reached over and put her hand on my leg, just above my knee. I got very still.

"Is this okay?" she said gently. Her finger was moving in slow, steady circles creating an explosion beneath my skin.

I nodded, at first unable to find words amidst the internal flood.

"Yes," I finally sputtered. "I—I like it." I couldn't reliably speak after that, could just sit there trying to stay cool, my every nerve cell thrilled and full of sudden curiosity, not fear—not yet.

We got to her house and shot baskets in her backyard. We played one-on-one even though she was three inches taller than me and got every rebound. It wasn't really about the basketball, not considering how much we bumped and tangled with each other. She did show me how to use my elbows—legally—on the rare occasion when I pulled down a rebound. She played at school but she hadn't been at tryouts because as a senior she already had her spot on the team.

On a drizzly Friday, a few days later, tennis was canceled. Neither of us wanted to go right home.

"Let's ride down to the river," I said, just to have something to do. We rode along River Road looking for somewhere to stop. The rain gave the river a muddy face.

"I know," I said, thinking I did. She turned the car around and followed my directions to an undeveloped road in Indian Hills. The brush was too thick on the side of the road to pull off. It seemed deserted, though, so we decided to stop. The drizzle made it especially quiet, kind of like being in a forest while still sitting in the car.

"How do you know this area?" she asked as she lifted the hand brake.

"I have old friends who live around here."

We sat quietly for a couple of minutes in the gentle rain, each of us with a hand on the other's thigh. Before I thought about it we were leaning toward each other in some kind of dream.

I'd been kissed by a boy before, more than a few times, and it always felt mechanical, like I was acting or guessing at what I was supposed to do. One guy nearly choked me to death when his hungry, searching tongue usurped all the space in my mouth. We'd been at a swim meet and he'd asked to take a walk, then he stopped and all of a sudden he was swan diving into my mouth, right in front of little kids who started groaning in amused disgust. My face turned hot from embarrassment and what I would later realize was anger. At the time I just pulled away and said I forgot something on the bleachers, then I hightailed it back to the pool to look for my friends.

With Donna, I had no feelings of awkwardness or confusion, not at the moment when we leaned toward each other, or when I felt the remarkable softness of the skin on her neck, her cheeks, the gentle give of her lips. For once in my life I didn't have to think, I *couldn't* think. I could only reach out, scoot over, run my hands through her hair, waves of something breaking inside me.

The car gave us a veneer of privacy. Except veneer is not very strong; a sense of motion lifted my head.

"Shit."

A cop car was silently pulling up beside us.

"Do you think he saw us?" I said, flying back to my side of the car, terrified that he'd spied us kissing.

Donna ran quick fingers through her hair as she rolled down her window.

"I don't know," she whispered.

He drove microscopically slow, his beady eyes glaring at us beneath the stiff brim of his hat. He didn't stop. Donna rolled her window back up, started the car, and waited for him to pass so she could turn around and get us out of there.

"Damn, that was close," she said, her hands shaking on the wheel.

We were both terrified of more things than we could name, like him tracking her license tag, him having a picture, him following us and knowing where we lived. Mostly we were scared he'd tell our parents, that our friends would know, that we'd be ridiculed and hated.

Paranoia is like wildfire, it just needs a match.

She drove around until we were both satisfied, like criminals in a movie, that he was not, in fact, trailing us. By the time she pulled into my driveway, her mood was lighter, which helped mine immensely.

"Even if we need a secret code I'll call you," she said, winking.

"Promise?"

"Of course, are you kidding? Let's do something tomorrow."

"Okay, good. Hey thanks," I said, narrowing my eyes to really look at her. "I had a great time."

She shook her head. "Go on."

After that day, we looked harder for places to park her car so we could be together, talking, kissing—there wasn't a safe place. Where do you go when you're a teenager—when you're not like *normal* people?

Sometimes on the weekend I spent the night with her. In the darkness, that being inside me directed my arms and legs, made me talk and hushed me up; it led me into a terrifying and thrilling world. To have Donna's hands, her eyes—even the *thought* of them—*on me*, ignited a million prickly points beneath my skin. I'd never known such attention and sensation before, nor did I recognize the playful, flirtatious creature that directed my winking eyes and ducking head.

The black night made it safe for us to explore each other's bodies, as did her silent walk across the room to turn the lock on the door. I floated in a sparkling pool after that, in full moonlight on midnight water, held only by her gentle hands, by her soft, generous kisses, by her arms around me and her voice swimming somewhere in my head.

All of the darkness inside me evaporated when her body was on top of mine. In a nanosecond it seemed the night was gone and that wrenching moment would come when she had to cross the room again and unlock the door. I'd drag myself to the other twin bed, the cold one, and we'd both try to sleep just as dawn began its unwanted invasion.

It was never long enough—the night—or those brief hours of fitful sleep. Morning would rudely spray the room, its arrival forcing me to realize that all of the night's darkness was still inside me. I'd awaken to a jungle of guilt so thick and dense I could barely breathe, let alone sit up. I hated myself, *hated myself. You CANNOT be this way.*

"What's wrong?" she said.

"I can't do this," I said, terrified as soon as I said it. "I—I just can't." The agony felt suffocating.

"Okay," she said, softly, putting her arms around me even as I stiffened.

"What if your mom comes in?"

She inched a little bit away but she kept a hand on my leg. She was sitting on the edge of the bed in her nightshirt and I was still under the covers. I made it a point to turn my eyes away from her long, beautiful legs. She had the grace of an athlete but I couldn't let myself think about that right then.

"Do you think it's okay?"

"It feels right," she said, half-smiling.

I examined the ceiling for awhile, my eyes hot and scratchy from lack of sleep.

"Have you ever done this before?" I said.

"You mean spent the night with someone—in the same bed?"

I nodded.

She looked out the window, now her turn to scan the nothingness for words. "No."

I felt so much younger than her sometimes, like now, even though only two years separated us.

"Ever kissed anybody?"

Sadness fell across her face.

"What, what is it?" I said; the thought of her hurting was unbearable.

"I . . . yes." She looked at me a long time, deciding whether to share something or not. In the hall, the bathroom door opened and closed. Otherwise the house was silent.

"Tell me," I said, my guilt now replaced by concern.

"A couple of years ago. She was . . . older than me." She turned her eyes away.

"You want to talk about it?"

She shook her head. "Maybe sometime. Thanks, though."

Her smile lit me up inside.

I spent the night with her as often as I could without raising Mom's concern and always awakened to the same quicksand of guilt. Donna would be confused and apologetic, though painfully tender. I'd say it was okay, it wasn't her, just me, that I couldn't do this anymore. She'd say okay, that we didn't have to, we could just be friends, but that wasn't possible, not really, because neither of us wanted to be "just friends."

Her Catholic mother always eyed us suspiciously; I could tell she didn't like me.

"You sure you won't stay for breakfast?" Donna said softly as we hugged for the last time in her room.

"No, I better get home." The mood that fell over me darkened everything, even her smile. I just needed to leave, needed to stop this thing inside me, but I couldn't stop it—I didn't know how.

The street stretched forever as I rode away on my bike. I forced a smile toward the woman shuffling down her driveway in her slippers to get the paper. It was an ordinary Saturday for most people, for normal people. I crossed Chenoweth Lane and coasted slowly down Oread, willing myself not to cry.

"Hi, Mom," I said, as I came in the back door.

"Hey, you're home early," she said, giving me a hug. She was in her Saturday morning buzz, a list of chores on the table.

"Yeah," I said, going for the cereal cabinet.

"Good, you can help me. You mind dusting and vacuuming the downstairs?"

"Okay," I said, leaning my head into the refrigerator. My arms and legs ached from fatigue. I'd have to wait until the afternoon to take a nap so she wouldn't realize that I'd been up all night.

Increasingly, I camouflaged myself by becoming more helpful around the house. My pattern of listening, deflecting, anticipating, and avoiding started in earnest after I met Donna. Mom knew we were friends but I minimized how much I saw her.

I hated lying to my mother—it didn't fit in with my got-it-all-together carbon-copy image. Always before I'd prided myself on being honest and I loved that my mother trusted me. Nevertheless, the lies fell out of my mouth like mist on a winter morning—I didn't have to try, they were just there.

At night I dried dishes while she worried aloud about Anne needing money. We never talked about the irony of Anne attending school with some of the wealthiest kids in the country—we never talked about a lot of things—until one night when the phone rang late. Then, all of a sudden, all Mom wanted to do was talk . . . with me.

13

Depending on whom you ask, a lifeguard
is . . . a public relations person who
promotes the facility.

American Red Cross Lifeguarding, p. 3

When Donna and I couldn't spend time together we were desperate to hear each other's voices. That desire overrode all sensible thought, especially when I made her promise to call me late at night. I foolishly believed that my parents would be asleep and I could pick up the phone without them hearing it.

Our house seemed unusually quiet at midnight: no television flickering, no dishwasher pulsing, no silver tray rattling. I leaned over the side of the bed with my hand on the receiver, waiting. To hear Donna's voice before going to sleep made me forget—or ignore—that other people, and their ears, also lived in my house.

"*Cathy*, come in here right now."

I'd just walked in the front door and reflexively glanced at Grandmother Frances as I crossed the room. Mom's voiced signaled PROBLEM.

She was pacing the kitchen like a feral woman, her eyes narrowing on me with laser intensity.

"What's going on?" I said, as nonchalantly as possible, remembering suddenly the click on the phone from the night before.

"Sit down. I—need to talk to you."

Her every edge shook—fingers, hands, neck, head. She fought with the cigarette lighter until finally the flame, smooth and perfect, obliged her. A burst of smoke climbed into the space between us, above the small table in the kitchen where we were both sitting.

The more restless she became, crossing and uncrossing her legs, the calmer I became. I turned into stone, glacial stone. *I am a rock. I am an island.*

"I—I think that . . . that *girl* has more feelings for you . . . than is . . . *normal.*"

"Oh, Mom," I said, trying to appear unruffled, casual even. I acted as if what she was suggesting was preposterous rather than a bull's-eye truth.

"No—I—she . . . talks to you . . . like a boyfriend would talk . . . to a girlfriend."

That same irritating smile came to my face, the one that showed up at the most inappropriate times.

"No, Mom, don't worry, it's nothing like that," I said a bit too quickly. Then I took an invisible breath and held it for a few seconds, puzzling over her words, pretending the concept had never occurred to me.

She was up and pacing the room again, talking about dating and what people think and that some people are, in fact, "strange" and they should be avoided.

Ice kept building beneath my skin. Her words bounced against an invisible frozen wall. I could not comprehend fully what she was saying, much less apply it to myself. All I knew at that moment was that she was very upset and I needed to calm her down and make her feel better.

She was staring at me, sucking hard on her cigarette, calling "that girl" abnormal and weird. I didn't have the guts to accuse her of invading my privacy, much less risk confessing my feelings.

I didn't have the guts for this conversation.

I leaned back in the chair, aware of my legs sticking to the wood from sweat.

"Really, Mom, it's nothing like that . . . we're friends." To Mom, I appeared unfettered. I was sixteen; she was forty. We were in the kitchen, her domain, site of countless past battles with my father. But she seemed uncomfortable in it suddenly. She was shaking so hard she didn't notice as ashes dropped from her cigarette to the floor.

"Why are you smiling—this isn't funny," she said, turning around quickly.

"I know it's not funny . . . you're obviously very upset." I bit on my cheeks in an effort to erase that pesky misplaced smile. "Mom, everything's okay. We're friends, from the tennis team." I soothed both of us so expertly. She wanted everything to be okay, always, no problems, not with any of her kids, not with me. And that suited me perfectly because the problem I had—me—no one could help with anyway.

"Well, why don't you ever call your friend Kelly? Or some of the other girls? You never see them anymore."

That racked me a little, confirming in some subtle way that I was supposed to be different than I was. I'd been so unhappy the entire year, so lost, until spring came and with it some reason to feel alive again. I couldn't tell her that. I couldn't risk her not under-standing, or worse, her ridicule. She was asking about my friends from last year at Meyzeek.

"It's hard, Mom, since we all go to different schools now."

"What about Dasmine?" she said, appearing visibly more calm now that we had entered a more acceptable conversational terrain. It occurred to me that the nicotine was an ally to me in this situation.

"There's a party this weekend—I was thinking of going," I said, feeling like a robot.

"Well, good," she said.

• • •

Later that night, I cried in my bed. I couldn't figure out what was wrong with me, why I was so deficient and malformed in the deepest parts of me. In the eighth grade, when I took that Confirmation class at church, I realized that I couldn't be perfect, that perfect doesn't exist, that only Jesus was *perfect*, and even he got mad. So I retreated to a determination of being good at everything I did—and so far I was succeeding.

I was making good grades, playing sports at school. I worked and saved money. I was doing everything right—except being interested, enough, in boys.

Maybe it wasn't a normal thing to think about dying as much as I did; I didn't know what went through the minds of other people. I knew that no one would have ever believed how often this girl with the all-American smile thought about killing herself. I didn't even tell Donna.

A strange logic had taken root in my head by then—if I could think about suicide, then I wouldn't really do it. That freed the tree inside me to follow its naturally crooked trajectory.

When I stopped long enough to ask myself why I wanted to see this girl, why I wanted to ride my bike to her house, to talk to her and be around her, why I wanted to *touch her*, I hated myself for wanting to. The guilt was seismic; the cracks in me unbridgeable. I tried not to think about it—I *couldn't* stop seeing her, there was no possible way I could *survive* that. I just had to be more careful. No more late-night phone calls. She'd graduated and was going away to college in one month and I couldn't fathom how I would survive.

On Saturday I stopped by Donna's before going to the party. We'd planned it and she was waiting for me, dressed in a button-down shirt and jeans, her skin wearing that just-showered scent. We embraced and kissed and every part of me longed to stay right there, in the precious privacy of her empty house. Her parents had gone out for the evening, as had her brother. Before my "talk" with Mom, Donna and I had been set on spending the evening together, if not the night—but now there was no way.

So we had to settle for ten minutes, which turned into twenty, then thirty. I glanced at the clock in the kitchen.

"I need to use your phone to call Lynn."

She dropped the phone book on the counter with a thud.

"I'm sorry I can't stay," I said, twisting with guilt from every direction.

"I know," she said. "It's okay."

Although it didn't feel okay, nothing ever felt okay anymore.

I sped down Brownsboro Road, hating myself for lying and wanting what was *impossible* for me to have. I willed my tears to stay unshed as I turned into Lynn's driveway.

"I'm so sorry I'm late," I said as she climbed in.

"It's okay," she said. "I was just worried you forgot." She flipped her hair behind her shoulder. "Your mom said you left a half an hour ago."

I hid my cringe from her. "I had to stop at the drugstore," I lied. "Whose party is this anyway?"

"Some kid from Ballard. I don't know him but everybody's going to be there," she said, leaning back in the Pontiac.

Lynn wore a short skirt with a black top, and white sandals. Her toenails were painted red. Her dark hair framed her face like a picture. I'd met her in Dasmine and liked her, even though we'd never gone to the same school.

"I'm guessing this is it," she said, when we came upon a line of cars parked half in the grass, half in the road. Up ahead we could see teenagers walking in and out of a large, two-story white house with lights placed along the front sidewalk.

I parked and slipped the keys in my pocket. I was wearing my yellow Ralph Lauren polo shirt with a pair of khaki shorts and a ribbon belt with lion belt buckles. That was dressed up for me.

"Hi, girls," Chandler said about one minute after we'd joined the masses of kids on the back patio. There were tons of people crowding in the house, which apparently had been vacated by the host's parents. I actually didn't know very many people and was delighted to see Chandler. "Can I interest you in a little something?" he asked.

"What is it?" I said, laughing at his manner. He was a tall, slender guy who wore oversized glasses and was always very friendly when I saw him. In his hand he held a blue plastic cup.

"Taste it," he said. "It's a 'cuba libre.'"

I took a sip and smiled. "Hmm," I said, approving.

"Coke and rum with a little lime and ice," he said, grinning in his lanky, nerdy way. Mom said his family was one of the wealthiest in the entire city. She'd taught him in the fifth grade at Chenoweth.

I didn't drink, not usually. In fact at school I took a stance against it in class discussion, but right now I gladly took the cup he offered.

"Cathy, how *are* you?"

"Hey, how's it going?" I said, hugging an old friend from Chenoweth, and then another. We talked of all those incidental things you say at a party—are you dating anybody, what're you doing this summer, how's your family, are you playing hockey in the fall? Soon Chandler had reappeared with another of his specialty drinks. We talked loudly over the stereo that was blasting into the backyard from the upstairs balcony. Someone had strung white lights along the rim of the large patio, which gave the night a particularly festive feeling. No one danced, though. Nor did they find their way into the swimming pool, at least not while we were there.

In these situations, and with the help of some drinks, the social genes in my DNA turned on automatically. My great-aunt, grandmother, and mother had all been crowned Carnival Queen at Centre

College, which involved all sorts of parties and a black tie ball at the coronation. My father had been president of his fraternity, the Phi Delts, at the time. It was just part of the blood in our family to know how to mingle and dance and twirl in the social swirl.

"Are you about ready?" Lynn said, surprising me a little. The last time I saw her she was making out with a guy in the backyard.

"Shouldn't I be asking you that question?" I said, laughing.

She blushed and said she had to be home by midnight. I glanced at my watch and realized it was already eleven-thirty.

"Who was that, anyway?" I said as we got in the car. I felt loose and chatty. No single thought could stay in my head longer than a millisecond. It never occurred to me to question whether I should drive the car.

Lynn told me she'd been hoping Bobby would be there—she'd met him a couple of weeks ago at another party. It was easier to listen to her and prod her to keep talking than to try and pretend I'd met anyone who interested me. There was only one, and I wouldn't dare mention Donna's name to anyone.

After that conversation with Mom I became much more spylike when it came to being with Donna. We had to wait a couple of precious weeks before I could finagle spending the night with her again. My lies increased, my helpfulness increased, my availability to Mom increased—so did my panic. I could not think about how I could go back to high school without Donna being there, so I didn't, I just put it out of my mind.

She did leave, one bleak day in August. I'd spent the night with her the weekend before, both of us somehow knowing that this would be the last time we would ever be together like this. In all truth, our infatuation had started stalling anyway, mostly because of the insurmountable realities coming at us from everywhere. Her pacing Catholic mother, my pacing smoking one. Her plans to go away to college, my sentence to two more years of high school. It would never work, couldn't work. We were from different worlds anyway. She didn't know any debutantes, had never heard of this clubby high school sorority I belonged to. She played sports, unabashedly, and eschewed the snobbery and prejudice so rampant in East End circles.

We never talked about any of that, just pledged our love and devotion. The words felt tinny in my throat, though, and I really wasn't all that surprised when her letters from school petered off by October. Initially, I raced home on my bike after field hockey practice to get the mail before Mom got home. Donna wrote a letter almost every day. But soon there were real live people—girls I couldn't think about—who were certainly asking her to go here, go there. She was in the grand ocean of college. I was stuck in the baby pool of high school.

We did see each other during her Christmas break. We embraced, we kissed, but it wasn't the same—which came as a relief to me, really. I had tried extremely hard in her absence to become more "normal."

Sometime after that I even met a boy who I wanted to spend time with, at least for awhile. He wrote poetry and played golf and was gentle and kind. He presented a corsage to me for his prom. On summer nights we'd drive through a fast-food restaurant for two cups of ice, then smuggle our red wine down to a hidden trail he knew on the riverbank. We'd drink and laugh and throw stones in the water and I'd have a special glow inside me knowing that this was the sort of thing my mother wanted me to be doing—for the most part, probably not the drinking. Whatever was between us was tepid and tame compared to the sensations I'd felt with Donna. But I pushed those thoughts away, far away. The past belonged in the past.

Mike went off to college a year ahead of me, which I was glad about. My senior year had finally arrived and I was totally focused on getting away from Louisville and the too-small house on Napanee.

That year the postman knew my name. He delivered colorful brochures of brick buildings and smiling students, of places around the country I longed to explore. We still didn't have much money, although we had more than when Anne had applied to college, thanks to Dad returning to the insurance business and Mom getting a principal position at a prestigious school in Louisville. Still, careers in insurance and education don't send you to Duke—from the moment I dropped my application in the mail, I was nervous to hear.

Every cell in my body wanted to leave, not just Louisville but the entire state of Kentucky. I loathed the idea of going to the University of Kentucky even as I knew, deep down, that I would probably end up there, just like most of the college-bound kids from my high school.

But every day when the brochures arrived, from cool places like Dartmouth and Oberlin, I let myself dream a little, indulged in wondering what it might've been like had my grandparents not died. That's a slippery game, though, because it quickly takes an unknown turn, inevitably winding up at the dead end where my parents likely wouldn't have met each other, which means the kid perusing college catalogs wouldn't actually have been *me*. Which would've been fine, if I'd been a different person, that is, but it's not exactly a choice you get—whether to be born and with what wiring.

So I just read the brochures and pretended. I sweated over that essay to Duke, where I applied early decision. In the meantime I sent two other forms, one to Kentucky and one to a school I knew very little about but where one of the cool girls on the swim team had gone, Emory University, in that giant city of Atlanta.

"Hey, Mom," I said one day as I was opening the mail. "Guess what?"

She was in her bedroom, changing out of her school clothes, a daily habit we all shared and had inherited from her.

"What?" Their bedroom was always neat and picked up, both of their antique dressers uncluttered and dusted. Granddaddy still stood on Dad's bureau, his arms outstretched at Lakeside. Mom was getting a little happier, less frenetic, less consumed with worry. Her new job gave her a whole world of problems she had to solve; it gave her two hundred kids to think about—and their parents.

"I got accepted to Emory." I held out the crisp, ivory-colored paper for her to read.

"Honey, that's terrific. I'm so proud of you," she said, hugging me, still holding the finely typed paper in her hand. For a moment, we both willingly loved that marker of achievement, that moment when possibility shone so brightly that the shadows of practical concerns, namely, how to pay for it, couldn't be seen.

That same smile of uncertainty found my face. Pride wasn't a feeling I knew how to actually own; it was something that deflected off me, and even in that moment, I wondered secretly if there had been a mistake, if they were hard up and needed to accept everyone who applied. I didn't say it, of course, because that would've sounded rude and ungrateful.

"We'll have to celebrate," Mom said, the realization of financial impossibility pulling some of the enthusiasm from her voice.

We were both holding out for a repeat miracle, for Duke to accept my early decision application and send me a fat scholarship, so the family could once again ride the high of a dream coming true.

Follow-up letters kept coming from Emory, from the friendly people in the admissions office, always on their crisp, clean paper, always worded in a kind, not too chatty tone. I felt encouraged by these letters. They made me feel *wanted*.

Sometime in November, as the day of notification from Duke

was approaching, I received yet another letter from Emory, this one encouraging me to apply for financial aid—my application was favorable and my chances of receiving scholarship money were high. And again, the tone was one of genuine interest in *me*, like I wasn't just a number or an SAT score, I was a real *person*.

"You know, Mom," I said that day in late fall, when the leaves had turned and fallen and been raked into little speckled hills, "it's going to be hard to turn these people down when I get accepted to Duke."

Fate surely laughed at that one, or maybe one of the ghosts, maybe Mama T, whose hearty laugh had traveled through the gene pool to lay dormant in my lungs, waiting for the time when I would be joyful enough to let it out.

The thin Duke envelope came not two days later—when I saw it, I knew. The letter's simple rejection confirmed all of my hidden fears; I really wasn't good enough or smart enough to be a doctor or to even get into the school where my sister was awarded a scholarship!

The strangest occurrence of all, though, was that reading the letter didn't bring the tears I'd expected—and feared—for two years. I only knew a strangely private sense of relief. I had no idea where I belonged, but somehow I knew it wasn't at Duke, even though it was an awesome place, one of those schools that made people around the East End go, "Oh, wow."

No one in the family said much, as the river of senior year kept gathering its force. Emory came through with a scholarship and loan combination that my parents said we could do—they could budget the monthly payment that was their portion and I could borrow in student loans what the school didn't cover. I was going to Emory University, a place not as flashy as Duke, but a *good school* nonetheless.

• • •

Everything was in bloom the day in May when Mom called me into their bedroom. She stood at the polished chest of drawers that once belonged to Mama T. The top drawer stuck a little when opening it, and I wondered if it had always done that, even when Mama T's hands loaded and unloaded its contents. Was the sound of old furniture sticking the consequence of age or had those wood creaks and moans always been there?

Even now that I was eighteen, a week shy of graduating, if a task pulled me into my parents' room, I would run my hand along the smooth, solid wood. *The real thing,* Mom so often said. Cherry wood darkens with age, she'd told me a hundred times. By the time I was a senior, the dresser was already so dark that the red in it only surfaced when the afternoon light landed on it as it was doing now.

I was curious and edgy as Mom reached deliberately into her jewelry box. These days Mom and I were operating on separate parallels. We had never again veered anywhere close to that shaky and scary conversation that happened when I was fifteen. I played up my few encounters with guys and played down my deeper curiosity about girls. For her part, Mom asked questions in a way that let me know what answer she expected to hear.

I was set to attend a few summer debutante parties—she hadn't pushed when I'd answered a firm *"No"* to the question of my being a debutante. It wasn't our family's kind of thing anyway, even though Dad had grown up in the middle of those Louisville social circles. We didn't have that kind of money and Mom wasn't all that taken with that kind of pageantry and social etiquette—she just didn't want her kids to miss out on anything.

It was okay that I was presentably going to the parties—it was even better that I could muster up a date. Mom didn't ask deeper questions and I didn't offer more revealing answers. I was going to college in the fall, getting out of this town and on with my life—finally. I wasn't thinking about anything else, especially how different I was, even from the people I'd known my entire life.

By eighteen, we both knew she had prepared me well. I had learned competency and practicality and hard-nosed diligence from her, the importance of achieving and taking advantage of the opportunities that come your way. She was never one to dawdle, or ponder about feelings—hers or anyone else's, including those of her children.

So any moment, like on this afternoon, when she suspended her motion to make some kind of real contact was extremely special. A mixture of relief and joy washed over me at having been noticed, of being *seen* by her. Or maybe I was the one who stopped long enough to see *her*. We were exactly the same height.

She pulled a diamond ring from the box on her dresser.

"My mother gave this ring to me when I graduated from high school. I want you to know how proud I am of you—and I want you to have it."

"Mom . . . ," I said, not knowing what to say or do.

"Here, try it on."

I slipped the white-gold ring on my stubby finger, amazed at how perfectly it fit.

"How does it feel?" she said, in the most tender voice.

"It feels fine. It's beautiful . . . wow. Mom, are you sure?"

"I've always wanted you to have it." Then she launched into the smattering of other "family jewels." "You kids won't inherit much."

"Oh, Mom, that doesn't matter, we have you and Dad."

We both gazed at the ring on my finger, its intersecting waves of small diamonds, the way it fit exactly to the contour of my hand. Mama T was standing there, too; I could feel her blue eyes, her pleased smile, her head tilted up since we would've towered over her five-foot-two frame. In that moment, my finger was my mother's finger, which was also my grandmother's, and in that moment, such a lineage brought me a pride so deep and entrenched, I couldn't imagine not having felt it before.

"Mom, thank you so much."

"You're welcome. Now, what I do is always put my rings in the same place so I won't lose them."

I'm sure my guarded expression returned, those teenage antennae poised to identify unsolicited instructions, no matter how reasonable or practical.

"Okay," I said, acting like I knew what to do with such an incredible jewel.

"Just don't lose it," she said, not pushing her point.

"I won't," I said, hugging her, then wandering out of the room, staring at this elegant ring that made my fat-knuckled athlete's hand a little less ugly.

"And don't play basketball in it," bellowed her voice that followed me down the hall.

"Yes, ma'am," I called back, hurrying upstairs to my room.

Somebody was looking out for me on those fuzzy weekend nights of freshmen year, when our sorority would "mix" with one fraternity or another, when someone would always be filling my cup with beer, when my hands would be held and released by sweaty fingers as we shagged around the frat house party room. Someone, *Mama T?*, kept an eye on that ring, the one that never—incredibly—was lost or misplaced for longer than a five-minute stretch.

I liked college at Emory, even as I tapped my fingers nervously in that initial Chemistry class, when the professor recommended we look to our left and right and said one of us wouldn't be taking Chemistry next quarter. Of the hundreds of self-declared premed students starting freshman year, a third of them would drop the goal and the class by next term.

I didn't tell my parents about all the wannabe doctors that weren't going to make it—they'd been too proud that day they drove onto campus, the wagon full of my clothes and my sister's hand-me-down stereo. Dad joked about "Sidney Silverspoon," some tan, blond guy zipping around campus in a white sports car. We'd ridden down fraternity row, past the Phi Delt house, although thankfully Dad elected not to go in to say hello. I could see the memories working on my parents as they laughed about Dad being president and Mom, the Carnival Queen and Phi Delt Sweetheart, eyeing the Betas, or better yet, them eyeing her. They wanted the same for me; I just wanted to make them proud.

We'd walked over to the gym, which amounted to a converted WWII airplane hangar, the indoor pool dark and small. It didn't matter that the pool was steamy and overchlorinated; I just needed to know precisely where it was.

A short man with a large, wrinkled head extended his leathery hand and introduced himself as Coach Smyke. We talked for a couple of minutes about the team and my previous experience at Lakeside. He invited me to come to a team meeting—I said I'd think about it.

My burgeoning sense of freedom, of finally busting out of high school and Louisville and that haunted house on Napanee Road, included being out of the pool, away from endless workouts and perpetual water in my ears. Truth was, since I'd quit Lakeside, whenever I did swim a few laps I couldn't bear how *slow* I was. I didn't confess any of this at the time, not with my parents standing there beaming at this man's interest in me.

I'd been nothing but possibility in those first shiny days at college; now that I'd graduated, I was nothing but a lifeguard. So much can change in four short years—and so little too. We didn't talk these days about wannabe doctors, especially since there was one living in the house, returned like a ghost that simply won't stay away.

July dragged on like a drunk in search of his bridge. Slow, suffocating, heavy. Maybe it would've been more merciful, in retrospect,
if fate had let me bomb out in that first Chemistry class, rather than
inch my way through the premed curriculum only to end up with,
shock of all shocks, a major in Chemistry in addition to Psychology
and on a waiting list.

I couldn't help but think too much, sitting in that chair, swinging my whistle. At twenty-two, I knew more than I cared to know,
especially about myself and the rotten things one person can do to
another. I'd left a few scars in my college path. The best way to avoid
getting hurt was to be the one to end it, whatever "it" was, and to
never let anyone know you too well.

After four years of college, I really had no one from that world I
wanted to call, even though I'd known and been liked by lots of
people. It never felt like people knew the real me, which meant I
could leave them without much longing or backward thought. But
that wasn't really it—I was trying to break free from the scummy
cove of my past. The problem was its waters kept getting deeper and
swifter and more difficult to maneuver.

14

A swimming assist may be used to help a
tired or distressed swimmer. Remember, tired
swimmers can become actively drowning
victims suddenly and without warning.

American Red Cross Lifeguarding, p. 141

By my sophomore year in college I had almost convinced myself that there wasn't something terribly wrong with me. Then I met Elaine.

She was a year younger than me, short and petite with long brown hair, and she liked the idea of "snuggling" in bed. In those late, dark hours, after the sorority-fraternity mixers were over and we'd consumed our share of beer and danced our share of shags, sometimes she'd come back to my room.

I would be suddenly awake then, thankful that my roommate was staying someplace else. And in the darkness something would loosen the vise grip I always held on my thoughts and words and actions.

Electricity traveled through my every limb, to my fingertips, which trembled in their exploration. There was an unstoppable river in me, one that I had kept dammed for all these years, only to find its current gushing through me, catching me off-guard—we were only going to "snuggle."

These became unmentionable secrets, these nights—there was no one to talk to, and nothing to talk about, as far as both of us were concerned. Sleep brought with it the twin curtains of denial and guilt, speaking out loud of this *thing*, of being *this way*, was unfathomable to me. It was a fluke, we decided, just something that had happened—it was just between *us*.

This was 1980, when Ronald Reagan defeated Jimmy Carter and the most important question on our dorm hall was, Who shot JR? A group of us ordered pizza every Friday night, snuck in some liquor, and howled at JR and his evil ways. There were no gay characters on television, only jokes and stereotypes; I was even careful not to voice my admiration of the Bionic Woman too loudly, less someone might think I was *that way*.

It would be after these *Dallas* gatherings, much later, when Elaine and I would sneak into my room, not together but separately, just in case anyone on the hall might notice. No one could know because what we were doing, sleeping in the same bed—kissing and touching and exploring and—what we were doing was wrong, but somehow the cover of darkness made it seem okay, or at least invisible, as if we became ghosts instead of confused and desperate girls. It was the shock of daylight that made things harder.

I hated myself, hated lying to my friends, to my parents, to everyone. *If they ever really knew me.* Keeping up the smile and the outer "I've-got-it-all-together" façade was getting harder and harder. Masks are like that; after a while, their weight starts pulling you under.

The thing is, I didn't know I was using a mask—all I knew was that on the outside I appeared happy and well adjusted and on the inside, I was hollowing out, disappearing. The fissure in me was deepening and I was about to crack. The one constant companion was my escape route: *I can always kill myself.*

I had to stop this thing with Elaine, reclaim my life trajectory— I wanted to be a doctor, to be normal. After months of unnecessary drama, my pulling away then changing my mind, her parents found out. She transferred and I never heard from her again.

It solved the problem of people talking about us in the sorority. I didn't care what people said about me, at least that's what I told myself. More than anything, I wanted the monster being living inside me to die, once and for all. The line of a song became my frequent companion: *I'm lost. Living inside myself, living inside this hell . . .*

Silver turns dark if you don't polish it regularly. Mom had given me a little silver cup from her father that I kept on top of the dresser in my dorm room at college, until it turned black. Not knowing what to do with it I stuffed it in my drawer.

Sometimes when I called home on Sunday afternoons, Mom and Dad wouldn't be getting along very well. He sounded hopelessly grumpy, then he'd get off the phone and Mom would report how critical and irritable he was. In her voice I heard anger and hurt, and the same futility I felt at twelve would rise like a tide inside me. I didn't tell her that, though.

"How are things with you?" she'd say after a few minutes.

"Fine. No problems," I said.

"Good," she said, her mood lighter. "I sure do miss you."

"I miss you too," I said.

I had wanted to tell them that I wasn't sure how I could pay this month's sorority bill but after hearing their voices, I decided against it. They were having a hard enough time with each other. Maybe I could add extra hours to my work/study job.

The sorority I belonged to—being from the East End of Louisville it would've been scandalous not to join a sorority—passed out bills every week on these little white scraps of paper. Most of the girls had bank accounts that received regular deposits from their parents, or so it seemed to me. I thought everyone was rich at Emory, especially in the sorority, except my friend whose father had died, and when I thought of her I just felt guiltier.

That Sunday in November I couldn't fake it anymore. The thoughts of killing myself, of ejecting out of the maze, now felt soothing, inviting even. When I hung up the phone my insides twisted at the sound of my parents' imprisonment—with debt, with each other, with the deaths that wouldn't let them go. In that moment, standing alone in my dusty dorm room, a heat rose in me that could not be iced—I wanted to *destroy* something. I wanted to scream and to hit, to do something that would crack open the walls that were collapsing against me.

I rifled through the medicine cabinet, past the toothpaste and deodorant, and stared at the bottle of aspirin. *It'll just make you throw up*, came an unwanted voice in my head.

I lurched around the room hungry to break something. In the next dorm room and all the way down the hall girls were talking on the phone and watching television and painting their fingernails and studying their damn chemistry.

I grabbed the shoe box of sorority receipts and bills, rummaged through my roommate's dresser for a match, then started lighting them, one by one, then in fistfuls. The flames made the diamond ring on my finger flicker in a dizzy pattern of color. They brought me to a strangely distant calm. To the paradoxical flat line, not of heat but of ice, of a river frozen shut, its smooth surface sealed, its hidden turmoil still oddly compelling.

The sizable mountain of fire made me blink awake. It was getting too big. Am I going crazy, starting fires and running my hands through the flames? I hot potatoed the mound into the sink, watched the water singe and smoke it, dumped the ashes into the trash can, paced around a couple more minutes, changed my clothes, and took off.

When in doubt—swim.

I swam until my arms were so sore I could barely lift them out of the water. I hadn't been swimming in such a long time, and I was slow, so incredibly *slow*. Still, I kept going. On Sunday afternoon no one was in the pool, except an old man, probably some nobel laureate in Chemistry for all I knew. I cried and I swam, lap after lap—and afterward I slept.

When I awoke that evening, the river had landed me safely on the banks of needing to get to the library, of needing to finish my Chemistry for the next day, of needing to not quit, no matter what. *We have to stick together—we're all we've got.*

Campus was already transforming into its holiday ghost-town ambiance on that Tuesday before Thanksgiving break. Most of its life had migrated elsewhere, north to the wealthy homes on Long Island or south to the sunny mansions in Miami. With no classes the following day, students were leaving in hoards for the airport, determined to beat the mad crush of travelers. My plan was to drive home to Louisville on Wednesday, through the twisting Smoky Mountains, a road I knew well from all the years of rotating into the copilot seat on our annual treks to Florida.

Late that Tuesday afternoon, as I pushed bunches of leaves with my shoes, everything seemed exaggerated—the brown scent of autumn, the emptiness of the buildings, the uncommon chill in the Atlanta air. It occurred to me that some students had no families to go to, or had families that were so wretched the students would choose to stay on campus during the break. There must've been *some* people who actually ate the turkey dinner advertised on the flyers stuck to the door of Cox Hall. Kids whose parents were divorced, or whose parents were traveling or working or generally just too busy to be bothered. Even now, with my parents fighting about money worse than ever, with alcohol no longer a convenient scapegoat, I still couldn't comprehend what our life would be like if my parents finally called it quits.

The leaves on the sidewalk in the quad were crisp in their death; colorful, daring in their majesty. They smelled of earth disrupted, of inevitability and decay. To crunch them gave me a faint sense of satisfaction.

Rounded old stone steps led to the front door of the psychology building. Inside, it took only a second to locate a sign announcing the student counseling center. Second floor. I'd made this appointment sometime after my pyro meltdown, and because they were so busy, this was the only time available. By four-thirty on the day before the holiday break, even the secretaries were gone, lights in the foyer were dim.

I knew I shouldn't be here, that I should've waited, that I should've known this would be a bad time. The glass door to the main office was open but the overhead lights were off. Maybe the lady forgot. I gazed at the papers on the desk, that strain of nosey curiosity rising in me. In such moments I'd always had the urge to pore through other people's stuff, to obliterate that line of privacy and respect. I never did because I knew it wasn't right, to steal Post-it pads and pens. Just having the thought proved that a badness lurked beneath the all-American smile that everyone else saw, the smile that despite my best efforts, was fading rapidly. *If they ever really knew me . . .*

"Hello?" A short, round woman appeared from a back office, not smiling.

"I'm supposed to have an appointment?" I said, my voice high like a little girl's.

"Oh?" she said, perusing a calendar book on the desk. "Oh, right. Come in."

If she told me her name, I immediately forgot it. We sat in a small office, made smaller by the stacks of books and papers and journals creeping toward me. There was barely space for two people in there. I was intruding.

"Why did you come in today?"

For a terrifying moment, my mind went completely blank. I could barely remember where I was, let alone say why I was there. Through the one unblocked window I could see the daylight slipping away, receding like a tide, taking with it all my usual bearings.

"I'm going home tomorrow—to Louisville, Kentucky—and I think—I'm afraid my parents might get a divorce."

Those words had been building up inside me like helium and just to say them out loud caused a tremendous reduction in pressure. The woman allowed no expression on her face, short of appearing somewhat bored.

"Why do you think that?" she finally said.

I launched into the whole story of my father's alcoholism, his sobriety, my mother's resentment toward him, their parents dying so young. I explained that things had been much better in the past few years in so many ways, except she hadn't changed as much as he had and he still wasn't making enough money, and on and on and on.

The psychologist offered little in the way of guidance or support or help. In fact, I have no memory of her saying anything, only of her sitting there, a tired woman ready for her workday to be over, for her holiday to begin. Maybe she didn't have a family, or anyone who loved her—maybe she thought I was just another spoiled, whiney kid.

"There's something else," I said, knowing there wasn't enough time for us to talk about it. If she sighed, I didn't notice, so intent was I on making myself continue. "I think I need to talk about something else, something about myself." I couldn't bring myself to confess the badness that was inside me, the badness that kept drawing me like a magnet to . . .

"After the break, why don't you call and make another appointment. We can talk about whatever it is then," the woman said, scooting her plump body forward so her legs could reach the floor.

"Okay," I said, lying, suddenly intent on getting out of the office, getting out of the building, getting off the planet. Outside, a battalion of tears rushed forward. Shame does that to you; it attacks swiftly, turning your face hot and red, launching an assault of tears, making your hands and fingers and knees shake. I hated myself, hated myself even more than I had an hour earlier. I wanted to die; I wanted to scream; I wanted to be somewhere—someone—else.

It really doesn't matter what you want, not when it comes to a lot of things. People can live their entire lives wishing that they had longer legs or thicker hair or the voice of a songbird. They can wish with every breath that this person or that one hadn't died. All the wishing in the world doesn't change the genetic facts, the gifts and quirks we're all born with. Nor does it change the twisting twirl of fate, of death's unpredictable, exacting aim.

Mom and Dad didn't get a divorce, not when I was ten or thirteen or nineteen. By twenty-two, when I lived with them after college, I figured they'd been through the worst of it and would probably stay married forever.

I was more preoccupied with the wrongness inside me. There'd been a couple of girls after Elaine with whom I'd ventured into the forbidden waters of touch. Each of these dramas ended pretty much the same way, with me or both of us too scared or too guilty to do anything but find a way to stop. I kept my heart wrapped in a coating of ice, careful not to let myself care too much about any of them for fear the ice, and thus my heart, might break. I focused more on trying to be "normal" and after graduation I'd pretty much decided that all of that taboo interest in girls had been just a phase. My more pressing concerns, anyway, were figuring out what to do with the rest of my life since lifeguarding didn't seem like a reasonable career option.

• • •

One evening at the Boat Club, after sinking for awhile, I walked under the road to the docks. Night falls late in Louisville in the height of summer. On this particular evening sunlight had turned the western sky a frightening red and orange. The brown water resembled blood pushing through a vein. I stepped away from the edge of the dock and sat down because all of a sudden I was afraid I might fall in.

The memory sped into my mind before I could turn it away. It was something I hadn't thought about in years and years and years, never realizing until that evening that there is something that can stare down death—fate.

I was young, too young, when a boy from another swim team started appearing at my side, requesting walks at swim meets, asking to visit while I was babysitting, inviting me to dinner with his family at the country club where they belonged. I was fourteen and incredibly uncomfortable with my body, with the curves that issued unintended invitations for whistles from the boys. These were those dark years when I was swimming morning and evening and sleeping or going to school in between—before I met Donna. Dad was still drinking, Mom was bordering on going to Our Lady of Peace, and the fun house floors in our house were undulating at a faster and faster pace.

Steve took me into a foreign place, not his country club, but into the world of being asked on a date, of being sought after by a boy. *Whatever you do, don't get pregnant*, my mother warned, in a tone of disguised desperation that I didn't understand. I didn't understand anything, nor did I have any particular interest in boys, not the kind I knew I was *supposed to* have.

He was a nice enough guy, lived in the rich neighborhood across from Brownsboro Road. When summer came and he invited me to go waterskiing on the Ohio River, I didn't hesitate. I'd been skiing only a few times in my life, enough to know how much fun it was.

"Can I go?" I said to Mom one day when we were in the kitchen, fully expecting her to say yes, to be extra excited because this was essentially "a date," something to reassure her that I was *normal*.

"Well," she said, pausing. There was an odd shift in her countenance. She left the cabinet open but stepped away from it, to the kitchen window, her gaze finding something invisible in the backyard. The room felt suddenly crowded and stuffy, as humid inside as it was outside.

"Your father might not like you kids being on the river."

If I'd have been my sister, I might've shot back a slew of mouthy words. *Father, what father? Who cares what the hell he thinks, anyway?* Red-Storm Rising could fire such spirit, surprise her opponent with the sudden passion that rose into her otherwise closed and serious face. Not me.

For a moment I didn't comprehend what Mom meant, why she was hesitating. Then I lowered my head, guilt filling my belly. How could I be so thoughtless and inconsiderate? I should've remembered what Mom and Dad so rarely talked about—Uncle Ches and the river.

"We'll be careful," I said, my voice small.

"I know," Mom said as faintly, her gaze now fixed somewhere in the past, pulled as it was sometimes by the undertow of memory. Despite the lines beginning to mark her face around her eyes, despite the pinched worry that rested so often around her lips, my mother was very pretty, stressed and increasingly brittle, but still pretty.

"You'll still have to ask your father," she said, as if talking from a daydream, her mind completely closed to my access.

Timing was absolutely everything when it came to Dad. For two or three days I wandered into the den casually, to place an imaginary thermometer in his mood. When I read grumpiness, I withdrew quickly. When I read potential bomb, when he was sitting in his den chair, quietly reading the paper, a drink on the table beside him, his ears alert to the happenings in the kitchen, I also backed away. I didn't want him to be too aware of my request.

I was waiting to find him in a distracted state, when he might be watching a golf tournament or some old rerun on television. Plus, I needed to be going somewhere, so that he and I wouldn't have time for much discussion.

Saturday afternoon presented itself, the day before I was supposed to go skiing.

"Oh, Dad," I said offhandedly during a commercial. I was standing behind his chair, near the back door, not far from the shelves that displayed our swimming trophies, Mom's picture with her father, and the silver bowl that read *Ches McCall.* "Mom wanted me to ask you if it's okay for me to go waterskiing on the river."

He acted at first as if he didn't hear me, as still as a wooden relic in a museum. From the side, I could see a rugged weariness to his skin, which was fleshy and blotchy. He was looking less and less like John Wayne these days, with his head low and his eyes distant and unfocused much of the time. I rarely looked at my father, really looked at him, and even now, I put my attention on the back door, trying to communicate hurry.

"Dad," I said, as softly as humanly possible.

"I guess it's okay," he said, irritably, spoken from his unturned head, his body still motionless in the brown chair, the voices on the television commercial providing an unlikely chorus. Only his hand moved to take a sip of his beer.

"Thanks," I said, making a rapid exit out the back door, to the shed, to my bike. I hopped on and rode away before either of them could give my request any more thought.

• • •

The ski boat was big, well kept—the kind of nice thing wealthy people owned with ease. I kept my T-shirt on over my bathing suit and laughed when I didn't know what to say. I watched and acted impressed with "my date" as he untied the lines and assisted the captain with our departure.

The other girl and I sat in the bow as we accelerated north toward Six Mile Island. From the water the riverbank appeared wild with trees and twisting roots. Lush bushes obscured the few houses and the slim road running alongside the river. From the land, the river could be viewed in smaller snatches, in jigsaw pieces glimpsed through tree limbs and brief openings. But once on the water, the expanse of the river itself opened up, as if it was a gigantic mouth, its water a swollen brown tongue.

Sunday was a good time to be on the river, the guys explained, less boat and barge traffic. The water near Six Mile Island was an eerie, artificial sort of calm. Except for the urgent, tea-stained current, the stifling humidity of July, and the river's unrelenting history, we could've been riding on a lake somewhere else, in another part of the country even.

I skied second, pleased with successfully crossing the wake a few times without wiping out, quick to put my towel around me as soon as I climbed into the boat and out of my life vest. My date went third, slaloming and eliciting excited screams from the other girl and me.

The trouble came when it was the boat owner's turn to ski.

He was a magnificent showboat, taking deep sharp cuts on his slalom ski, flying across the wake like a champion. We owned the river in those few moments, shouting and clapping at his spectacle. I even lowered my towel, at the insistent urging of my date, so I could shake my fists and clap my hands freely at the ski show taking place.

Then, suddenly, the boat swerved out of control. I slammed

against the seat. My knee scraped against a fiberglass edge. Back and forth we swerved. To the right, to the left. The sides of the boat were over our head one way then the other. The three of us kept smacking into each other, into the seats, the sides of the boat. We grabbed at anything to avoid falling out.

I didn't know what was happening. Time sped up and slowed down all at once. My date lunged for the safety cord in the ignition. The motor deadened and the boat kept deeply rocking, eventually settling into a deceptively gentle sway.

"What the hell happened?" the guy on the ski yelled.

"I don't know," Steve yelled back. "Are you okay?" His voice was shaky, his blond hair still wet and sticking up from his head.

"I'm fine," the skier yelled, beginning to swim toward the boat.

"How about you?" Steve asked me in a softer voice.

"Sure," I said, that stupid grin coming to my face. My knee was bleeding. He handed me a towel and put his arm around me for a second then went to help his friend into the boat. The other girl was unharmed, just quieter than she had been before. We all were.

No one could say what had happened—it was just one of those things, one of those unexpected moments when the river opens its palm, grabs whatever it can get ahold of, and yanks.

"Sure you're okay?" Steve asked, moving closer.

"Of course," I said, forcing a coolness to disguise my fear. "I thought it was kind of fun . . . something different."

From his expression I knew I'd said an idiotic thing. Thankfully the boat owner was taking off his vest, talking about how wild it looked from where he was. We were all reassured by his return to the controls and by the lower speed he used on our ride back to the dock.

Sitting on the same dock, eight years later, I stared north in the direction of where it had happened. Something about the stuffy July air, about how the river changes its face in darkness, brought tears to my eyes. The uncle I never knew died in a boat like that, probably not far from where our boat nearly flipped. A shiver crossed over my shoulders. I hugged my knees tightly against me, not wanting to be so close to this beautiful killer, yet not wanting to leave either.

Dad's older brother, Ches, was a senior in medical school at the University of Louisville during the summer of 1954. He and some of his buddies were out on the river, horsing around, sitting on the back of the boat, doing backflips into the water. It was like most July days in the Ohio Valley—hazy with arresting humidity.

These were fortunate young men, privileged—they were adorned with society's shiniest dreams. In 1954, they had the right last names and the right skin color. They would be the city's doctors and lawyers one day, its bank presidents and influential business leaders. Every door in America was wide open to these men, but they weren't contemplating such matters. They were simply carousing on the water, one of the best places to be on such a sticky, unforgiving day.

Afternoon leaned toward evening—the time came to head in for the day. Maybe the heat had finally worn them down, maybe the beer cooler was empty, maybe a summer storm was creeping in from the west. Maybe they had to get home and showered before dinner, the bachelors in the group needing to pick up their dates. At twenty-five, Ches already had a wife and two sons, ages two and six months. He was taking a break from his studying, out for a relaxing afternoon on the river.

He wanted to try one last flip off the stern. His buddy at the wheel didn't hear him. Ches flung his body into the water just as the driver shifted the motor into gear, just as the propeller engaged.

The muddy-colored water swallowed him instantly. Stunned at first, these usually easygoing guys screamed his name, over and over and over. Nothing.

His body was just gone, and with it his movie star smile, his long pianist fingers, his champion golf swing, his future career as a surgeon. For three days the river kept that body captive, hidden in its dark, blurry currents. For three days Granddaddy and the Coast Guard dragged the river in search of the firstborn son. For three days young Curt, my future father, then nineteen, stumbled along the banks, his best friend, Paul, and others stumbling beside him.

Curt had called Margaret Anne, my future mom, even though they'd agreed to date other people that summer, and she drove from Danville to be with him, to sit on the high banks, to stare once again into the blank, empty eyes of unexpected death. They scanned the greedy, urgent water for a clue, a body, an explanation. She understood more than anyone that there wasn't anything to be said.

There were minutes and hours to endure. She sat on the bank in the deadening humidity, unafraid to look into Curt's foggy brown eyes, to wrap her arms around him in the few moments he let himself cry. She sat and waited and stared at the river when he needed to scour the banks again with Paul.

The river produced the body finally, not far from the scene of the accident. Hidden in a snarl of roots and bush limbs, the handsome young man was not recognizable. The boat propeller had cut through his neck, an instantaneous death. A closed coffin.

By mid-July I'd stopped asking about any mail from Emory or Louisville Medical Schools because the answer from Mom or Dad was always the same. I was still dodging making plans for summer's end, and my parents were still being considerate about not asking.

Sometimes instead of driving, or when Mom needed the car, I rode my trusty ten-speed bike to work, down the long steep hill, along the lush, overgrown road, through the wealthy neighborhood of Indian Hills. The road was so steep it required no acceleration, only coasting, the kind of descent that can be tricky on a bicycle. Usually a chicken, I challenged myself to ride without braking, to lean into the curves, to see if I could make it all the way to River Road without pedaling. Often, I could make it beneath the overpass, the river coming into swift view in the near distance. I'd pedal then, turning right onto the narrow two-lane road, sprinting the half mile or so to the first parking lot of the club. When large trucks sped past me and honked, my heart zipped into fast motion—only a few times did I have to steer off the road onto the gravel edges to avoid getting hit.

Occasionally, I'd heave up that mammoth hill after work, but most of the time Mom would pull her big wagon into the lot to give me a ride home. She was like that, always there, ready to help in any possible way she could.

Once in a while I'd take the car to work, if I had a split shift and she didn't need it in the morning. The day of the miracle was a day like that, in late July, when I worked early then had a break in the middle of the day.

I trudged into the front door, glad to be out of the thick July haze, planning on napping that afternoon with the attic fan turned on.

"Cathy," Mom said, bristling, not with anger but with excitement. "You got a phone call." She met me in the living room. "A woman from Emory."

I peered into Mom's eyes to see what she knew.

"She wouldn't tell me anything," Mom said, hurrying into the kitchen, to the notepad by the phone. "She wants you to call her."

Hope, or something, started making my heart beat faster.

"Is it okay? Should I call her now?" I was thinking about how expensive it was to make a long-distance phone call in the middle of the day.

"Of course. Here—here's the number."

I dialed the number and stepped into the dining room, where Mom was standing and watching me intently. The serving table and silver tray rested behind her. My back was to the cherry hutch. The room felt electric, not stuffy necessarily, but . . . well attended, as if Mom wasn't the only one watching me stand there, the phone cord extending from the kitchen into the border territory.

I asked to speak to the woman whose name Mom had printed neatly on the paper.

"Is this Catherine West McCall?"

"Yes, ma'am."

"I'm calling to tell you that you've been accepted to Emory Medical School, to begin classes in August."

"Oh, my gosh, really—are you sure?" I couldn't think.

The woman chuckled. "Yes, we're sure. Congratulations. You've been first on the waiting list for a couple of weeks now. Do you accept?"

"Yes, ma'am, of course."

"Good. You'll be receiving a letter in the mail in the next few days; we just like to call first. It'll have scholarship and financial aid information, too."

"Thank you," I said. "Thank you very much."

"You're welcome, dear. We'll see you in August."

I hung up the phone and stared at Mom, stunned. "I'm in."

"*Oh, Cathy,*" she said, her arms flying around me. "*I am so proud of you.*"

I hugged her, and smiled and cried, disbelief crashing through me like an ocean wave.

"I can't believe it," I said. "I'm going to medical school."

"That's right," Mom said, pulling her raised arm down like a basketball player who has just made a slam dunk. "Way to go!"

We hadn't ever talked about how I might pay for medical school, except that everyone told me I could borrow the money. I told Mom that the woman mentioned something about financial aid—Emory had been so generous to me in college, maybe they would be again.

"Don't you worry about that," Mom said, her excitement electric. "Where there's a will, there's a way!"

15

If you approach from the front,
you may be confronted face-to-face
with a panicky victim.

American Red Cross Lifeguarding, p. 147

August 1983, a new start, another chance. Terrified as I was, they'd let me into the ivory gates, and so long as I kept my head down and my eyes focused, I could do it, I knew I could—I had to.

Determination, like a river current, can carry you a long way, as long as you watch for jutting trunks and submerged logs, for sudden jerks that can throw you out of the boat and into the propeller blade. From the beginning, I laughed easily at jokes and met interesting people from around the country, some of whom had traveled all over the world. If I was nice enough, maybe they wouldn't know what a fake I really was.

One Monday afternoon, a few weeks after classes started, my handsome lab partner, Duncan, and I were sitting outside after Gross Anatomy lab. A group of six of us shared a tall, capable cadaver we named Abe. Of the six, we paired into twosomes and divided the body that way, so we worked as a team, but most intensely with our individual partners.

Duncan and I had just finished a three-hour dissection of the right shoulder and arm, paring away the skin, delineating the muscles and major tendons, exposing the deeply hidden nerves. It was hard, smelly work.

The warm sun and clean air pushed the formaldehyde from my nostrils as I sat on the steps, trying to stretch my back. Duncan was cute, well mannered, funny. He mentioned my making dinner for him sometime. I laughed, much to his confusion. When I jokingly suggested that *he* make dinner for *me*, he just sort of frowned.

"It doesn't work that way," he said.

"Sure it does," I said, smiling, faking my way through the conversation, glad when I saw a friend and could beg my good-byes to run and catch up with her.

We labored well together, he and I, but it honestly never occurred to me to want to spend time with him outside of the lab. I started medical school determined to be *normal*, not *that way* anymore. More than anything, I didn't want to flunk out—so I kept my head down and my eyes on my books.

"How's it going?" Mom asked on one of our Sunday phone calls. "Is it really hard?"

"Not especially, it's more the volume. Lots of memorization."

"Oh. What about the people? What are they like?"

"Some nerds, but a lot of them are really nice. One guy's father used to be a senator."

"In the U.S. Congress?" Dad said.

"I think so."

"Wow," he said. "That's neat."

"Are any of them, you know, handsome?" Mom said, her voice pitch rising a tad.

"I'll see you later, honey. Love you," Dad said.

"Love you too, Dad."

After the click I could hear Mom's voice more clearly. I was standing in my tiny, second-floor studio apartment. Shirts and jeans and books and albums covered the floor. I turned my gaze out the window, to the oak trees whose leaves were beginning to explode with yellow and orange.

"Oh, I don't know," I said. "I might have dinner with my lab partner, but really, Mom, I think everybody's studying pretty hard."

"I'm sure." She then told me about Curtie starting to date a new girl and that Anne was still seeing that guy, "who I don't think is very good for her. Well, I've got to go," she said. "I sure am proud of you."

"Thanks, Mom."

"You need anything?"

"I don't think so."

"Okay, keep up the good work. I love you."

"I love you, too."

I hung up the phone and walked numbly into the small kitchen, where I had a couple of pots in the cabinet, some milk and Cokes in the refrigerator. Most nights I bought a salad, or drove through Wendy's. I didn't even cook dinner for myself, let alone for some guy.

Truth was, I knew I'd never have dinner with Duncan, knew I had no desire to. I didn't think about it, though, not specifically like that. It never occurred to me that he might be attracted to me. Guys were my friends—like my brother and father—people to joke with and work with and talk to. But like my mother, I wanted the plot line to be different, wanted the river to turn north, not south. I wanted it, but at the same time, I didn't really—at least not enough to make dinner.

Back on campus in med school, and with the real excuse of needing to study all the time, I pulled away from people I knew in the sorority and especially from the girl I'd spent the night with many times the year before. Even though we were still on the same campus— the medical school occupied the central district—we might as well have been on different continents. I had promised myself that I would not get distracted.

I'd finally been allowed into that revered kingdom of *Medicine*, away from the manufactured crises of the sorority and into the real world of life and death. If I worked hard and didn't quit, then someday I might be one of those fast-moving residents dressed in a short white coat who flew into the bookstore from time to time to buy breath mints.

I walked into the Anatomy building and never looked back. What followed were a few months—essential, focused months— where I studied and made good grades, where I began to make new friends and to believe that maybe I could be a doctor, and be *normal*, after all.

I smacked the Anatomy book closed and leaned back so that I was completely stretched out on the floor. The carpet felt plush and smelled like lavender. We were one week away from the Thanksgiving holiday, which meant first-semester exams were looming.

"You want to just spend the night here?" Elizabeth said, nudging me to turn over so she could rub my shoulders.

"That feels so good," I said as she kneaded my neck and back muscles through my long-sleeve T-shirt. "I still have my contacts in," I mumbled, already half asleep.

"I have an extra case," she said. "I think I even have an extra toothbrush—unused."

"Hard to pass on that," I said, chuckling when she jabbed me playfully.

Elizabeth and I had become study buddies, which was a real boon for me since she was one of the smartest people, not just in the class but on the planet.

"C'mon, you wisecracker," she said, giving me a little shove in the back.

In a matter of minutes I was dressed in a borrowed T-shirt and sound asleep in her double bed.

The next thing I knew, I was lying on my stomach. It took me a second to realize that it was morning and Elizabeth was running her foot up and down the lower part of my leg. It took me another few seconds to comprehend why she was doing it.

I kept my body very still, feigning sleep. An ancient *No* echoed faintly in the deep crevices of my mind. Every part of me was now alert and charged and debating.

If I was ever going to stop my encounters with women, now was the moment. It was a choice that wasn't a real choice at all, like standing still in the sand as the ocean waves rush across your ankles. After the third or fourth wave, the sand beneath your feet gets pulled away and you have no choice but to follow the force of the water.

I turned my head.

She stopped her foot. Her hair was mussed from sleep but her doe eyes seemed bigger and darker and deeper than I'd ever noticed. She was quite pretty.

"Are you okay?" she said.

"I have fought this thing for so long," I said. It seemed she was holding her breath. I closed my eyes.

"I just can't do it anymore—can't fight it anymore," I said, reaching for her, closing my eyes to her embrace.

That moment marked the beginning of the end of my charade. More than falling in love, we sort of fell into each other emotionally, and physically. We discovered a compatibility, she and I, in our uneasiness with being considered—or considering ourselves—*gay*. We weren't, of course; this was just something between us. Never mind that we confessed over wine one night to each having had previous experiences with girls.

To know a place well, like a river finding its bed, is to know where to start coasting in preparation to turn onto your hometown street.

Chenoweth Lane felt as familiar to me as breathing. The fine brick houses and raked lawns were the same, exactly the same. When I passed the white picket fence I flipped my blinker and slowed down, took a left on Napanee, even paused at the stop sign in front of our house, our same little redbrick house, its black front door recently painted and looking stylish.

"Come see the dining room," Mom said, after I'd been home a couple of minutes, having been greeted with a plate of homemade chocolate chip cookies and an enormous hug. The flavors of love—hamburger browning, bread warming—spread through the house, which seemed surprisingly bright and cheerful, somehow less small.

"Do you think it's too dark?" she asked of the deep burgundy paint that brought the antiques—the table and hutch and cupboard—to life.

"No, it looks great," I said. "Seems bigger."

"I think so too," Mom said, zipping into the kitchen to stir the spaghetti sauce. Gray hair bunched in waves on her head. Her face bore a few more wrinkles but otherwise she buzzed around with the same humming efficiency.

From the doorway I studied the dining room a little more closely—the difference was more than paint. It took me a moment to identify that one of the biggest shifts turned out to be a relatively simple one. Instead of leaving the dining room table in its usual position—its flaps open and ready to be set for eight—Mom had lowered the sides, making the table long and narrow. It required remarkably less space, which had the effect of making the room feel more spacious.

"Hey, Miss Bug," Dad called, coming in the front door and right to me with arms outstretched, not taking off his coat. He smelled of smoke when we hugged. "Any trouble driving?"

"No problems at all," I said.

"Good, good." These days he had that happy golf energy most

of the time; it was actually part of him, this glow, and it had little to do with playing golf. As he hugged and kissed Mom, I marveled at how they could be so enraged at each other, then the next day proceed as before, laughing even.

"The house is looking good, Dad," I said.

"You like it? Your mother's done a great job," he said, taking off his coat.

"Well." Mom launched into telling us about the lady from her school who came out to give her a few suggestions. Dad sweetly admonished her, reiterating the compliment, wanting her to *hear* it. In that moment, incredibly, they'd forgotten about me, not unlike when I was young and spying and they pretended they didn't see me. Except this was everything unlike those times. They hugged and talked and checked in with each other in a private, end-of-the-day way.

I glanced through the expanded dining room again. *The ghosts.* Maybe they visited less often these days.

After the holiday Elizabeth and I spent all our time together even though we barely talked about our relationship with each other and we definitely didn't tell anyone else. Although Elizabeth and I became incredibly close, as classmates and colleagues and simply as friends, we never uttered the word *lover* or applied it to ourselves. Yet to anyone peeking in the window, or listening through the phone line in the middle of the night, that would've been the first word to come to their mind.

Denial blooms with companionship, in that it's easier to ignore the truth if others close to you are doing the same. But there are only so many hours of darkness in any given twenty-four hours. The business of dealing with daylight, and guilt and future and . . . reality . . . always comes forth. The guilt not just about making love to a beautiful woman but about being deficient—not being good enough—became increasingly unwieldy for me.

"Oh, Cathy, you get so black," she said to me once, as I sat on the floor in her apartment, my agony visible. "It scares me."

I sensed that I had to cover up the darkness inside me, keep it hidden, even from her. It was my first hint that maybe everyone *didn't* live so closely with the idea of their own death.

Elizabeth was bright and talented and lovely. Our connection deepened over the next couple of years. So did our mutual paranoia and struggles with our sexuality. Point blank, neither of us wanted to be gay, nor could we see any way that such a life would be accepted by our families or by society. The physical part of our relationship waned beneath this pressure, and beneath the later, more mature realization that we were better friends than lovers anyway.

We were both looking for ourselves, and for a way to fit in, in between cramming for Microbiology and drawing maps of the cranial nerves. The similarity of our struggle bound us tightly together. After we stopped kissing we remained the closest of friends.

She loved the water, too, and we'd road trip to the ocean or to the lake every time we had the chance. Atlanta is the largest landlocked city in the United Sates, but that never stopped me and my friends from driving five to ten hours just to find the sun and sand and salt water.

At the midway point of school, in the summer of 1985, I spent a couple of weeks at home, swimming at Lakeside, basking in the admiring gazes that came when Mom told her friends I was in medical school at Emory. That summer Anne was living in Midway, Kentucky, no longer seeing "the guy who wasn't good for her." Instead, she was going to the races at Keeneland, falling in love with a horseman, contemplating marriage.

Curtie had just graduated from college and gotten married a week later. He was living in Louisville with his new bride and his new job at the bank.

Our parents stayed in the house on Napanee Road, just the two of them—and the ghosts, of course, but now that Dad was sober the silver tray never rattled in the middle of the night, at least not whenever I was home from school.

Even though Anne, Curtie, and I were now all well into our twenties, Mom, still aka the Little General, kept up her full steam worrying about us, her "kids." She reported on the phone to me about Anne's latest news (*Why don't you call her?*), and then the details of Curtie's marriage and career moves. *We have to stick together—we're all we've got.*

As a family, we rocked along. Truth was, though, I was drifting further away than any of us realized. My being in medical school created an aura around me, not unlike Pigpen's dust. It gave me a reason for not dating, for not getting married, for my life being essentially on hold.

I was less penetrable, less reachable, less knowable than ever. I had it all together, *my daughter the doctor*, and in those first couple of years of medical school, I hadn't realized how quickly the family sun was setting on my hero's shield.

The crack in the glacier started paradoxically with a lightning zap. I returned to Atlanta to begin my third-year rotations. School would be vastly different from now on—the time had come for all of us to formalize our impersonations of being doctors, to have actual patients assigned to us, to follow around the residents and attending physicians, to be posed stupefying questions, to endure the humiliation of not knowing the answers.

The zap came on a clear, breezy Saturday afternoon when I was hitting tennis balls with a woman I'd just met, Jackie. She was involved with one of my good friends. I dared not utter the word *lover* out loud, but Jackie seemed capable of saying anything with ease.

"Nice shot," she said after I blasted one that she hit into the net. All three balls awaited retrieval, one on her side, two on mine. We both approached the net. "You have a great forehand," she said, winking. "I thought you were a swimmer."

"I am . . . or was. I mean, I can still swim."

She cocked her head to the side, one hand on the net. Her eyes, dark as unlit charcoal, held mine.

"How long did you swim?" she said, her body still and focused completely on me.

"Uh, let's see," I said, consulting the blue Atlanta sky. "Ten years."

"Wow, why'd you quit?"

Her perception—and proximity—unnerved and excited me.

"It's a long story," I said, dodging.

"I'd love to hear it," she said, not moving, her eyes opening me like eager fingers lifting the cover of a new book.

I bent down to pick up the two balls on my side.

"Want to hit me some at the net?" she said easily.

"Okay," I said, unsure about what was happening.

We talked while we hit a few forehands and backhands, then we'd walk to the net in search of the balls, but really to be closer, to continue our conversation. The breeze made it impossible for anyone walking by to hear what we were saying, or so I told myself.

"Ever been in love?" she said in one of those net moments.

"I don't know—sort of, I guess."

She laughed and when she did, her thick dark hair fell away, revealing her pearl-skinned neck.

"When were you first involved with a girl?"

I glanced around even though the breeze had gusted up and there was no one close to us. A lanky guy walked in long strides over by the road but there was no way he could hear us.

She followed my gaze. "No one can hear us," she said, not quietly.

"I'm . . . it's just . . ." I pursed my lips in an assessing pause. "It's not the kind of thing I tell just anybody."

She smiled and tilted her head, her eyes studying me all the more intensely.

"You want to go have a beer?" she said.

"Sure," I said, ignoring the slippery feeling of my feet on that first patch of ice.

I kept answering her questions—there were so many. And she answered mine.

In her nearby apartment we drank a beer, then another. Our flirtation deepened; it tasted delicious and dangerous. I leaned against a doorjamb, acting cool. Her stories fascinated me. Another beer. We laughed, we clinked bottles. We stood too close.

We had to stop this, we knew, but neither of us moved away, not until we made plans to get together again, maybe a little more tennis.

And thus the treason began, slowly from a physical standpoint, but instantly in the emotional terrain of the heart. We connected again and again, giving lip service to her involvement with my friend, while in reality already trampling all over something I would later learn to call a boundary.

It was messy, the unfaithfulness of Jackie, encouraged by me, my disregard for friendship, the rudeness and insanity all excused in the name of love. After a few months of tears, hurt, flat wrongdoing, there came a time when Jackie and our mutual friend no longer slept together, a slippery time when our affair became, what? Just us.

And this Jackie person was already more herself in the world, unafraid—or at least less paranoid than me—about being, you know, *gay*. Suddenly, I no longer cared what anyone called anything, I could see only her bottomless eyes as I fell deeper and deeper, reaching toward whatever was pulling me into her affection, into her web, into however she wanted me to be.

School, family, friends—life—all became secondary, peripheral. I had a single oxygen supply, and she had thick brown hair and
a quirky smile. Bam, just like that, I was out for the count.

"What's going on with you?" Mom said that winter on the phone.
    "Nothing. Why?"
    "You're never there when I call."
    "Mom, we have weird schedules," I lied.
    "Well, how come your roommates answer the phone?"
    "I don't know. I'm sorry," I said, kicking a pile of socks into the
floor of my closet. "How's Anne feeling?"
    "Not great, but she's not complaining. Why don't you call her?"

The news of Anne's pregnancy barely landed on my radar screen, so
immersed was I in the soap opera of my life, in this completely new
world of being *in love*. I abandoned everything and everyone, which
included spending precious little time at the house I shared with
two med school friends.
    One of them called my room "the mausoleum." The bedroom
stayed neat, which was the surefire mark that I stopped in and out but
never stayed for any appreciable period of time. There weren't even
any piles on the desk, which was a makeshift contraption, a large
piece of veneered board supported by two metal filing cabinets.
    I was so lost in orbit I didn't know what was up and what was
down. The piles—bills, schedules, clothes—collected in the backseat of my Toyota, and in the front seat, on the floorboards, everywhere. Where I slept was the least of it, sort of.
    I saw my housemates only in passing, on the weekends or in the
hospital. In Jackie's apartment, I became my own version of a piece
of furniture, even though sometimes I had to hide in the bathroom
because she lived in campus housing and wasn't supposed to have
anyone living with her, certainly not a *lover*.

She and I worked and studied and played basketball on Saturday mornings in an intramural league. Mostly, though, I did whatever she wanted to do and I pushed out of my head the questions of what people thought about me, about *us*.

"People don't care," she said one day when we were walking in Lenox Mall.

"Then why are they looking at me?" I said. I'd lived the previous ten years believing that whenever anyone looked at me they were thinking negative things—I looked like a boy, I was fat—they wondered silently if I was *gay*.

"You're unbelievable," she said, shaking her head in a tender way as she turned into a store. I trailed her like a puppy dog, a cute, bright one who carries her own leash in her mouth, ready at any moment to give it over, wanting her master to take the reins and direct.

So long as I kept my view solely on Jackie, it was easier to ignore that people might be staring at me, which they weren't doing, of course, but homophobia turns the lens inside out, like looking through binoculars backward; everything that's big seems small, and vice versa.

Our time together wasn't exclusive by any means—Jackie, among other things, was a social wonder. She knew everybody. We followed local bands to bars in places like Little Five Points and Buckhead, where I'd know a few people and Jackie would know half the crowd.

We even went out to the suburbs one Saturday night, early on, north of the city, into a neighborhood of oversized, immaculate houses. The wide roads curved gently around brushed, well-tended lawns. It reminded me of the Louisville neighborhoods of my youth, the ones across Brownsboro Road, where the rich people lived. That might've alerted me to what was about to happen, but I wasn't accustomed to paying attention to my hunches and fears.

"Are you sure this is the right place?" I said, glancing at the eventless street, expensive cars lining one side of it.

"I've got the address right here."

"Who *are* these people?" I shifted in the passenger seat while Jackie pulled the car to a stop.

"I told you, friend of a classmate." She threw a smirk at me, one I interpreted as interest. "You're nervous, aren't you?"

"No," acting cool. In reality my heart was bouncing wildly out of rhythm. Heat rushed up my torso to the tips of my ears and I was deeply grateful for the darkness.

I followed her up the front walkway, feeling strangely out of place, like I'd been dropped back about ten years, into a high school party being given, with tacit parental consent, by one of the liquor-pouring sons of the East End set.

And damn if I wasn't right—sort of.

The front door opened into a number of people—women—standing in a richly carpeted great room, in the kitchen, down the hall. There was notable laughter and that buzz that forms when groups of people—women—are talking at the same time. In their twenties, thirties, and forties, these weren't grad students, these were real-world people, gay people, *lesbians.*

But they were so pretty! Not all of them, but many of them, with their coifed hair and gleaming lipstick. They leaned sexily in tailored slacks and skirts, silk blouses, fiery necklaces, glinting bracelets.

Jackie ducked discreetly to me to ask if I was okay, which is when I realized I must've been staring, my mouth hanging open, my own stereotypes exploding like a bomb inside my chest. These women were . . . *gay?*

Jackie's friend began introducing us. Some women extended their hands in kindness, others nodded in a cool, surveying way. I felt younger than most of the others, could feel I was being "checked out," was ghastly unable to find that sorority girl ease I'd developed early in life. In other words, I couldn't speak.

Then Jackie was making excuses for my sudden onset of shyness—"This is her first gay party" she said, just as the hen cackle in the room subsided—or so it seemed to me.

"You're coming out! Welcome!" exclaimed the friendly hostess, a blonde with black mascara and hints of powder on her face. She was older than my mom!

"Thank you," I mumbled, aware of the well-meaning chuckles rippling through the group.

We didn't stay all that long because we really didn't know many people, and as students, we led a life quite different from this affluence. Still, the curtain had been lifted for me, and I was quiet as we sped south on the highway toward the pub in Little Five Points, quiet and secretly thrilled.

16

The cross-chest carry is used primarily for an active victim. It is designed specifically for the comfort of the victim and is difficult to use for long distances, even by well-conditioned lifeguards.

American Red Cross Lifeguarding, p. 145

On some days the surface of the Ohio River can resemble a plate of glass; perfectly smooth and still, it becomes a painting, a mirror, a mirage. No malice lurks in such peaceful moments—the current moves forward like a ghost, unseen. But a river by nature is always breaking things, rubbing holes into rock, pushing its weight against obstinate riverbank mud, lapping and swirling against tangled, exposed roots. The water runs in constant, if sometimes unacknowledged, motion.

On such days, its work occurs underneath the surface, which is what it was doing that morning in December when I drove down River Road, past the Louisville Boat Club, out near the bend where Uncle Ches drowned. My throat felt hot and swollen. A few days earlier I'd been rounding at Egleston Children's Hospital on the final day of my third-year pediatric rotation. That morning in Louisville I just needed someplace to go so I cruised along the river for awhile and then went home.

Grateful for the empty house, and especially that Mom was still out shopping, I headed straight for bed. The memory of our clash from the previous evening ran around in my mind like a frightened creature too confused to know how to stop.

"What's the matter with you? Why don't you call anyone while you're home?" she'd said.

"Who, Mom?" I'd said with a sharp bristle in my voice.

"I don't know." She snapped the lid on the round Tupperware of leftover casserole. "Sarah, or Lynn. Maybe Kelly's home."

I shook my head.

"What's wrong with my just wanting to spend time here?"

"Nothing." She shook her head slightly. "It's just . . ."

"What?" I was daring her to come right out with what she was thinking—that she thought there was something *wrong* with me. I stood planted in the border territory. Every time she looked at me, I felt criticized. Dad was at work.

"You just don't seem . . . you're not yourself," she finally said, hands on her hips, her tone nearly accusing.

"Yes, I am, Mom. I just feel sick. I'm sorry."

The evening dragged on interminably. After two bowls of ice cream, I'd said good night. This morning I'd been determined to go "do something," so I went for a drive, then, feeling crummy, just came home. I had nowhere to go, no enduring friend in Louisville to call now that I was home for Christmas. It made me too nervous to even think of calling Donna—and everyone else from high school didn't know the true me. Neither did my mom or dad or anyone in my family.

I climbed the stairs slowly and crawled into bed. My room looked the same as always, slanted ceilings and an area rug the color of a bluejay's back. Over the years we'd moved the twin beds into different configurations. Now they jetted into the room from the left wall, separated by a single bedside table that was crowded with throat lozenges, a box of tissues, a bottle of cough syrup, a sticky spoon. One floor down revealed the Christmas tree and the stockings Mom knitted with our names on them hanging beneath Grandmother's watchful face. Mom had placed some greenery along the mantel, and the little man once again adorned the back of the toilet in my parents' bathroom.

None of it helped lift me out of my achy funk. For the first time in my life the decorations and worn-out songs grated on me; they didn't mesh with the hospital work I'd just finished—taking care of bald little kids battling leukemia. A few hours of solitude this morning only made me crave more. That and I was as desperate for Jackie as thirst is for water.

Downstairs the front door opened. *"Cathy."* It was Mom.

"I'm up here," I yelled back.

Bags were set down and I listened to the familiar staccato gait climb the steps.

"What's wrong?" she asked, a look of mild exasperation on her face.

"I don't feel very good." I felt like a piano was sitting on top of me and my head hurt.

"Do you have a fever?" She leaned over and put her hand on my forehead. "You don't feel warm."

"Maybe I picked something up in the hospital."

She stood a minute more, in that familiar pose of problem-solving thought. It felt like her eyes had X-ray capabilities, that by looking she could both assess my degree of illness and also see right through to the ache in my heart.

"Let me see your throat." I opened wide like many times in my childhood. A deep sigh fell out of her. "You do have some white patches and it does look swollen. I'll bring you up some chicken soup in a little while," she said.

"Thank you," I said, my eyes moistening.

No one understood depression in those days, or that the body physically revolts and becomes susceptible to the weakest little germ when placed under too much stress. What was my stress? Only the increasing insanity of appearing one way during the day at the hospital, competent, bright, compassionate, then another way after hours, dependent, needy, fearful. My legs and arms and head felt full of thick, black mud.

My parents had no idea of Jackie's importance to me—at least I didn't think they did. I'm sure Mom noticed that I spoke with her on the phone several times during the holiday break. After a grumpy week in bed I started feeling a little better and decided my mood had been, at least in part, from the flu. By the time my departure for Atlanta was imminent, though, the gulf between me and my parents felt oceanic.

Beyond Napanee Road, life was expanding and me with it. I became more and more comfortable moving around town with Jackie—going to restaurants and bars, noticing men and women, wondering who was gay and who wasn't.

I still talked to my parents religiously on Sundays.

"What did you do this weekend?" Mom asked.

"A group of us went to hear Amy and Emily at the Little Five Points Pub last night."

There was a slight pause. "Oh. Was it fun?"

"Yeah, it was great."

"Do any boys go out with you girls?" Her voice was tinny and strained.

"Mom," I said. "I spend time the way I want to. I enjoy going out with my women friends." That was as honest as I could be—at least I wasn't lying.

"I was just asking," she said, her voice closing down on me.

We bumped along like that, Mom and I; we'd been bumping like that for years. In those earlier days of our easy-flow conversations, when she was wrecked with frustration and concern about Dad, about how to provide more than everything to her three kids, in the days when I was her carbon copy, her second chance, her bright-eyed-has-it-all-together-born-twenty-one daughter, we were fine.

Then, I had to grow up.

I had to be the me that neither of us wanted me to be.

For years, none of us McCalls understood the prominent space our family allotted to denial. Dad figured it out first. By quietly changing his attitude and perceptions, by quietly applying honesty to himself, he ripped the curtain of denial that shrouded all of us—but we each had our own individual robes of it created by then.

The experts don't call alcoholism a family disease just to be kind. Making up reality—rather than accepting it—can become a way of life, had become *my* way of life. It is a costly way to live, though, because its weight, like glacial ice, just gets heavier and heavier. In my third year in med school, after seeing Jackie for several months, I started dismantling my own denial, albeit slowly. I made a concerted effort to limit my lying, to stop being quite so deceiving when it came to my personal life. I began dropping my Houdini tricks in conversations with my mother. She'd never asked for my dishonesty, for my disappearing acts, in the first place. She didn't like it, my new honesty, I could tell, but she did keep calling—at least for awhile.

In the spring, Mom made her annual pilgrimage to the Mecca of Ormond Beach, Florida (*it's cheaper than Our Lady of Peace*) and Anne, seven months pregnant, joined her. From our earliest days we McCalls resembled loggerhead turtles returning to the same beach year after year. Mom and Anne encouraged me to drive down from Atlanta.

"Jackie and I can be there by midday Friday," I said to Mom on the phone.

"Okay," she said, her voice a bit distant.

Denial is as pervasive as an oil slick, and just as obstinate.

I hadn't felt nervous about Mom and Anne and Jackie meeting each other until the moment Jackie and I pulled into the condominium parking lot. I'd just assumed that they would all three like each other because they were each important people to me—and then I hadn't thought about it again. See how denial works: don't look, don't think.

Heat rose from the blacktop when I stepped from the car and stretched.

"Should we unload now?" Jackie asked.

"Let's go say hello first. They're probably by the pool."

Jackie tipped up on her toes as she sometimes did when she was nervous.

"I'm so glad you're finally going to meet them," I said, touching her shoulder briefly then pulling my hand away.

"Me, too," she said, her voice not especially full of enthusiasm.

They were right where I knew they'd be, lounging on chairs in the grassy area between the pool and the beach. When we approached, Mom jumped up with arms outstretched.

"Hello," she said, hugging me tightly. "I'm so glad to see you."

"Same here," I said, the scent of sweet coconuts encircling me. I stepped closer to Anne, who resembled a sea lion happily basking in the sun. "Don't get up," I said as I bent to hug her.

She smiled. "Okay."

"Mom, Anne, this is Jackie."

Everyone said hello in a congenial enough manner and then we stood there for a hot, awkward moment. The air carried that thick salty feeling.

"How was the trip?" Mom said, holding her hand over her forehead to shield her eyes. She wore a blue-and-pink two-piece bathing suit, the kind with a skirt on the bottom half.

"Easy," Jackie said, pulling on her shirt for relief from the heat.

"Let's see that's one aaa-dult and three children," Anne said in an exaggerated country accent, to which Mom and I laughed. Jackie just looked confused.

"It's an old joke," I said, realizing suddenly that there was no way to translate the memory to her of that endless night when we were kids and Mom was tired and the oldest living desk clerk in the Confederacy rented us the last hotel room on I-75 between Atlanta and Lake City.

Another parched moment dragged on.

"What room are we in?"

"Here, let me show you," Mom said. "You need anything?"

Anne shook her head. "Maybe some water."

Mom led us around the edge of the pool to a short walkway. Some little kids shouted "Marco . . . Polo . . . " from the water.

"This is a nice one," Mom said, referring to the condo. She'd stayed in several different ones in the complex. "I like that it's on the first floor. You can park right out here," she motioned just before opening the door to the unit.

It had your basic galley kitchen, living room opening onto a patio and a hallway toward the bedrooms. Down the hall Mom turned into the first doorway on the right.

"I have you girls in here," she said of the small bedroom with twin beds. I glanced at Jackie, whose eyes were unreadable.

"I hope this is okay," Mom said, her voice a little tense.

"Mom, it's great. We're just glad to be here." The room felt stuffed with moisture and heat and fibrous air.

"You can use this bathroom. Anne and I can share the master," she said in her typically efficient manner. "Okay?" she asked, expecting affirmation.

"Great," I said, obliging. I was aware of Jackie somewhere behind me.

"You all need any help unloading?" Mom was at the freezer putting ice cubes in a blue plastic cup.

"No, we're fine. We'll get the car and change and be out in a minute."

"Okay," she said, now holding two cups, standing at the door.

"Here, I'll get that." I opened the door.

"Thanks. See you out there," she said, and she was gone.

That's when I noticed that moist feeling I associated with being indoors in Florida, that faint whiff of mildew that seemed to permeate every thread of fabric.

"Are you okay?" I asked Jackie, who was glancing at a handwritten list on the table.

"Sure, fine," she said, although she didn't seem fine.

I walked over and put my arms around her.

"This is okay, isn't it? That we're here?"

She shrugged.

"Except for the twin beds, I know," I said. "C'mon, let's get the car so we can change and go in the ocean." That made her smile.

"I thought you'd never ask," she said, squeezing my side affectionately.

The front door opened and I jerked away from Jackie.

"I forgot my visor," Mom said, pausing to look at us for a second then pulling the hat off the counter. She turned and left without another word. Only the scent of coconut oil still lingered.

"Think she saw us?" I said.

"No," Jackie said, her voice holding a note of defeat. "You know she probably knows, anyway."

"You mean about us?"

"Yes."

"I don't think so—not my mom."

We started walking to the car. I was careful to keep my voice so quiet that even Jackie, walking right next to me, could barely hear.

"Why do you say that?" I asked.

"C'mon, Cath, they're not blind." She opened the hatchback of her car as my frown deepened. "It's not like you wanted to bring a guy with you for the weekend."

"Mom doesn't think about things like that—I don't think she has a clue," I said.

"You're so paranoid—I mean, what would be the major problem?"

"What do you mean?"

"If she knew?"

I shook my head, too afraid to answer that question. "I'll get our crackers and drinks from the backseat," I said, needlessly, just to change the subject.

Despite the beach and the cold ocean water, the entire two days felt like I was skipping barefoot on hot blacktop. There was no outright display of intense emotion—that was always reserved for McCall family members only—but neither was there much ease either.

"How do scallops sound for tonight?" Anne said as she squirted more lotion on her arms.

I glanced to my left at Jackie. "That okay?" I said quietly, as if she hadn't heard or needed me to translate or something. She nodded.

"Wonderful," I said to Anne more forcefully. Mom was lying with her eyes closed in the chair between Anne and me. Jackie was next to me on the end.

Anne had been telling me about the farmhouse she and her husband had bought and the plans they had for renovating it. The conversation waned now, as if she'd reached a point where it took too much energy to come up with more to say.

"You want to go for a walk?" Jackie said. I looked from her to Anne, torn. Mom had lifted her head. With her hand shielding the sun she glanced from Anne to me, seeming to consider the proposal.

"Go ahead," Anne said, maybe sensing my dilemma, maybe not. "I might go for one in a little while."

"I think I'll wait, too," Mom said, leaning back again.

"Does your family always work that way?" Jackie said to me when we were safely alone, a quarter mile down the beach.

"What way?"

"You know, everyone doing everything . . . together." Her tone didn't sound malicious. In it I heard that there must be something wrong with our family.

"Well, we're pretty close." I gazed at the muscular breakers and thought of my brother and sister and I braving those waves all day when we were kids. "I never really thought about it."

"You seem so . . . focused on them," she said, not looking at me. "Hey, look at that," she said, pointing to a large mogul of sand far away from the water. It turned out to be a sand sculpture of a giant, curving snake.

"It's incredible," I said. I almost added my desire to tell Anne and Mom about it so they would walk this way to see it but I kept that last thought to myself.

We were careful not to touch each other, of course, although I gave no thought to the easy choreography with which Jackie and I shared our space—the little bedroom, the bathroom, the backseat of Mom's car on the way to dinner the next night. At twenty-five I was still terribly naïve about the subtle dance steps of intimacy, about what we reveal about ourselves through body language and other nonverbal expressions. I'd always been a naturally affectionate person, yet I gave no thought to my perceptive sister probably picking up on my stilted ways around Jackie.

"Hey, sis, come here," Anne said the next morning, after all four of us had been resting in our sun goddess poses for awhile. She placed my hand on her belly.

"Wow," I said.

"Can I?" Jackie said, lifting out of her chair, too. An expression of sheer wonder spread across her face and Anne laughed. Jackie sat on the edge of Anne's chair and kept her hand on Anne's pregnant belly for quite awhile, mesmerized. Anne seemed to get a kick—so to speak—out of Jackie's fascination with the baby.

By Sunday afternoon it felt like we'd been in Florida for a month, and not in a relaxing way. I don't think I took a full breath the entire weekend, at least not until we drove out of the parking lot on our way back to Atlanta. I even forgot to walk down to the ocean to kiss it good-bye before we left.

"You're pretty tied to your family," Jackie said as we crossed the state line into Georgia.

"I guess," I said, not understanding anything anymore.

That was April 1986, twelve years after the tornado crashed through Louisville, eleven years after my father erected an effective blockade to the invasion of alcohol, and ten years after I'd kissed a girl for the first time. I had just over a year left in medical school and the time was approaching when I needed to decide what kind of doctor I was going to be. I already knew, although I didn't like admitting it, especially to my mother. *What, you're not going to be a real doctor?* I'd always known what interested me the most about people: why they do what they do.

I was destined to follow Freud from the time I was in seventh grade and my teacher had us write a story about a typical day in our future. At the time, at that sagelike age of thirteen, I could already feel the falseness in my words. I described waking my children, getting them dressed for school, cleaning up the kitchen, kissing my husband good-bye, then going off to work as a child psychiatrist. There was a slight eeriness to the feeling at the time, writing those words, hearing the faint yelping of the me trapped so far inside that I could easily ignore her, turn her into a foreign being, some *thing* to be hushed and criticized and silenced.

Nearing the end of that third year of med school, in addition to selecting a specialty, I also had to begin thinking seriously about where to do my residency training in Psychiatry. Of course, I couldn't see past Atlanta, as much as a part of me, buried deep, deep inside, longed for the adventure of living somewhere new. Not without Jackie, though, and she had one more year of graduate school.

"Don't base your plans on me," she said, ever so casually, a few weeks after our stifling weekend in Mecca.

"I'm not," I said, my voice that of a child's. I was sitting on her couch with my feet on the table.

"You know," she said, stopping her tidying to look at me. "I have to remind myself that you're responsible, that you pay your bills and get yourself to where you're supposed to be." A thoughtful expression came onto her face, one that suggested mild distaste.

"What do you mean?"

"Well, you're just always . . . here."

"I like being with you," I said, pouting.

"I know, I know, that's great. I just have to remind myself that you do have a life, too."

The small space of her apartment had seemed to be shrinking of late.

"Funny you should mention it. I do need to run home for a little while," I said, getting up, "to responsibly pay a few bills."

She shook her head and put her arms around me. "You know what I meant," she said, although I didn't really. I knew how warm her body felt, how much I could just stay and suggest we take a nap. But she'd already talked about needing to go to the library. I was slow, but I could eventually get a hint.

"Meet you back here later?" I said, kissing her, holding her, foolishly, slavishly, not wanting to let go.

"Sure," she said, her mind already gone to somewhere—or someone—else.

• • •

It was a gorgeous afternoon, sunny and new. The flowers on campus sprinkled yellows and reds and purples around the sidewalks. I drove the few minutes to my house and bowed ceremoniously upon entering when one of my roommates stared at me in mock disbelief.

"I know, you're glad to see me," I said.

"Always," she said, laughing.

We were sitting around, catching up, when the phone rang.

"It's your mom," she said.

"Great." I hopped off the couch. "I'll take it in the mausoleum." I hustled down the hall, my step and mood light.

"Hi, Mom."

"Hi. I can't believe I caught you at home," she said. "Is it pretty there?"

"Yes, ma'am, it's gorgeous."

As she described the dogwoods coming into bloom in Louisville, I pictured her standing in the dining room beside the cherry hutch, gazing out the front windows of the living room, watching the world go by.

The dust on the hardwood floor in my room was so thick I could make circles and squares and triangles in it from where I sat, which was on the floor, leaning against my bed. It was a blessing that my mother couldn't see the dust through the phone line.

"So what have you been up to this weekend?" The slight tilt in her voice alerted me.

I told her that I'd gone out to dinner the evening before, after going to the Piedmont Arts Festival with friends, that it had been a lovely Atlanta day.

"Did any boys go along?"

I sat up straighter and bent my knees.

"No, Mom. I've told you I enjoy what I do—that I like—spending time with my . . . friends."

"Well . . . I was calling to see when you're planning to come home."

"Umm."

"For the baby."

"Yeah, I know. Um, when's Anne due again?"

"The first week in June. You're out in June, right?"

"Yes, ma'am. I—Jackie and I were thinking about going to the Outer Banks for a week or so."

The density of the pause, of the silence—so rare—should've been a signal to me, but how do you measure that which is invisible, regardless of its weight?

"*Cathy . . . are you gay?*"

I turned into ice. No breath, no motion, no sound. Four words, then . . . nothing.

"Cathy?"

"Mom . . . ?"

"Are you?"

"If—if you're asking me if I'm involved with a woman—the answer—is yes."

"OH MY GOD." She started screaming and yelping in her crisis voice, saying words like *strange* and *weird* and *what's wrong with you* and a host of syllables that broke apart somehow in the cable line connecting us.

"Mom, try to calm down—"

"I can't calm down! Have you told your brother and sister—I'm not telling them, I'm not telling anyone! OH MY GOD, WHAT'S WRONG WITH YOU?"

That's when I noticed everything in the room as if for the very first time. The dirt and chipping paint on the windowsill, the wooden box on my dresser, the tangle of necklaces hanging from the corner, tennis shoes and loafers and Top-Siders in a teepee on the floor of the closet, the brown cork bulletin board above the desk, a rotation schedule and a misplaced red ribbon from somewhere sticking to it.

I noticed, too, the smoothness in my voice, the clarity of my enunciation, the deliberate selection of my words.

"Mom, try to take a breath. Is Dad there?"

"He's not home. OH MY GOD. I'm not telling him."

"Mom, it's okay, you don't have to tell anybody. It's okay, really, just try to calm down." She was so upset; I could see her pacing and fuming and searching the rooms of the house for a clue, for an explanation, for something she could use to reach inside me and rearrange the loose screws, the malformed joints that were causing her daughter to speak these outrageous things.

"Your father's coming in the door now!" She was crying hard in that shrieking yelp that came out only in times of sudden change. Job losses, accidents, deaths—times like those. My honesty had once and for all burst the family bubble, that myth that we lived by, that we were all happy and well-adjusted and *together*, that we'd made it through Dad's alcoholism intact and unscathed. The dreams—and the plans—that she had for me disintegrated in that single conversation; they burst into flames, then turned to ash and floated in all directions, disappearing, never to be seen or touched or proudly displayed again.

"What's happened?" I heard Dad's voice in the kitchen. Mom was still crying and yelling.

"Here, it's *Cathy*," she said, the disapproval in her voice slicing through the ice around my heart, which was fluttering out of control.

"Miss Bug?"

"Hi, Dad."

"Are you okay?"

"Yes, sir."

"What's going on?"

"Well—Mom asked me if I was gay . . . and I said . . . 'If you're asking me if I'm involved with a woman then the answer is yes.' "

Another interminable silence stretched the distance from four hundred miles to four million. I imagined his brow furrowed, his lips pursed in thought, his eyes darting back and forth but not really focusing on anything.

"Well—we don't have to understand it, but I guess we have to accept it."

All the ice inside me turned into a river at that moment, a river of relief and fear and uncertainty.

"I know Mom's really upset," I said, holding the gully washer of my tears back.

"Yeah, I better go see what I can do."

"Okay, Dad, thanks. I love you."

"We love you, too, honey."

I stood up like a robot, closed my door until it clicked, then fell onto my bed just as the dam was breaking. Years of self-hatred and guilt, of telling her I had no problems, of keeping the strange beast that was the *real* me covered in the camouflage of good intentions— they all cascaded down like a great flood.

What have I done?

From the time I was a young child I could cry, not openly in front of other people, but in the solitude of my private world. I would hold it—still do—until I could be alone, and then the dam would crash open, great waves would surge upward. I'd barely be able to catch my breath and still the salty water would pulse forward. The waves could convulse through my body, rearrange me. I was four and waking up from a nap, realizing I'd missed the trip to ride on the train, experiencing for the first time in a visceral way what it felt like to be *left*. Or I was fourteen, my brother twelve. He stared at me as if he didn't recognize me, fire burning in his eyes, "I *hate* you," he screamed, and up the stairs I ran.

Or, now. Twenty-five—exposed, disdained, and so, so *stupid!*
What have I done?

Darkness crept into the room unseen; it merged with the black juice
spewing from that inner abyss. Time—minutes, hours—flowed by;
I still couldn't move, couldn't get off the bed. I wanted to stay there
forever, until my flesh disintegrated, until I became a skeleton wor-
thy of the grave.

All I could do was reach for the phone—for the first time grateful to get Jackie's answering machine. Said I'd talked with my mom,
would tell her all about it tomorrow, that I was beat and I was going
to sleep—not to call.

Daylight brought its miracle, its insistent reminder that no one had
died, that the Earth was, in fact, still spinning. The next day, I ventured into a world of different colors, a world where everyone on
the sidewalks of campus and in the hospital cafeteria, everyone who
looked at me *knew. Cathy, are you gay?*

Except my patients in the hospital. This month I was on general
surgery. The patients and their loved ones looked at me with hope
and appreciation or with downcast, frightened eyes. Most of them
copied the smile I offered, which helped me as much as it did them.
By day's end I was ready to tell Jackie about the conversation.

She was delighted, insisting from the outset that I was too tied
to my family, too worried about what they and other people
thought about me. I didn't know what I was; I just knew, deep down,
that I was terrified.

17

Recent studies on cold-water survival have found
that some people who are presumed dead after
being underwater for an extended period of
time may retain enough air in their lungs and oxygen
in their blood stream to sustain life and
prevent brain damage.

American Red Cross Lifeguarding, p. 210

Within twenty-four hours Mom called back, for a brief few minutes, to inform me that she had told Anne and Curtie.

"This is the craziest thing I've ever heard," she said. "You can't know what you're doing."

She started crying again and exited the conversation before I could find words to explain what I hated about myself. At least, for years I'd hated it, or resisted it or whatever words you want to put to the lies we tell ourselves, even as we do things that we pretend we're not doing.

The days stretched out of shape after that, growing wide and interminably long. All the usual places I went on campus—the sidewalk past the cafeteria, the circular drive around the student center, the downhill descent toward the new multimillion-dollar gym—became foreign places, large and wide and strange. No trace of the original pool building, that humble old airplane hangar that doubled as a gymnasium. That girl who arrived on campus so bright-eyed and full of dreams, the one who led her humble parents around the quad, past the stone buildings to the modern Chemistry structure, past the famous hospital and into the leafy estate of the university president—

she was gone, that girl, gone the way of the old gym, flattened and remade, no hint of the original anywhere in view.

It didn't occur to me to go swimming, even though Emory had built a gorgeous, state-of-the-art natatorium. I was so disoriented, so wrenched from the familiar, that I forgot about swimming. Some of the old songs still played over and over in my head, though, like *I'm lost, living inside myself. . . .*

After that conversation with Mom, I spoke to no one in my family. She sounded so hurt and angry, so crushed by the revelation of the true me. Before that fateful exchange, I'd talked with Jackie about possible scenarios of "telling" my parents but she never harbored the same dilemma. Hers had been a less ordinary childhood, where she was passed between different families. She'd grown into one of those remarkable people who sort of raise themselves, but who also feel no strong connection with their family. From the beginning, she wanted me to just tell them about us, and put the onus on them to deal with it.

So the mulling, before and after the conversation, had been mostly private and internal. I trudged through days at the hospital, one patient after another, but my mind was elsewhere, sunken in the returning murk of complacency. I couldn't muster real interest in much of anything, stood dumbfounded and humiliated when attending physicians and residents asked me questions I couldn't answer. *I'm not smart enough to be a doctor*, I thought, even as I was impersonating one, complete with stethoscope and white coat.

My haven was Jackie's tiny apartment.

"Oh, you're here," she said, somewhat surprised that I was sitting on the couch one afternoon.

"Dr. Bennett finished rounds early," I said, starting to get up. She crossed the small space and kissed my cheek, her motion suggesting hurry.

"I've got to meet my study group at the library in fifteen minutes," she said, making a goofy face that seemed sort of conflicted and sort of not.

"Oh," I said, knowing I needed to read but not particularly wanting to.

She was already putting some things in her backpack. "I'll be back late—don't worry about waiting up," she said.

"Okay," I said, now standing, not really sure of what to do.

She stopped for a second and gave me a hug. "You okay?" she said, not really wanting to know.

"Sure," I said, turning my long face away.

"We do have a huge project coming due," she said, defensively.

"I know. Good luck with it," I said, my enthusiasm lacking.

"Thanks," she said quickly and was gone.

I sensed something was changing between us, but I couldn't put my finger on what it was. The space of her apartment just kept shrinking. That she was inching away from me, from my suffocating pull on her, was an insight that wouldn't reveal itself to me for several more months. I had my own crisis going on and it felt like Jackie—or at least her apartment—was the only place I belonged; I couldn't risk losing that.

I'd heard stories about people whose parents disowned them when they found out they were gay. Even though I knew this was a theoretical possibility in my family, it wasn't until that unstopping river of days after my phone call with Mom that I began to seriously consider losing contact with them. *We have to stick together—we're all we've got.*

The silence from Kentucky tumbled forward. It was like rocks on a riverbed, unseen yet disturbed, piling on top of one another, each confirming the fear that I really was the crack, the defective link, the one responsible for our family breaking apart.

No one called. Derby had passed, and outside the Atlanta air was filled with the soft opening of full-blown spring, of painted grass and colorful petals. I was walking through each day separated by a pane of glass, unable to see or hear, to touch or smell—I was unable to *feel* anything.

That Saturday, nearly two weeks later, I stopped by the mausoleum, nodded to my roommates, got some clothes, and headed back toward campus, to Jackie's apartment, where I sat, inert as a table. I didn't know what *to do*.

Except I was in a free fall—free finally from the bind of deception, free now to be in the world as myself. What I hadn't ever counted on was the fall.

"Oh, quit worrying about it," Jackie said, finally, to my fretful moping.

"Right," I muttered. "I'm too tied to my family." *But what if I never see or talk to them again? What if they don't love me anymore?* I couldn't say that out loud, sitting in her cramped kitchen/living room, staring at a textbook but not seeing it, doing nothing but taking up space. I was falling through a black hole, sinking to the depths of a dark, unbearable place. I glanced outside, unable to absorb the coaxing sun, unable to muster any desire to go do anything. I just sat there on the sofa like a zombie, a robot, like a lost child.

The phone rang, one of my housemates. "Your sister called, thought you'd want to know."

"Thanks," I said, hanging up.

"Think I should call her back?" I heard myself say, recognizing that old being inside me who put fingers to my vocal cords and strummed, the one whose origin I didn't know, who had sent me flying down the hall all those years earlier toward that senior in high school, toward my first crush, toward—go ahead and admit it—my first *girlfriend*.

"If you're going to keep obsessing about it, you might as well," Jackie said.

It had been nearly two weeks. My hand shook as I dialed the number, my heart falling ever faster in its free fall.

"Hello?"

"Anne?"

"I'm so glad you called," she said. The love in her voice wrapped around me like a hug. I couldn't say anything.

"Cac, are you there?"

"Yes," I said, holding in the tears that were hanging in my eyes. "I guess—Mom told you."

"Oh, Cac, I tried to call you but you weren't home." She paused. "I think it's wonderful—it just makes you more you. It's so good to hear your voice."

"It is?"

"I was afraid you would cut us off."

"Me, cut *you* off?"

"I'm just *so* glad you called."

I took a breath and noticed how a sun ray was throwing a spotlight onto the corner of the couch. Outside, the wind jostled the leaves, making their shadows skip on the fabric.

"How are Mom and Dad doing?"

"Well, it's hard for them. Mom said Dad's been crying in his sleep."

That was a fist in my gut.

"I'm so sorry," I said.

"Don't apologize—you haven't done anything wrong. It's just a shock to them . . . they need time."

"Yeah," I said, my voice fading, the descent beginning again, the phone line stretching a thousand miles, our family taut and again at breaking point.

"Cac, it's okay. It just makes you more *you*," Anne said again, as if she could read my thoughts. "I love you—and I always will."

"What . . . do you think I should do?"

A few seconds of silence ticked off. I just kept staring at the busy spot on Jackie's sofa, unaware of anything in the world at that moment except Anne's voice.

"Can you come home?"

"You think that would help?"

"Yes. You could fly into Lexington and we could drive down together."

We talked about the upcoming Memorial Day holiday, and as we did, the shadow leaves skipped around on top of the couch.

"Okay. I'll look into it," I said.

"Check on flights and call me back. I'll talk to Mom and Dad," she said. "Cac, you're important to our family; just don't cut us off, okay?"

"I would never do that," I said, the tears coming again. "I love you, Annie."

"I love you, too."

When I hung up, it felt like I had been holding my breath for two weeks, for ten years really, like I was bursting through the surface of a pool, of an ocean.

"I'm glad I called," I said to Jackie, who was rinsing a couple of dishes.

"Feel better?" she said, peering around the corner of the cabinet, her tone surprisingly sweet.

"Yes," I said. "You think I should call right now for flights?"

"Might as well."

Later that night, after the flurry of plan making, when I was lying in bed, Jackie asleep beside me, the waves came again. Dad was crying in his sleep. Mom couldn't even talk to me, she was so upset, so *mad*. Never in my life had she and I gone two weeks without talking—what if something happened to one of them?

I couldn't even fathom Curtie's reaction. What if he just didn't talk to me anymore? We'd been inseparable as kids, but as adults he'd veered sharply right—a banker, a churchgoer, an involved young Republican. Once I developed enough wherewithal to form an opinion, I gravitated as far, if not further, in the other direction.

Curtie wouldn't understand this, would need to hide me. In one brief exchange with Mom, I'd become a big, fat skeleton he'd need to keep hidden in *his* closet.

I rolled away from Jackie, who was sound asleep. I needed to be alone. Maybe I *should* stay away from them; wouldn't that make things easier for everyone? But I never wanted to do that. I didn't want to keep lying, which was driving me further away, keeping us on the fake, mirror surface of things. Relationships based on dishonesty can't deepen; I was beginning to figure that out.

I slid out of bed and stepped into the small bathroom. The tile felt hard and cold. There was nowhere to sit but on the toilet. I should've been relieved, and I was, but the tears that came carried fear, waves and waves of it. I didn't know how to be honest, not really, not about myself, not even *to* myself, much less to my family. What if I couldn't do it? What if they wouldn't want me anymore?

It all happened so fast, really, the yanking back of the curtain, the Houdini—me—ripping off my mask, or rather Mom putting her fingers to it and me going along. None of us was prepared, not for the depth of my lying, for the mammoth nature of the surprise. After having been honest with my mother that day on the phone, there was no way I could go backward.

Denial is a one-way ride, a one-act show—there's no turning around, no backing up. Once the jig's up, it's up, like Mom finding out that Dad was taking checks from the back of the checkbook and not recording them. There came a point where no amount of lying could get the tellers at Liberty Bank to cash his ten-dollar check, no amount of promises could make Mom give him one more chance. He had to do something new.

The only thing left to try was honesty. It was the same for me. I didn't want to manipulate or deceive Mom, or anyone, anymore. The truth was that being attracted to women felt natural to me. No amount of lying or hiding or pretending was ever going to change that.

From the airplane window I was glad to not be flying over the Ohio River, to not be seeing the thick, mud-packed water curving like a snake along the edge of downtown. Lexington, instead, offered a sea of green pastures, neatly marked by white fences and steeple barns. The buildings seemed small and few compared to the glass-and-steel monstrosities of Atlanta.

For once I was glad I didn't have to deal with the ghosts as real people, although who knows, maybe one of them would've been as cool about all of this as Anne was being. You can never know the answers to such questions—life just would've been different—it wouldn't have been this life, if they had lived.

The plane window felt cool against my forehead as I leaned against it, curling into myself, suddenly not wanting to be here at all, but to be in the bubble of Jackie's apartment, in the fantasy world where I had to do nothing but exist. I couldn't let myself think about who she'd be spending time with in my absence, that she'd never been faithful in any of her many previous relationships. She loved me; she said she did. And I loved her desperately. But love and need aren't the same thing.

Anne hugged me at the gate for a long time, despite her ever-growing belly.

"You doing okay?" she said.

"I guess," I said, feeling younger and not at all equipped to be the grown-up I had inadvertently—at age twenty-five—declared myself to be. "How about you? I can't wait to see your house."

"Well," she said, sighing in that gentle way she had, as more of an extended breath. "It's kind of a mess. We're trying to get the drywall and painting done before the baby gets here."

"Sounds impressive."

"Don't get your hopes up," she said, rolling her eyes.

Their farmhouse was in Midway, Kentucky, which was, as its name implied, approximately halfway between the towns of Lexington and Frankfurt. It was quite a bit closer to Lexington than Louisville, which explained why I could return to Kentucky via a side entrance instead of having to land immediately on the main stage.

She showed me the neat old house, told me how they planned to redo the bathroom and kitchen, that they still had this and that wall to knock out. My sister could do things like that, picture how something would look in the abstract, see the potential of things. I nodded as if I could, too.

"Let's go see the horses. I have to put some medicine on Lefty's shoulder."

Lefty, a muscled thoroughbred they rode for fun and for polo, trotted to the fence as soon as he saw Anne waddle toward the field.

She rubbed his neck and head, leaned in and hugged him. At the encouragement of my sister, I put tentative fingertips to the white streak on his long nose, but that was as close as I got.

"It's all right, he's a good boy," she said. "He won't hurt you."

"Oh, I know," I said, trying to act nonchalant, trying to hide my fear.

She rubbed his head between his perked ears.

"How are Mom and Dad doing?" I asked.

She let out a long sigh. "They're still pretty upset." Anne expertly examined the gash on Lefty's shoulder before squirting some medicine into it. "I suggested maybe they go talk to a counselor." At that she glanced my way then refocused on the horse.

"You think they will?" I was wearing a bright yellow shirt that I'd bought while shopping with Jackie. It felt stiff against a gust of wind.

"I told them I know someone at the university here." She patted Lefty on his good shoulder and stepped back. "Mom wondered if you would go."

"With them?" I said, my eyebrows shooting up.

"No, no, I don't think so, just by yourself." Anne had started walking back toward the house. "Let me show you my garden," she said, brightly.

"I . . . can't change this about myself," I said as I followed her.

She stopped and turned around. "I know," she said. "I had friends in college who were gay."

She said the word so easily, even though she and I had never had a conversation like this, not about relationships. Suddenly I realized we were friends. I understood in a new way that she was only two and a half years older than me, that there wasn't much difference between twenty-five and twenty-seven.

She started toward the flowers. "He's not that kind of guy—the counselor."

"You think it would make Mom and Dad feel better if I went?"

She nodded. "I do. Might make it easier for *them* to go."

"Okay," I said, pursing my lips, pushing away thoughts of that wretched therapy appointment in college. "Not this weekend?"

"No, no. It'll have to be this summer when you're home." She pointed to where she hoped to plant some tomatoes and vegetables, and proudly uttered names of several blooming plants that I promptly forgot. "Mom might bring it up tomorrow," she said. "Just wanted to give you a heads-up."

"Okay, thanks." I stood with my hands in my pockets, watching the wind ruffle the rolling pastures in our view. "Have you talked about tomorrow otherwise?"

She shook her head. "No, we're just meeting at the house about eleven."

It was my turn to exhale loudly. She turned her nurturing gaze toward me and put her hand on my shoulder. "I'm really glad you're here."

"Me, too," I said, leaning, like Lefty, on the strength of her love.

18

❋ ○ ❋ ○ ❋ ❋ ○ ❋ ❋ ○ ❋ ❋ ○ ❋ ❋ ○ ❋ ❋ ○ ❋ ❋ ○

In a passive drowning situation, the victim
suddenly may slip underwater, making no
attempt to call for help, or may float facedown
on or near the surface of the water.

American Red Cross Lifeguarding, p. 96

Approaching the Cannons Lane exit, off I-64, on the other side of the interstate, I could see the back nine of the golf course at Big Spring. Lush trees formed a wall of green and beyond the branches a couple of golf carts moved down the fairway. They might as well have been on another planet. Cars raced past them in both directions, never noticing the ease—promised or imagined— that lay along the brushed putting greens and trimmed fairways.

We passed it quickly, slanting onto the ramp, then turned in the opposite direction to make our way along the edge of Seneca Park. Soccer players raced toward us on a dash for the goal. We turned right, drove past Erhler's. I wanted a double-dip chocolate chip ice cream cone, but I kept silent.

The light in the heart of St. Matthews was red.

"You know, I've never had a White Castle hamburger," I said, glancing at the square white building that sat next to the railroad tracks.

"Really? You've never had a Slider?" Anne said, extending the word in a way that surprised me and made me laugh. "We used to go in there in high school, after parties. We had a *big* time," she said, again exaggerating her accent.

Thoughts of high school started pulling me into the chute, the tunnel, into that black swirling current of past.

"I've had their fried-fish sandwiches," I said, grabbing for any words that would keep me from sinking.

"Gross," Anne said, grimacing, just like when we were younger.

We crossed the tracks and chatted about how a few small businesses now occupied some of the houses in those first couple of blocks of Chenoweth Lane. Really, we talked about nothing important since neither of us knew what to say.

I felt a little as I had at Meyzeek when we waited before school like cattle nearing the plank. I didn't recognize how much I was holding my breath.

"That's such a pretty house," I said of my favorite, right before we reached Napanee. Set a good distance from the road, it had a lovely white picket fence and green shutters.

"I know," Anne said, flipping on the blinker. She drove slowly down the block, paused at the Oread stop sign, then pulled into the driveway behind both of my parents' cars. "Okay. Here we go," she said, leaning over to give me a quick hug.

Everything—the walkway, the front stoop, the boxwood bushes—was unchanged, and yet it all seemed oddly new to me, like I was seeing it not for the first time in years but for the first time in my life. I was walking into the house without feeling my feet on the ground, only the faintest sensation of a push, a phantom hand on the small of my back, urging me to follow my sister inside.

"Hello?" Anne called.

"Hey," Mom said, walking into the living room from the kitchen, her voice heavy and tired. "You feeling all right?" They embraced in front of the cherry desk with Mama T's picture on it.

"Hi, Mom," I said, taking a tentative step.

"Hi, Cathy," she said, her voice flat, her eyes narrowed. She stepped over to halfway hug me, then turned quickly. "Come on in. Curtie just called. He'll be here in a minute."

Surprisingly, the house seemed airier—the ghosts had cleared out, or maybe it was the gentle feeling of spring. I felt like a stranger, like a guest, hesitant, self-conscious, careful to step lightly.

"You want a Coke or something?"

We'd followed Mom into the kitchen, which seemed to shrink with all three of us in it.

"Hi," Dad said, appearing from down the hall.

"Hey, Dad," Anne said, hugging him.

"How're you feeling?" He was gentle around Anne's belly.

"Doing fine," Anne said, breezily, all of us grateful for her ease at that moment, pregnancy and all.

"Hi, Dad," I said, wanting to cry, to apologize for causing them all this heartache and pain.

"Hi, honey," he said, giving me an awkward hug. I felt like I'd been branded with a large scarlet *L* on my forehead. It was as if I wasn't completely there, since the girl who had lived here in this house with these people wasn't really me and now that I was here, I didn't fit in, I didn't say and do the things they expected me to say and do. I could see my sudden foreignness reflected in their eyes. I didn't know where to stand.

The minutes ticked along slowly as Mom and Dad inquired in more detail about Anne's sleeping and eating and how the house was coming along. I slipped into the bathroom and sat there, head in my hands, trying to take deeper, slower breaths, telling myself it would be okay, that it was good that I was here, that I had to walk back in there.

From the bathroom, I took the long way to avoid the kitchen. I padded through the living room, past the desk and the silent eyes of both grandmothers, into the haven of the border territory, the dining room. It allowed for easier movement, now that Mom had put the flaps of the central table down. Running my hand along the richly polished cherry hutch strengthened me enough to step a little closer to the doorway. I lingered there, on the edge of their conversation, participating with my interested nods and smiles—I didn't know what to say.

Curtie hurried through the front door. "Sorry I'm late." He hugged everyone, including me. He'd become so handsome. He was restless, though, chafing against the restrictive, hierarchical system at the bank. At twenty-three, my brother, Jack Benny—self-employed from the time he was nine years old—was already outgrowing his career. Mom had told me all about it several weeks ago, when we were talking on the phone like we always did, about Anne and Curtie and Dad and her, about everyone in the family, except me.

Curtie didn't say much; nor did he look at me directly. I could see that he was upset, ashamed of me even. He had a closed expression in his eyes, like his stomach hurt.

"Let's go in the den," Mom said.

So there we were: the five of us. *We have to stick together—we're all we've got.*

No one turned on the television.

Anne and I sat on the small, rattan two-seater couch in front of the old heater. Mom sat across the room from us, on the upholstered couch that was under the window. Dad and Curtie were in the chairs to my right, in front of the double trophy shelves that still displayed our most impressive swimming prizes and Uncle Ches's silver bowl.

We sat for a few seconds without anyone saying anything— probably an absolute first in our family, considering we regularly interrupted each other, finished one another's sentences as a matter of course, and generally talked at the same time. Not today.

My heart was so far up in my throat I wasn't sure I *could* speak. I kept reaching for my glacial cover, my cool, has-it-all-together façade. It was harder to find in the presence of such heat and light, with all of these knowing eyes seeing me as if for the first time.

"I know this is really hard," I managed to utter, just as Dad cleared his throat.

"I wanted to say a few things," he said, holding a small stack of wrinkled, yellow legal pad pages. "I've had to ask myself what I could have done differently—and you all know there's a lot of things." He then started reading a list of regrets he had, times when he should've been here for us and wasn't. "There was that Christmas Eve when I came in so late. I knew you all were worried the moment I saw your faces but I couldn't let it show, how much I cared; I was too filled with guilt. The time I never showed up to take you to the fair. How impatient I would get when you were little." Big tears hung in his eyes. Anne and I glanced at each other briefly.

She had sat up when he began to speak, my self-appointed protector, ready to walk the fire line for me, if necessary. But now she leaned back a little, as we all did, listening to this man tell us how much he loved us, had always loved us, how much he wished he could get those years back. His guilt was something you could almost see, like cold air on a winter morning, except it was a sun-washed spring day. We all sat in a respectful, sniffling silence until he finished.

"Dad," I said, willing my voice to be firm. "I appreciate your sharing but this is not your fault in any way. It's not because you did or didn't do anything. It's just . . . the way I am, the way I've always felt."

I could feel Curtie's greenish eyes frowning at me.

"What?" he said, not believing me.

"It's . . . what's natural for me." I didn't know how to explain what I'd not quite figured out myself.

"I don't agree with it," Curtie said, meaning homosexuality.

"It's okay—you don't have to," I said.

He squinted at me for a moment then slumped back, falling into his large frame, his head shaking slightly.

"I just don't understand it. You've never had any problems," Mom said.

"Mom, everyone has problems," I said, my Sigmund-nature surfacing.

She shook her head, staring as if she didn't recognize me, as if she suddenly didn't know this imposter of her daughter. Yet there seemed a genuine desire in her eyes to get to the bottom of this, as if it—I—was a puzzle that needed to be solved.

"I've . . . never been able to *tell* you, to let you know when I had a problem." Tears started climbing unexpectedly into my eyes.

"What do you mean?" she said, her voice quivering. She hadn't really wanted to release those words, but they escaped anyway.

"I always tried not to cause any problems. Like . . ." I glanced at the slanted ceiling for a second, hoping to read a secret script from somewhere or someone. There was only the blank white wall in between the darkly stained beams.

"I can remember a pair of shoes I had, that were wearing out on the bottom, and thinking I needed another pair, but not wanting to tell you because we couldn't afford it. I didn't *really* need them—I could keep wearing the ones I had."

"Oh," Anne said, putting her arm around my shoulder.

"What are you talking about?" Mom said. "I bought you shoes."

"I know, Mom, I know you did. It's—it's not about that, about the shoes." I had trouble keeping the pain from rising out of me, the tears from bursting out. "It's about my not being able to tell you how I was feeling—that's the problem I had, that I couldn't be honest, not with you—about how I was feeling."

"I can understand that," Dad said, his voice calm like Anne's.

"Well," Mom said, seeming to decide not to say the thing that had vaulted into her thoughts.

Another silence descended. I wanted to make her and Dad and Curtie feel better—that felt familiar. What felt so tentative and fragile was my trying to stay true to myself and open with them at the same time.

"I just don't get it. You're only twenty-five years old—how can you possibly know?" Mom added. She was twisted up, her legs sharply crossed, her hands locked around her legs.

"I—I don't know how, Mom, I just do."

She sighed heavily, holding her tongue, her disappointment spilling into the room like a river, like a flood, like the time we had two feet of water in the basement and still it kept coming.

"It's that girl—"

"Mom," Anne said, her voice steadying all of us.

"No one's making me be this way." She was speaking of Jackie, wanting it to be her fault, like it was some disease I had picked up. I wanted so badly to cry, to scream out, to fall on the floor and receive their stones. To be causing this strife, this pain in them, was nearly unbearable, and yet still I felt a steady, invisible hand resting on me.

I bit the inside of my mouth. "I've felt this way for a long time . . . I just didn't want to . . . accept it." I glanced up briefly and saw Mom squinting at me hard. Curtie looked frustrated and uncomfortable.

"Well," Mom said, exasperated. "Anne said she knows a counselor—a psychologist—in Lexington."

"He's very nice," Anne said quietly to me as I nodded.

"Will you go talk to him?" Mom continued.

"Yes, ma'am, I'll talk to anyone you want me to." A current of fear and sorrow rushed through my stomach. "I . . . this isn't something I'm just choosing," I said, my voice flimsy.

Curtie crossed his arms and made a noise but when we looked at him he didn't say anything. I couldn't explain it to them, not in a way that they could understand. Despite my long struggle, I didn't understand it myself, not really. But if I shared my fragile understanding with them then they would just think I was confused, that I wasn't really gay at all. I felt caught in a wordless twirl, on one of those saucer rides at the fair that spin you around until your brain breaks into jelly.

Dad cleared his throat again. "We don't condone this."

"I know."

We all gazed around at each other, and away, too, our eyes dragging the room for words that would pull us through this storm, words that would bridge this undeniable crack. We wanted words that would carry us away from this new, foreign terrain and back to the place we once lived. They wanted me to be the girl they loved and were so proud of; I wanted them to still love me, in spite of my . . . deficiency. Then there was Anne, who didn't see me as deficient at all, but somehow—miraculously—she saw me as just being *me*.

"I'm really sorry," I said because I couldn't not say it; the silence in the room was too hard to bear. I was reaching as far as I possibly could and still they were hundreds of miles away.

"We love you," Dad said, his voice softening, his brown eyes moving from Mom to Curtie to Anne and back to me. Curtie and Mom both nodded and Anne put her hand on my arm and kept it there. My resolve started melting. It took everything I had to hold in my tears.

"I love you all, too," I said, my eyes leaking.

"We will always love you," Dad said. "It's just going to take us some time."

An exhale helped steady me. "I understand," I said, my voice shaky. "It's taken me a long time." Recognition lodged in his expression. He slowly nodded his head in a thoughtful, regarding way.

Mom had her lips pursed, making herself not say the things that must've been flying through her head. Same with Curtie. He sat with his arms crossed over his chest. They both directed their eyes toward the carpet, not really looking at it.

The happy spring breeze rustled branches and new leaves. It shimmied through the screens, as if the ghosts were doing everything in their power to assure each of us that this would all turn out just fine. It didn't feel that way at the moment, not easy and light anyway.

Anne turned a little to be looking directly at me.

"I think it's an honor to know this about you," she said firmly, for the benefit of the others as much as me. "Like I've told you, I think it just makes you more you—and you're so special."

I took as big a breath as I could and looked at each of them, albeit briefly.

"I just really appreciate you all being here. I know this is really hard." Words abandoned me after that.

There didn't seem to be any words left in the world. Mom and Curtie spoke with their presence, with the frowns that covered up their hurt and confusion. Still, they were here, as committed to family as anyone can possibly be.

Family means no one quits on each other, no matter what.

I couldn't take in the full impact of that insight right then—I was too concerned with what I should say or do next, how I could possibly make this better or easier while not lying to them anymore.

The breeze and the ghosts darted between us.

"Hup," Anne said, sitting forward suddenly, a hand naturally falling to the side of her stomach. "Feels like somebody just woke up. Here," she said, reaching for my hand, "I think that's a heel."

I felt a little nub and smiled. Anne was trying to smile, too, although she was clearly uncomfortable. She nodded at Curtie.

"Come here," she said, and he obliged, his tall body bending gently as she placed his big hand on her belly.

His eyes opened wide with the same expression of wonder he'd worn when he was four. He looked from Anne to me with a huge grin on his face. We both smiled back.

Acknowledgments

Water moves through any number of mediums, through salt wave and storm cloud, through lake ripples and the urgent pace of a river current. Ice, fog, rain, dew. Water's secret, like my family discovered, is to never stop, to never quit, to never abandon the work of transforming. A person, a family, can fight against change, sink beneath it, float on its surface, but to give up on the power inherent in change is to give up on living. And because change, like water, can be treacherous, it is imperative that you keep an eye on each other—always. As a family, we have never closed that watchful eye, even as we have continued to emerge as individuals, with challenging differences and reassuring similarities.

These days I wear two rings, one on each hand. On my right is the one my mother passed on to me from Mama T. Its interlacing diamond curves often elicit comments from cashiers and receptionists. They mark it immediately as an heirloom, often leaning over to study its intricacy more closely.

The other ring also attracts compliments, although it is much simpler in design. Made of white gold, this slim band ring has intersecting lines of gold that resemble a kind of lattice. My life partner,

Barbara, and I designed and exchanged rings with each other to create a physical symbol of our love and commitment. This year, 2006, marks our eighteenth anniversary.

This book would not have been written without Barbara's belief, encouragement, and honesty. Her love is a pure gift in my life.

Nor could this book have come into being without the courage and participation of my family; to each of them I owe my greatest thanks.

There are few people as tenacious in their loving as my mother is in hers. She is friend, buddy, confidante, and elder. She and my father still harbor a remarkable sense of wonder about life, which continues to be inspirational and sustaining. As is my father's honesty, gratitude, and good humor. He is a wise friend, and as good a listener as there is.

Among the many aspects of life about which we have no choice, who your siblings are is one of them. To walk through life flanked by a sister like Anne and a brother like Curt is one of my life's greatest blessings. Anne's love and her regard for the gift of Barbara in my life (and in hers) have only deepened with time. She has enriched our lives with a beautiful niece and nephew, Cate and John.

As for Curt, after dealing with his own pain and shock about my sexuality, his support has emerged in many forms. The truest measure of his and his wife Isabella's embrace is their insistence that Barbara and I be involved as fully as possible in the lives of their four children: Wylie, Meg, Ches, and Jack.

So you see, this story really does have a happy ending, at least so far. Does that mean that when we gather, it is all bliss and ease? Heck no, we're a family. We interrupt each other, step on each other's emotional toes, offer too much unsolicited advice—some get frustrated, others shake their heads in consternation. We laugh a lot, too, and cry, sometimes more than others.

As to the ghosts, they walk among us still, but in new and surprising ways. Never dreaming they would, my parents have both lived longer than their parents did, which has required that they reorient to the fact that they are not only alive and well but also still married! Recently, Mom shared some of her thoughts about her father-in-law, Granddaddy.

Granddaddy's death was so hard because he was the last one. Before that, I always felt like if I got in trouble, I could lean against him. He was like a warm wall, that strong and that supportive, and then he was gone—they were all gone. Now I realize, all these years later, that that's what I want to be, a warm wall that my kids, and my grandkids, can lean against.

The ghosts appear in other ways, too. There is that certain head tilt of my brother's son, Ches, and the laughter that peels out of his daughter Meg's mouth, so similar to my laugh and to my mother's and my grandmother's. Family pictures, old and new, confirm the handiwork of genetics. Grandmother Frances's eyes have made their way into the faces of my sister's children, her coloring and red hair affixed this time around to my nephew John. These are pictures we can gaze upon and ask questions about, both of my parents now able and wanting to talk about the past.

There are others to thank for their assistance in the creating and birthing of this book. Fellow writers and colleagues at the University of North Carolina at Wilmington: Sarah Messer, Janet Ellerby, Lindsay Aegerter, Barbara Waxman, Philip Gerard, Denise Gess, Stan Colbert, Clyde Edgerton, Rebecca Lee, Michael White, Terry Tempest Williams, Lia Purpura, Dana Sachs, Brad Land, Elizabeth Humphrey, Meredith Anton, and Mark Basquill.

Special friends and early readers deserving of thanks include Martha Wisbey, Luleen Anderson, David Purcell, Steve McDaniel, Karen Werhle, Ann Rea, Janet Blanchard, Susan Ray, Belle Hart, Darren Hart, JoAnn Wilkes, Kristi Gottlob, and Gail Anderson.

I am deeply appreciative for the careful reading and invaluable guidance I have received from my agent, Dena Fischer, and for the help from Amy Rennert. In a similar vein, I thank my editor, Julia Pastore, for her regard and precision, and for her genuine interest in this work. The team at Harmony Books has been superb.

I must also thank my two canine writing companions, Mason and Hattie, whose presence and gentle snoring have been more helpful than they know.

And there is one last thank-you, to my neighbor, the Atlantic Ocean. My lifelong dream of living near the ocean came true when Barbara and I finished our schooling and moved to the coast of North Carolina. Now I no longer have to plot and plan and wait for the next time I can get to the beach. Instead, I go anytime I want to—to bodysurf, to walk, to gaze at the water, to listen. I still stand at its edge and lean against that same old pull around my ankles. I don't bend over to kiss my friend the ocean good-bye anymore, though, because now when I walk away, it stays with me.

A Note on the Type

The text of this book was set in Centaur, an old-style, or Venetian, typeface designed by Bruce Rogers for the Metropolitan Museum of Art between 1912 and 1929.